# BATMAN '66

VOL. 5

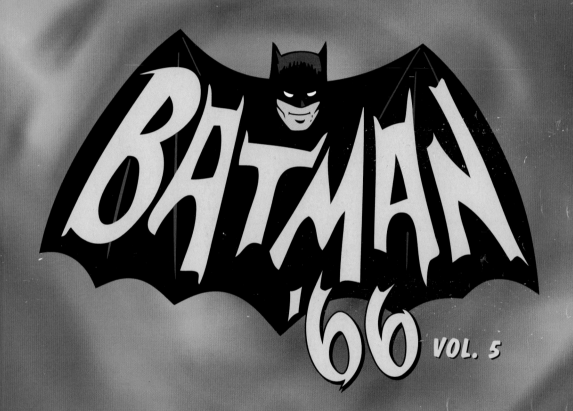

# BATMAN '66 VOL. 5

Written by
**JEFF PARKER**
**RAY FAWKES**
**GABE SORIA**
**LEE ALLRED**

Art by
**BRENT SCHOONOVER**
**GIANCARLO CARACUZZO**
**JON BOGDANOVE**
**LUKAS KETNER**
**TY TEMPLETON**
**JESSE HAMM**
**SCOTT KOWALCHUK**
**DEAN HASPIEL**
**JONATHAN CASE**
**MICHAEL ALLRED**
**CRAIG ROUSSEAU**

Colors by
**KELLY FITZPATRICK  FLAVIA CARACUZZO**
**ROBERTO FLORES  OMAR ESTEVEZ**
**TONY AVIÑA  SCOTT KOWALCHUK**
**ALLEN PASSALAQUA  JONATHAN CASE**
**LAURA ALLRED**

Letters by
**WES ABBOTT**

Cover Art & Original Series Covers by
**MICHAEL & LAURA ALLRED**

BATMAN created by BOB KANE with BILL FINGER

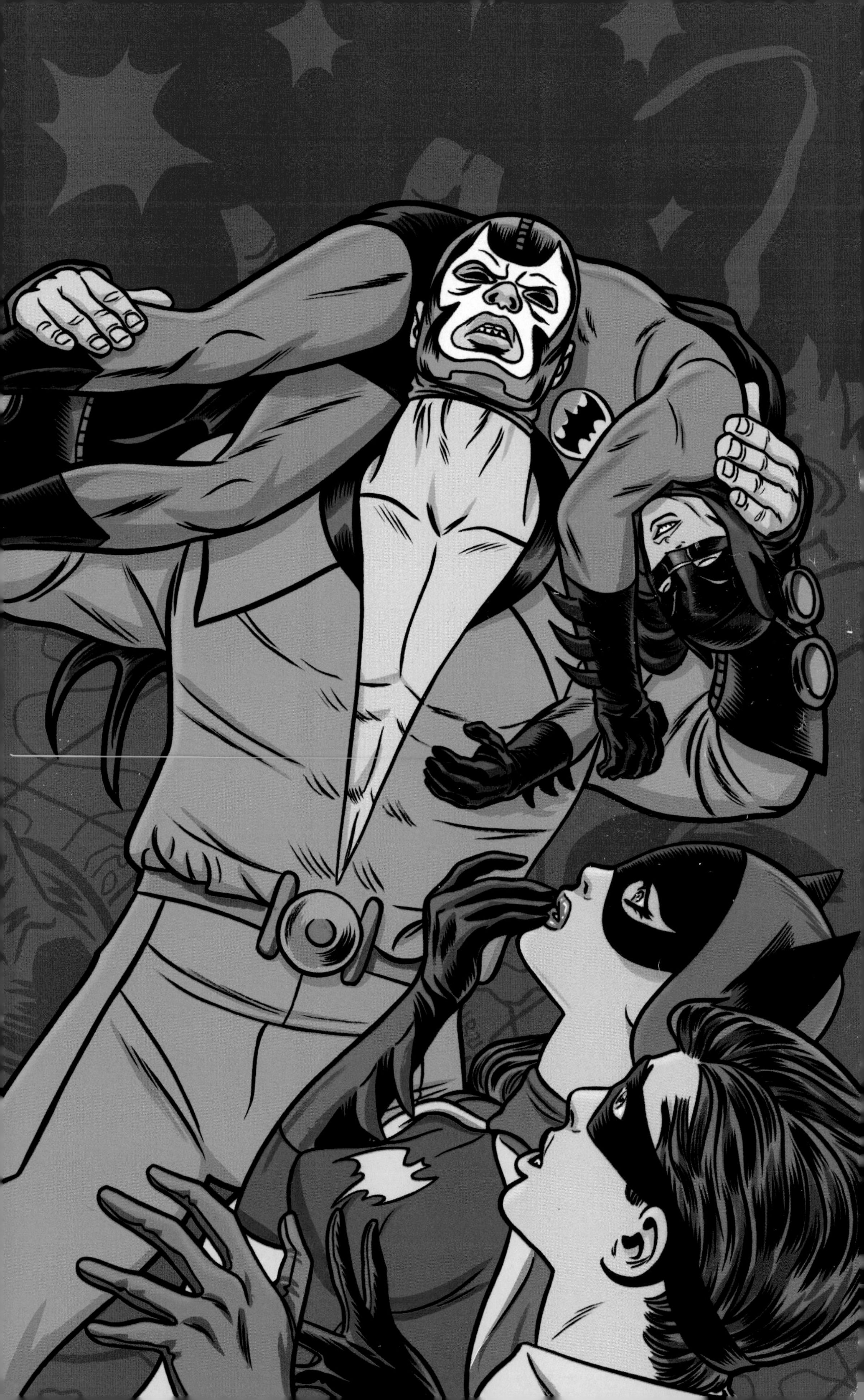

# TABLE OF CONTENTS

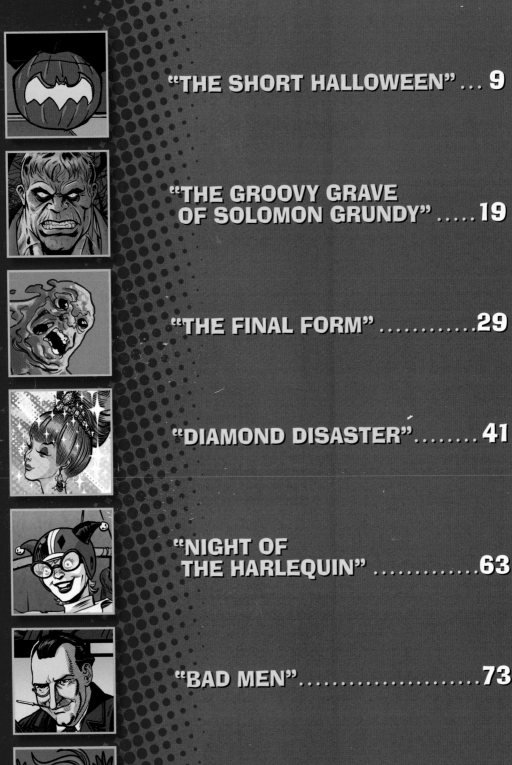

**BATMAN '66 VOL. 5**

Published by DC Comics. Compilation and all new material Copyright © 2016 DC Comics. All Rights Reserved. Originally published in single magazine form as BATMAN '66 23-30 and online as BATMAN '66 Digital Chapters 46, 58-73. Copyright © 2014, 2015 DC Comics. All Rights Reserved. All characters, their distinctive likenesses and related elements featured in this publication are trademarks of DC Comics. The stories, characters and incidents featured in this publication are entirely fictional. DC Comics does not read or accept unsolicited submissions of ideas, stories or artwork.

DC Comics, 2900 West Alameda Ave., Burbank, CA 91505
Printed by LSC Communications, Owensville, MO, USA.
11/4/16. First Printing. ISBN: 978-1-4012-6483-3

Library of Congress Cataloging-in-Publication Data is available.

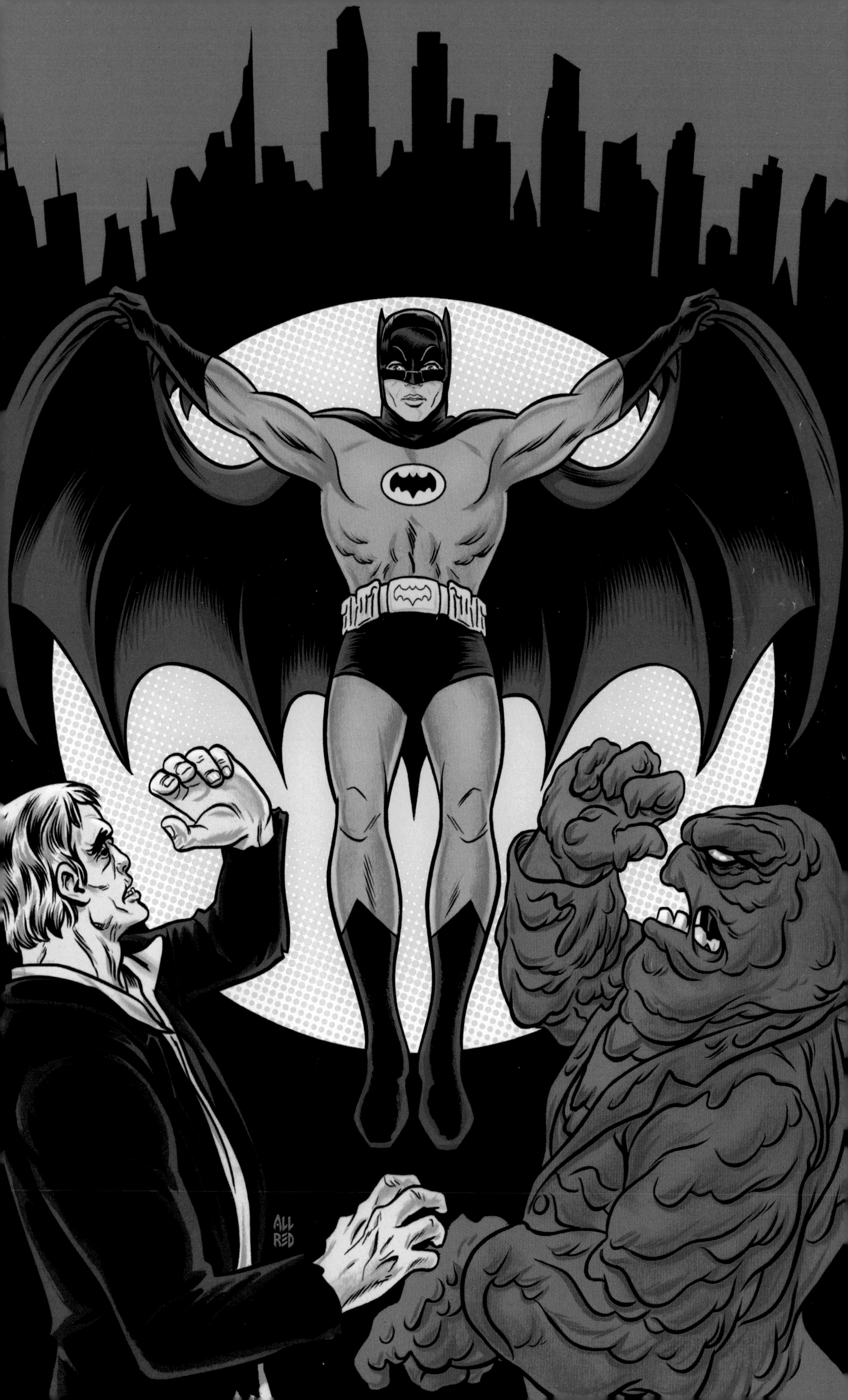
ALL
RED

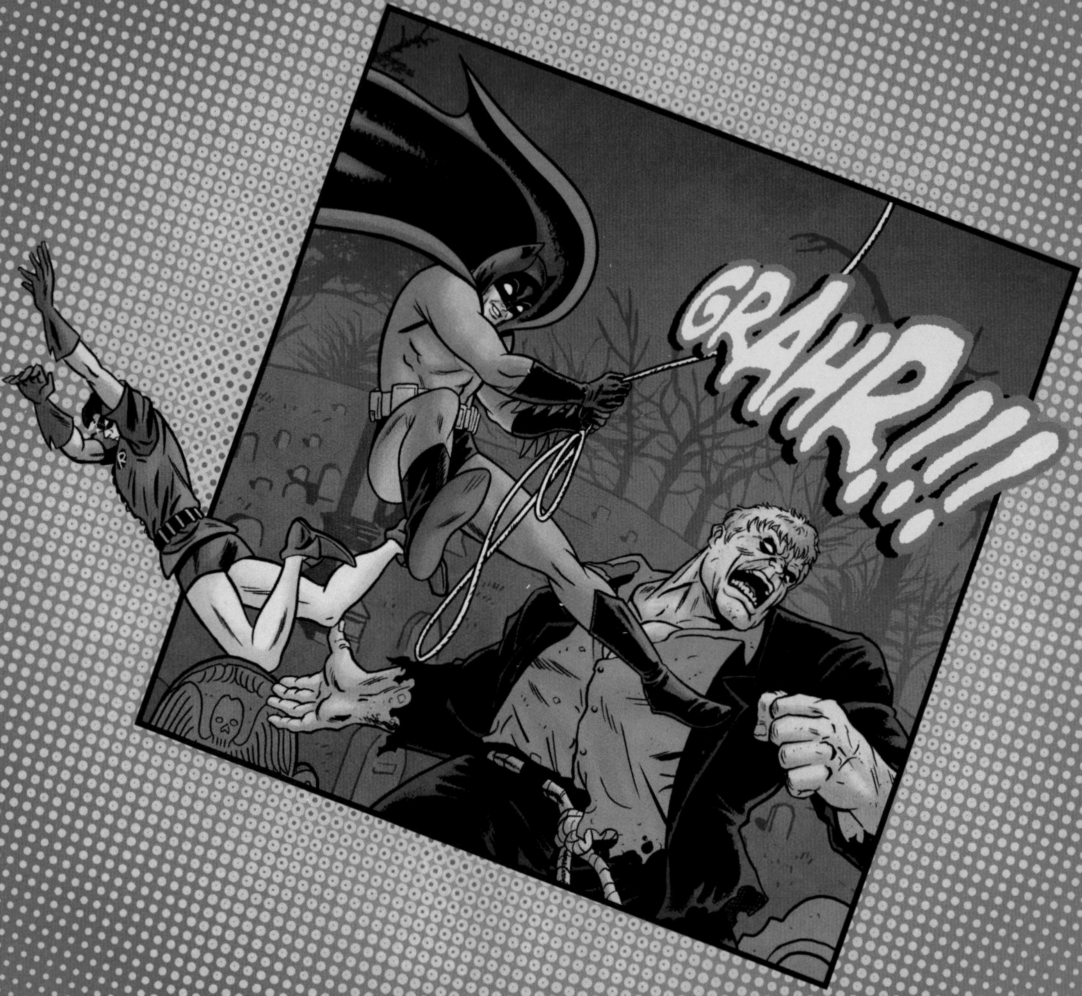
GRAHR!!!

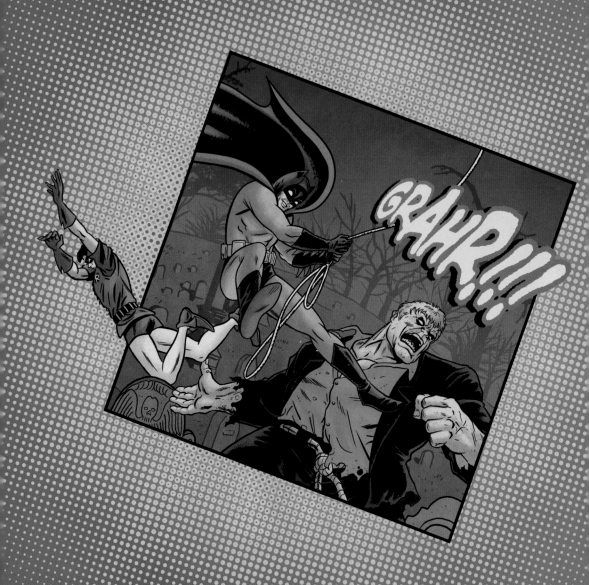

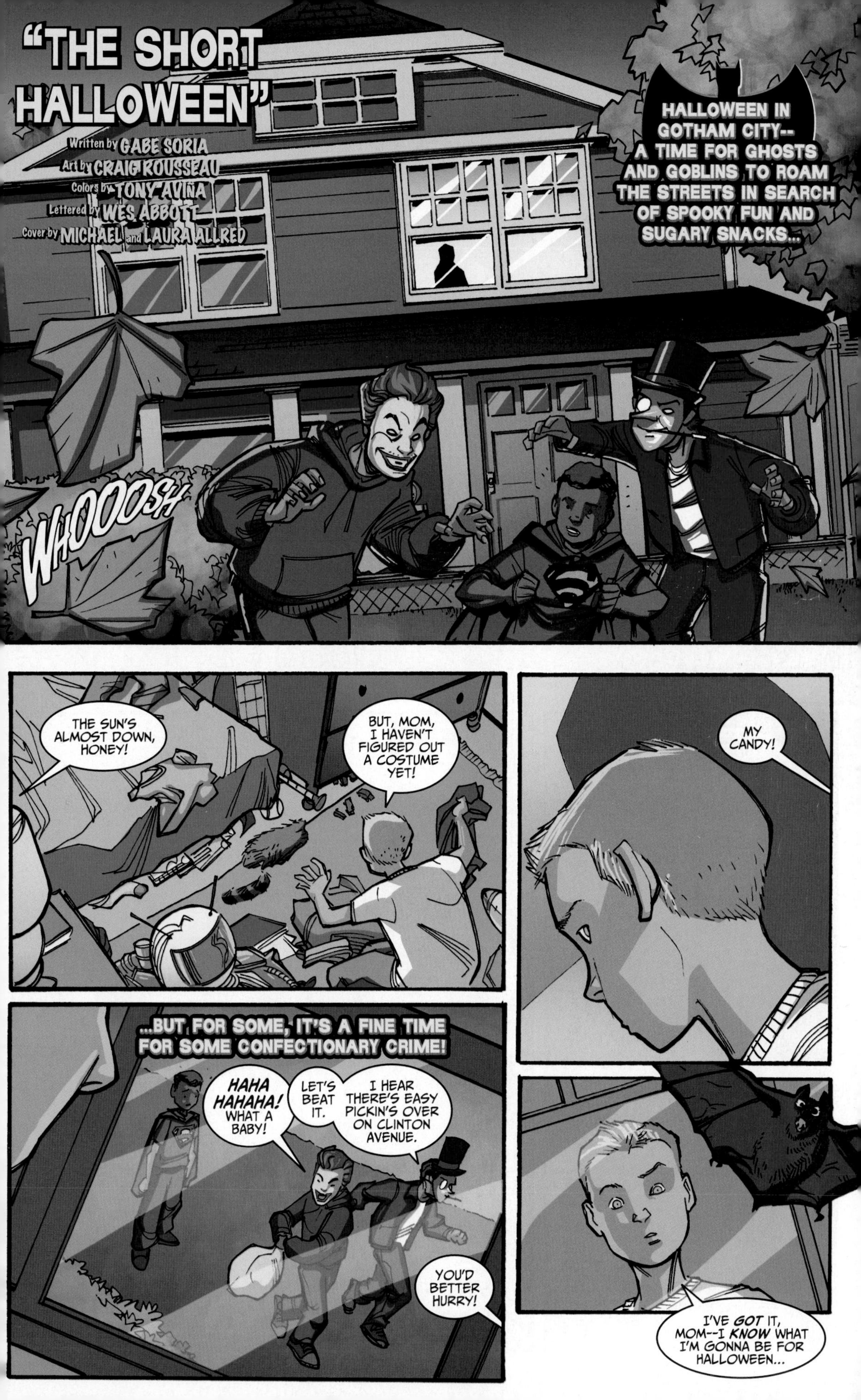
"THE SHORT HALLOWEEN"
Written by GABE SORIA
Art by CRAIG ROUSSEAU
Colors by TONY AVIÑA
Lettered by WES ABBOTT
Cover by MICHAEL and LAURA ALLRED
HALLOWEEN IN GOTHAM CITY-- A TIME FOR GHOSTS AND GOBLINS TO ROAM THE STREETS IN SEARCH OF SPOOKY FUN AND SUGARY SNACKS...
WHOOOOSH
THE SUN'S ALMOST DOWN, HONEY!
BUT, MOM, I HAVEN'T FIGURED OUT A COSTUME YET!
MY CANDY!
...BUT FOR SOME, IT'S A FINE TIME FOR SOME CONFECTIONARY CRIME!
HAHA HAHAHA! WHAT A BABY!
LET'S BEAT IT.
I HEAR THERE'S EASY PICKIN'S OVER ON CLINTON AVENUE.
YOU'D BETTER HURRY!
I'VE GOT IT, MOM--I KNOW WHAT I'M GONNA BE FOR HALLOWEEN...

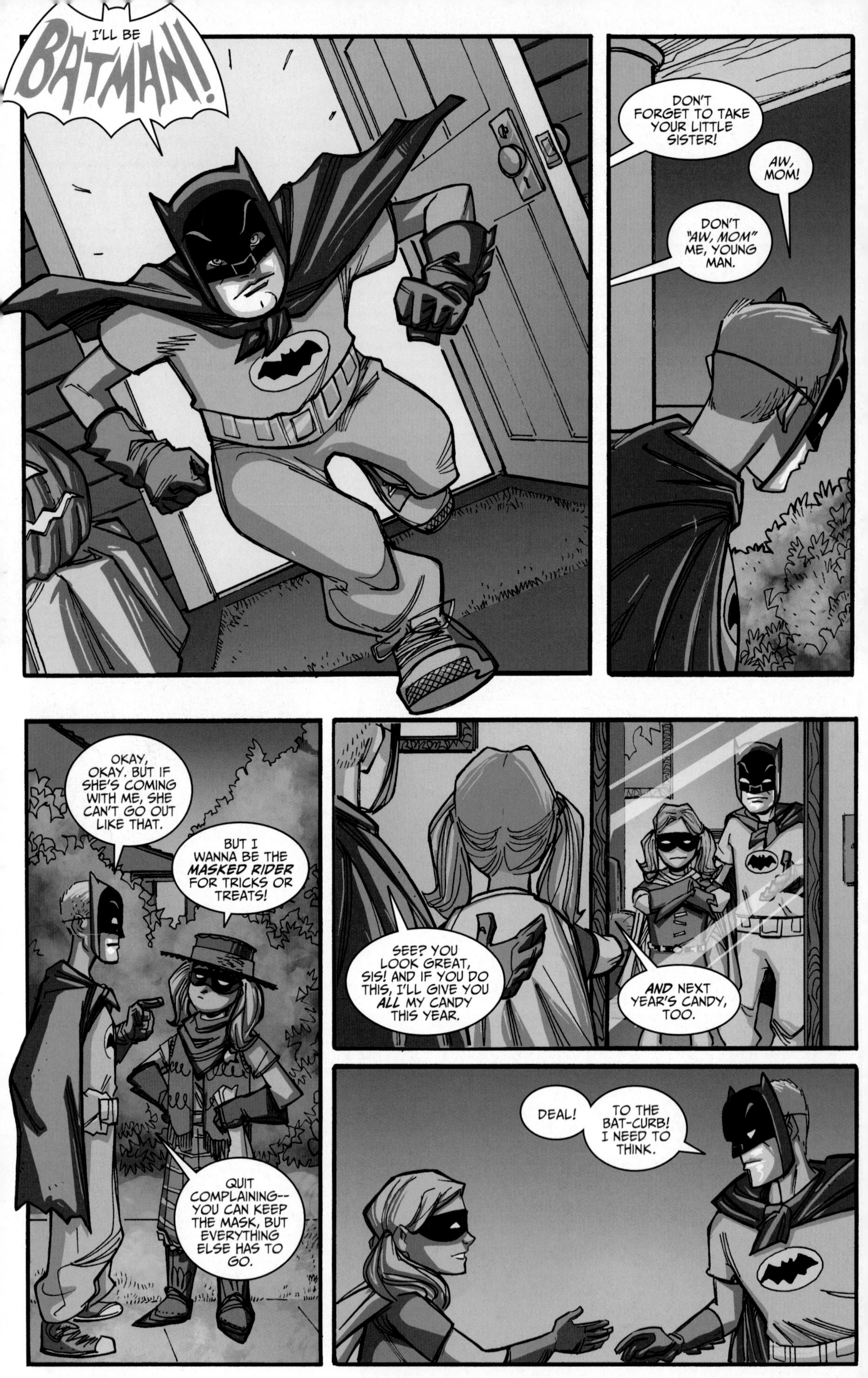
I'LL BE BATMAN!
DON'T FORGET TO TAKE YOUR LITTLE SISTER!
AW, MOM!
DON'T "AW, MOM" ME, YOUNG MAN.
OKAY, OKAY. BUT IF SHE'S COMING WITH ME, SHE CAN'T GO OUT LIKE THAT.
BUT I WANNA BE THE MASKED RIDER FOR TRICKS OR TREATS!
QUIT COMPLAINING-- YOU CAN KEEP THE MASK, BUT EVERYTHING ELSE HAS TO GO.
SEE? YOU LOOK GREAT, SIS! AND IF YOU DO THIS, I'LL GIVE YOU ALL MY CANDY THIS YEAR.
AND NEXT YEAR'S CANDY, TOO.
DEAL!
TO THE BAT-CURB! I NEED TO THINK.

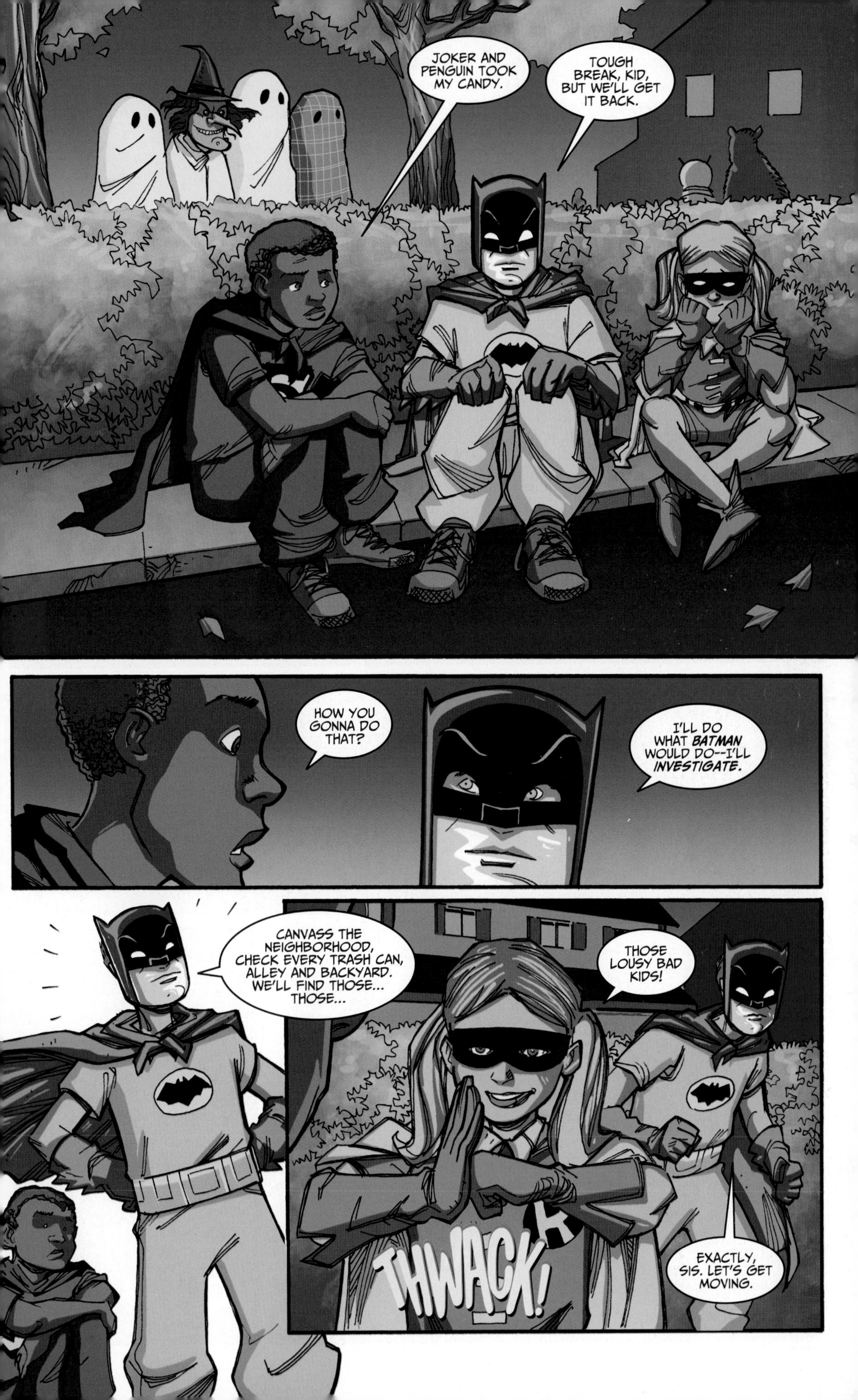
JOKER AND PENGUIN TOOK MY CANDY.
TOUGH BREAK, KID, BUT WE'LL GET IT BACK.
HOW YOU GONNA DO THAT?
I'LL DO WHAT ***BATMAN*** WOULD DO--I'LL ***INVESTIGATE***.
CANVASS THE NEIGHBORHOOD, CHECK EVERY TRASH CAN, ALLEY AND BACKYARD. WE'LL FIND THOSE... THOSE...
THOSE LOUSY BAD KIDS!
THWACK!
EXACTLY, SIS. LET'S GET MOVING.

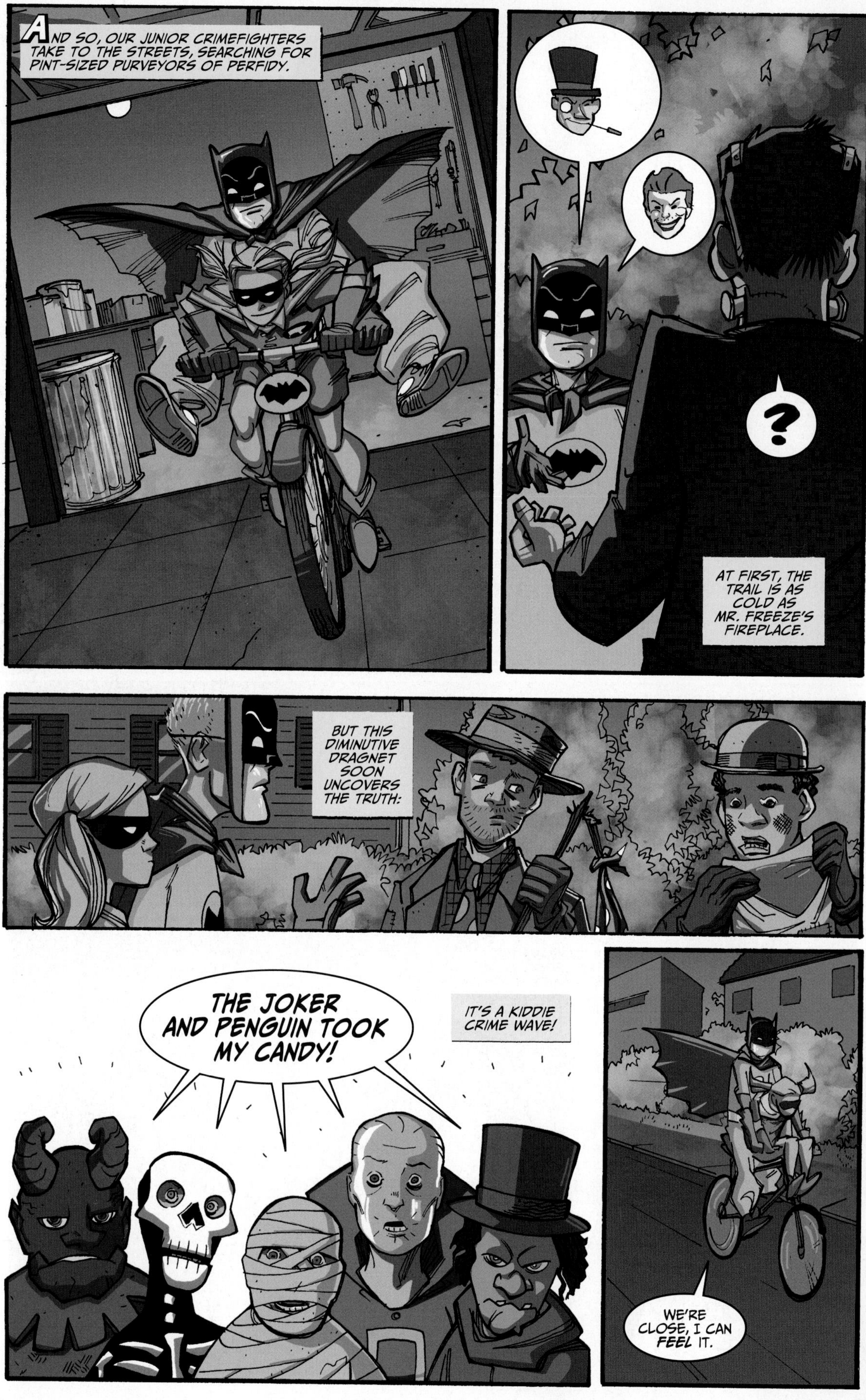
AND SO, OUR JUNIOR CRIMEFIGHTERS TAKE TO THE STREETS, SEARCHING FOR PINT-SIZED PURVEYORS OF PERFIDY.
?
AT FIRST, THE TRAIL IS AS COLD AS MR. FREEZE'S FIREPLACE.
BUT THIS DIMINUTIVE DRAGNET SOON UNCOVERS THE TRUTH:
THE JOKER AND PENGUIN TOOK MY CANDY!
IT'S A KIDDIE CRIME WAVE!
WE'RE CLOSE, I CAN *FEEL* IT.

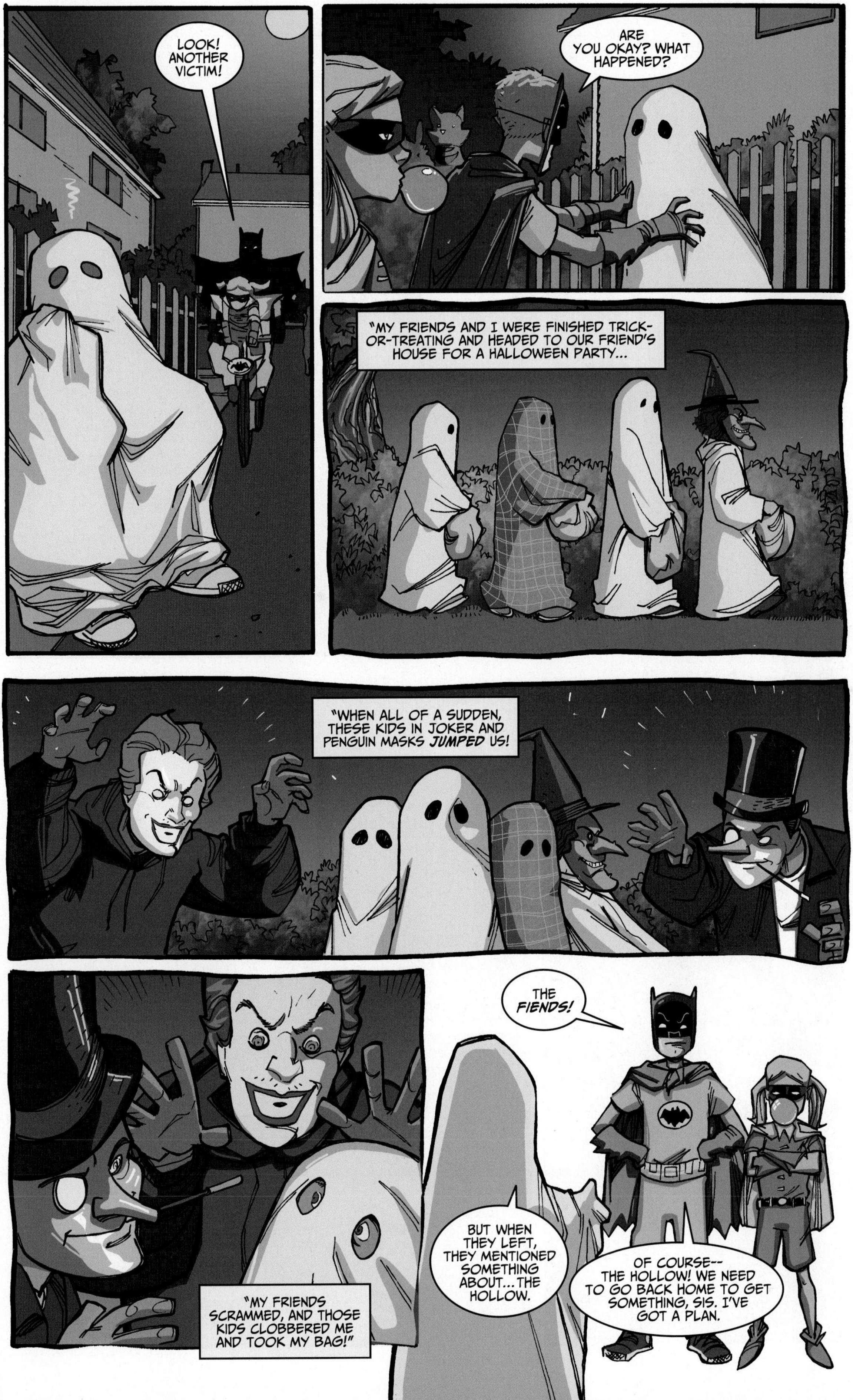
LOOK! ANOTHER VICTIM!
ARE YOU OKAY? WHAT HAPPENED?
"MY FRIENDS AND I WERE FINISHED TRICK-OR-TREATING AND HEADED TO OUR FRIEND'S HOUSE FOR A HALLOWEEN PARTY...
"WHEN ALL OF A SUDDEN, THESE KIDS IN JOKER AND PENGUIN MASKS JUMPED US!
"MY FRIENDS SCRAMMED, AND THOSE KIDS CLOBBERED ME AND TOOK MY BAG!"
THE FIENDS!
BUT WHEN THEY LEFT, THEY MENTIONED SOMETHING ABOUT...THE HOLLOW.
OF COURSE-- THE HOLLOW! WE NEED TO GO BACK HOME TO GET SOMETHING, SIS. I'VE GOT A PLAN.

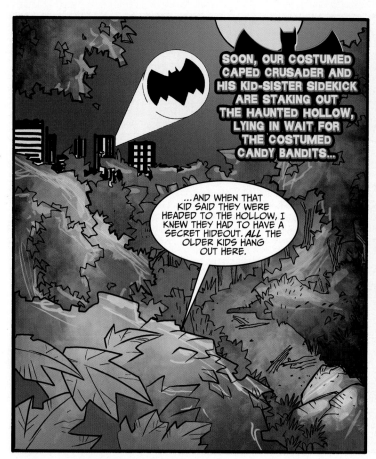

SOON, OUR COSTUMED CAPED CRUSADER AND HIS KID-SISTER SIDEKICK ARE STAKING OUT THE HAUNTED HOLLOW, LYING IN WAIT FOR THE COSTUMED CANDY BANDITS...

...AND WHEN THAT KID SAID THEY WERE HEADED TO THE HOLLOW, I KNEW THEY HAD TO HAVE A SECRET HIDEOUT. *ALL* THE OLDER KIDS HANG OUT HERE.

IT'S SPOOOOOOKY.

DON'T WORRY, "OLD CHUM."

NOT EVERYBODY HAS AN OLDER BROTHER BATMAN TO PROTECT THEM.

LOOK-- THERE THEY ARE!

READY, ROBIN?

YOU BET, BATMAN.

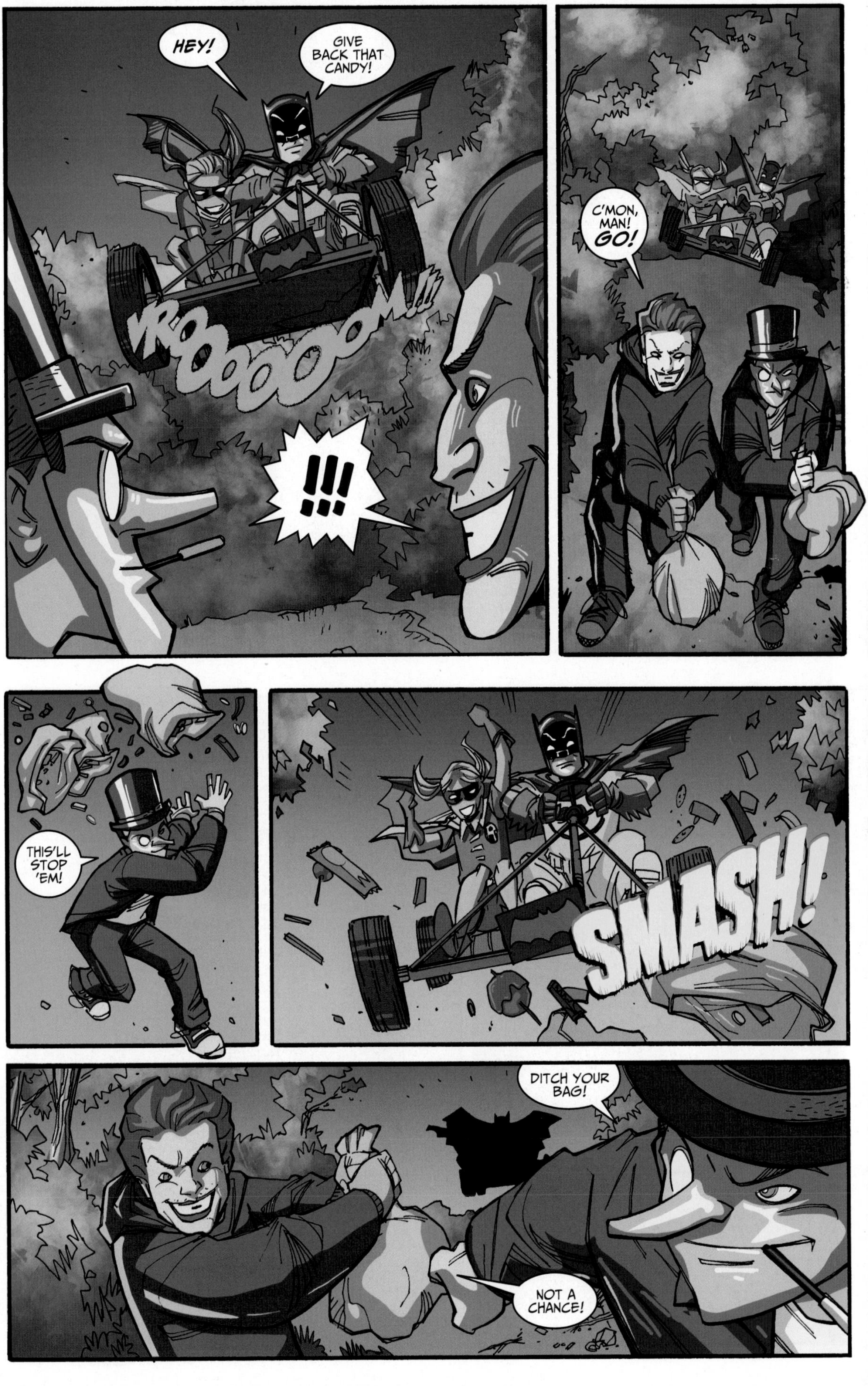
HEY!
GIVE BACK THAT CANDY!
VROOOOOOM!!!
!!!
C'MON, MAN! GO!
THIS'LL STOP 'EM!
SMASH!
DITCH YOUR BAG!
NOT A CHANCE!

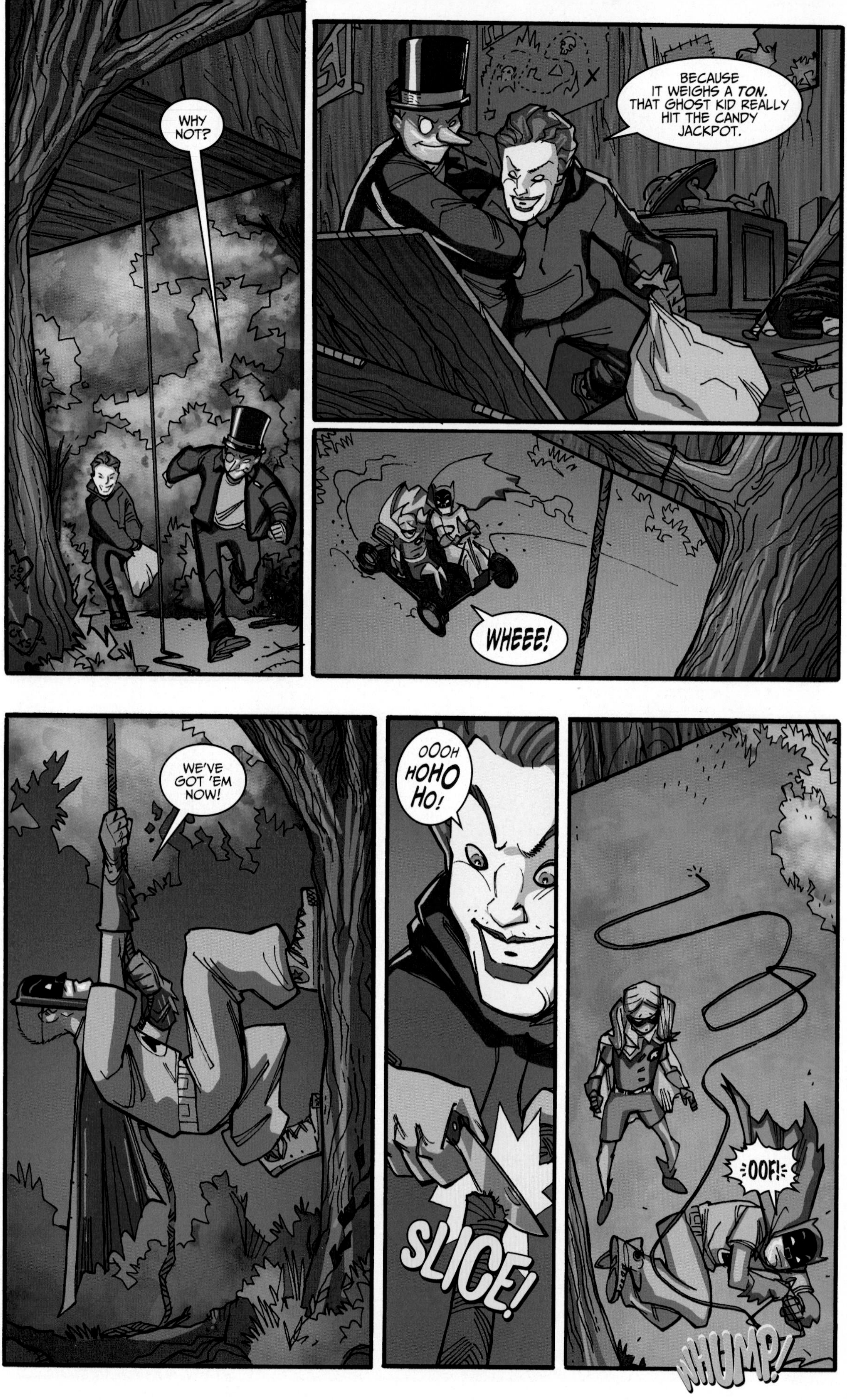
WHY NOT?
BECAUSE IT WEIGHS A TON. THAT GHOST KID REALLY HIT THE CANDY JACKPOT.
WHEEE!
WE'VE GOT 'EM NOW!
OOOH HOHO HO!
SLICE!
OOF!
WHUMP!

HA! WHAT ARE YOU TWO TWERPS GONNA DO NOW?

YOU'LL NEVER BE ABLE TO CLIMB THIS TREE! AND WE'VE GOT ENOUGH CANDY UP HERE TO LAST US A *WEEK!*

UM, I DON'T KNOW ABOUT THAT...

HE GOT ROCKS. A BUNCH OF *ROCKS!*

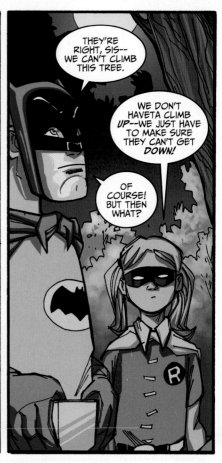

THEY'RE RIGHT, SIS-- WE CAN'T CLIMB THIS TREE.

WE DON'T HAVETA CLIMB *UP*--WE JUST HAVE TO MAKE SURE THEY CAN'T GET *DOWN!*

OF COURSE! BUT THEN WHAT?

THEN...

...WE CALL IN THE *AUTHORITIES!*

THWACK!

LATER...

HA... HA?

YOU THINK THIS IS FUNNY? I'LL GIVE YOU SOMETHING TO LAUGH ABOUT!

NORMALLY, I WOULD *NEVER* TELL ON ANOTHER KID, BUT THOSE GUYS WERE JERKS.

AND THEY COULD'VE BEAT US UP.

THAT, TOO.

BUT NOW WE MISSED TRICKS OR TREATS!

THERE'S ALWAYS NEXT YEAR, SIS.

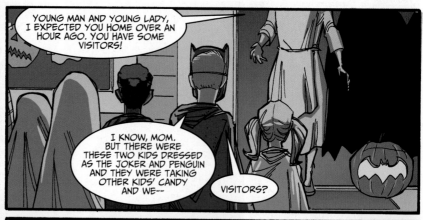

YOUNG MAN AND YOUNG LADY, I EXPECTED YOU HOME OVER AN HOUR AGO. YOU HAVE SOME VISITORS!

I KNOW, MOM. BUT THERE WERE THESE TWO KIDS DRESSED AS THE JOKER AND PENGUIN AND THEY WERE TAKING OTHER KIDS' CANDY AND WE--

VISITORS?

TA-DAA!

BATMAN!

IT'S AN HONOR TO MEET YOU YOUNG HEROES. WE'VE HEARD ALL ABOUT YOUR EXPLOITS.

ROBIN!

YOU PROBABLY KNOW THAT ALL THE CANDY GOT RUINED. SOME BATMAN I TURNED OUT TO BE.

BUT YOU TRIED YOUR BEST IN THE PURSUIT OF JUSTICE, AND THAT'S WHAT MATTERS.

AND WHILE THE JOY OF CRIMEFIGHTING IS ITS OWN REWARD...

HOLY ALL HALLOWS EVE, BATMAN! LET'S JUST GIVE THEM THE CANDY!

FROM ALL OF US HERE AT BATMAN '66, HAVE A BAT-TASTIC HALLOWEEN!

THE END

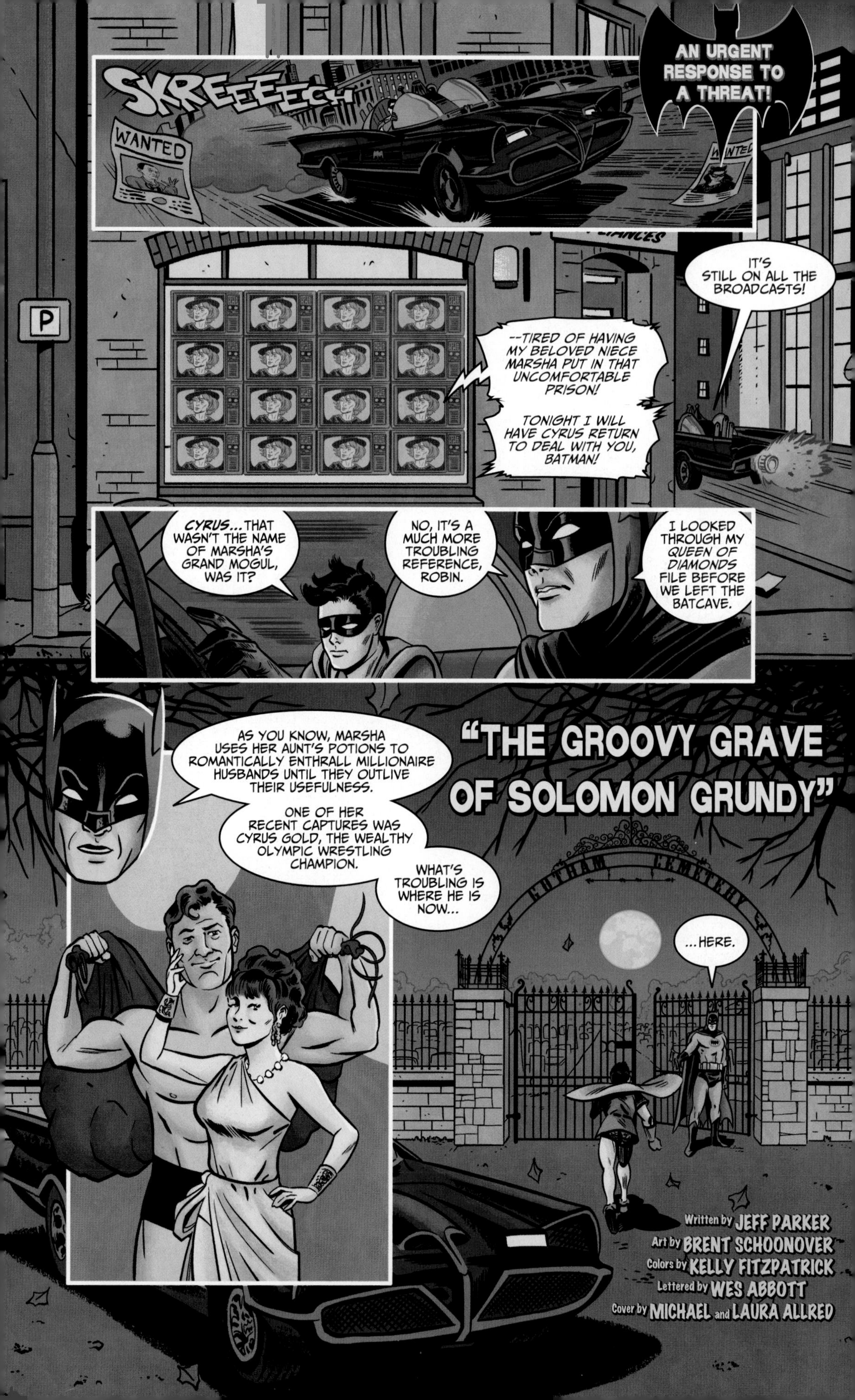
SKREEEEECH
WANTED
AN URGENT RESPONSE TO A THREAT!
WANTED
--TIRED OF HAVING MY BELOVED NIECE MARSHA PUT IN THAT UNCOMFORTABLE PRISON!
TONIGHT I WILL HAVE CYRUS RETURN TO DEAL WITH YOU, BATMAN!
IT'S STILL ON ALL THE BROADCASTS!
CYRUS...THAT WASN'T THE NAME OF MARSHA'S GRAND MOGUL, WAS IT?
NO, IT'S A MUCH MORE TROUBLING REFERENCE, ROBIN.
I LOOKED THROUGH MY QUEEN OF DIAMONDS FILE BEFORE WE LEFT THE BATCAVE.
AS YOU KNOW, MARSHA USES HER AUNT'S POTIONS TO ROMANTICALLY ENTHRALL MILLIONAIRE HUSBANDS UNTIL THEY OUTLIVE THEIR USEFULNESS.
ONE OF HER RECENT CAPTURES WAS CYRUS GOLD, THE WEALTHY OLYMPIC WRESTLING CHAMPION.
WHAT'S TROUBLING IS WHERE HE IS NOW...
"THE GROOVY GRAVE OF SOLOMON GRUNDY"
GOTHAM CEMETERY
...HERE.
Written by JEFF PARKER
Art by BRENT SCHOONOVER
Colors by KELLY FITZPATRICK
Lettered by WES ABBOTT
Cover by MICHAEL and LAURA ALLRED

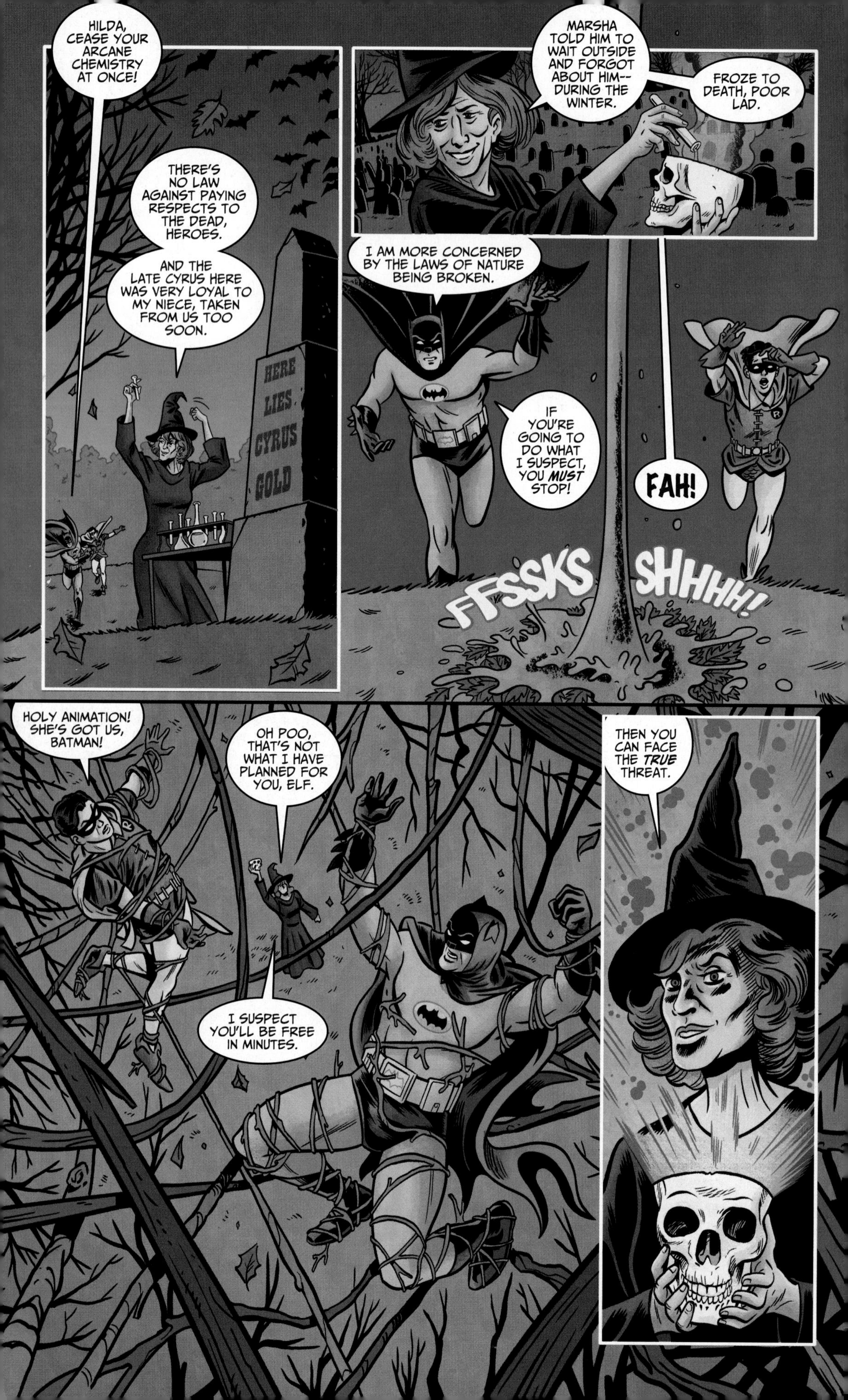
HILDA, CEASE YOUR ARCANE CHEMISTRY AT ONCE!
THERE'S NO LAW AGAINST PAYING RESPECTS TO THE DEAD, HEROES.
AND THE LATE CYRUS HERE WAS VERY LOYAL TO MY NIECE, TAKEN FROM US TOO SOON.
HERE LIES CYRUS GOLD
MARSHA TOLD HIM TO WAIT OUTSIDE AND FORGOT ABOUT HIM-- DURING THE WINTER.
FROZE TO DEATH, POOR LAD.
I AM MORE CONCERNED BY THE LAWS OF NATURE BEING BROKEN.
IF YOU'RE GOING TO DO WHAT I SUSPECT, YOU *MUST* STOP!
FAH!
FFSSKS
SHHHH!
HOLY ANIMATION! SHE'S GOT US, BATMAN!
OH POO, THAT'S NOT WHAT I HAVE PLANNED FOR YOU, ELF.
I SUSPECT YOU'LL BE FREE IN MINUTES.
THEN YOU CAN FACE THE *TRUE* THREAT.

FIRST, AS THERE'S NO TIME FOR DIGGING, I OPEN A PATH THROUGH THE SOIL...

...ABOUT 1.3 QUARTS OF FUMING SULFURIC ACID INTO THIS SOGGY GROUND SHOULD REACH THE COFFIN!

VSSHH

SHE'S CRAZY!

STILL, YOU MUST APPRECIATE THE APPLICATION OF SCIENTIFIC METHOD, ROBIN.

SHE'S ASSESSED THE DENSITY OF THE GROUND, *AND* WHAT QUANTITY OF SO3* WILL REACT WITH WATER TO REACH SIX FEET AND PENETRATE A CASKET LID.

*SO3 = SULFUR TRIOXIDE.

ALL CHILD'S PLAY COMPARED TO THIS PART, BATMAN.

THEY BARRED ME FROM TEACHING FOR USING *THIS* KIND OF ANCIENT CHEMISTRY!

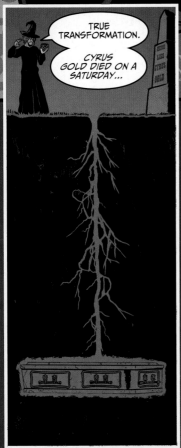

TRUE TRANSFORMATION.

CYRUS GOLD DIED ON A SATURDAY...

HIS POOR CURSED SOUL BURIED ON A SUNDAY...

YOUR OLD LIFE'S GONE, COME BACK TO US NOW!

STRONGER, VENGEFUL... NEVER TO DIE AGAIN!

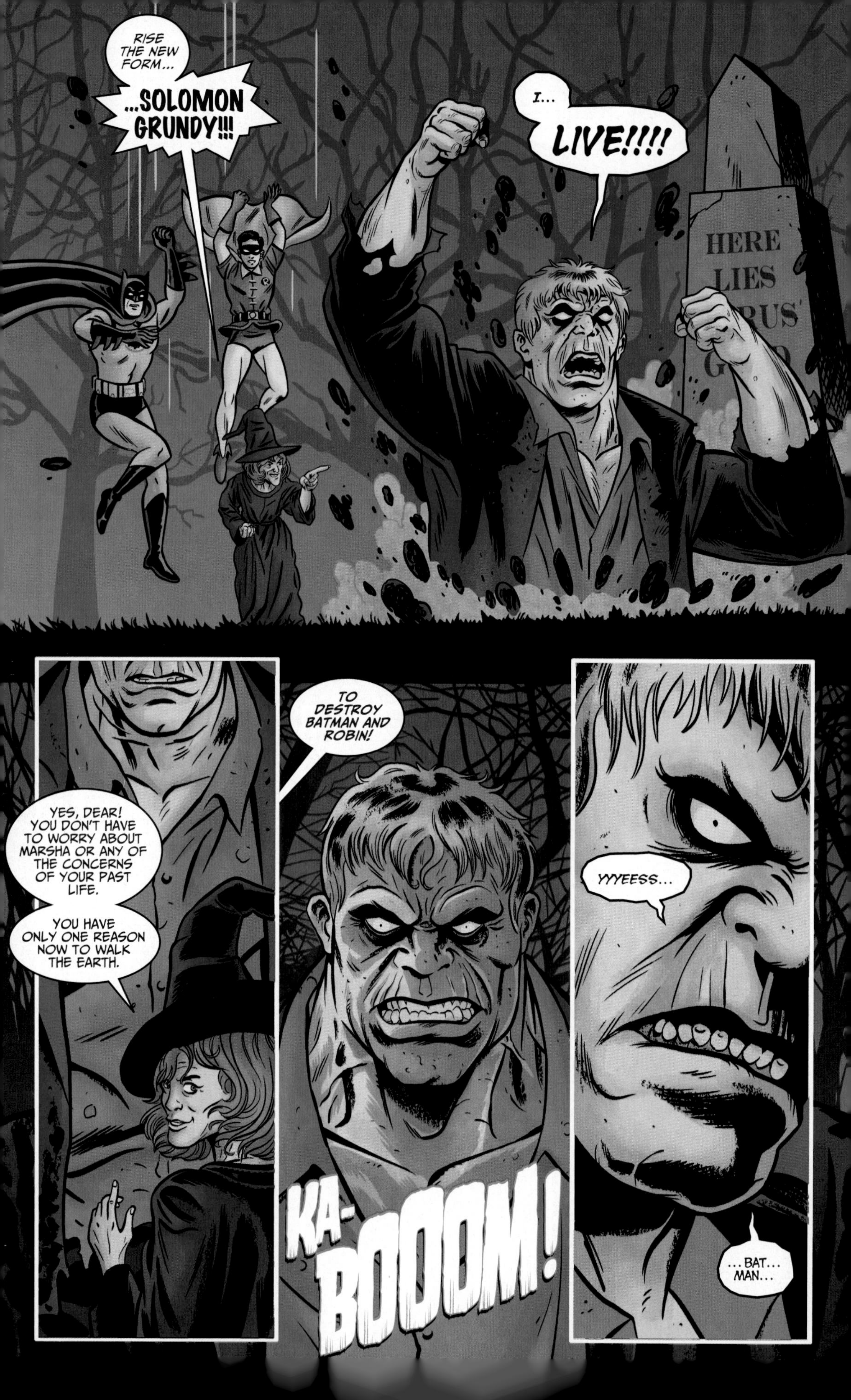
RISE THE NEW FORM...
...SOLOMON GRUNDY!!!
I...
LIVE!!!!
HERE LIES
YES, DEAR! YOU DON'T HAVE TO WORRY ABOUT MARSHA OR ANY OF THE CONCERNS OF YOUR PAST LIFE.
YOU HAVE ONLY ONE REASON NOW TO WALK THE EARTH.
TO DESTROY BATMAN AND ROBIN!
KA-BOOOM!
YYYEESS...
...BAT... MAN...

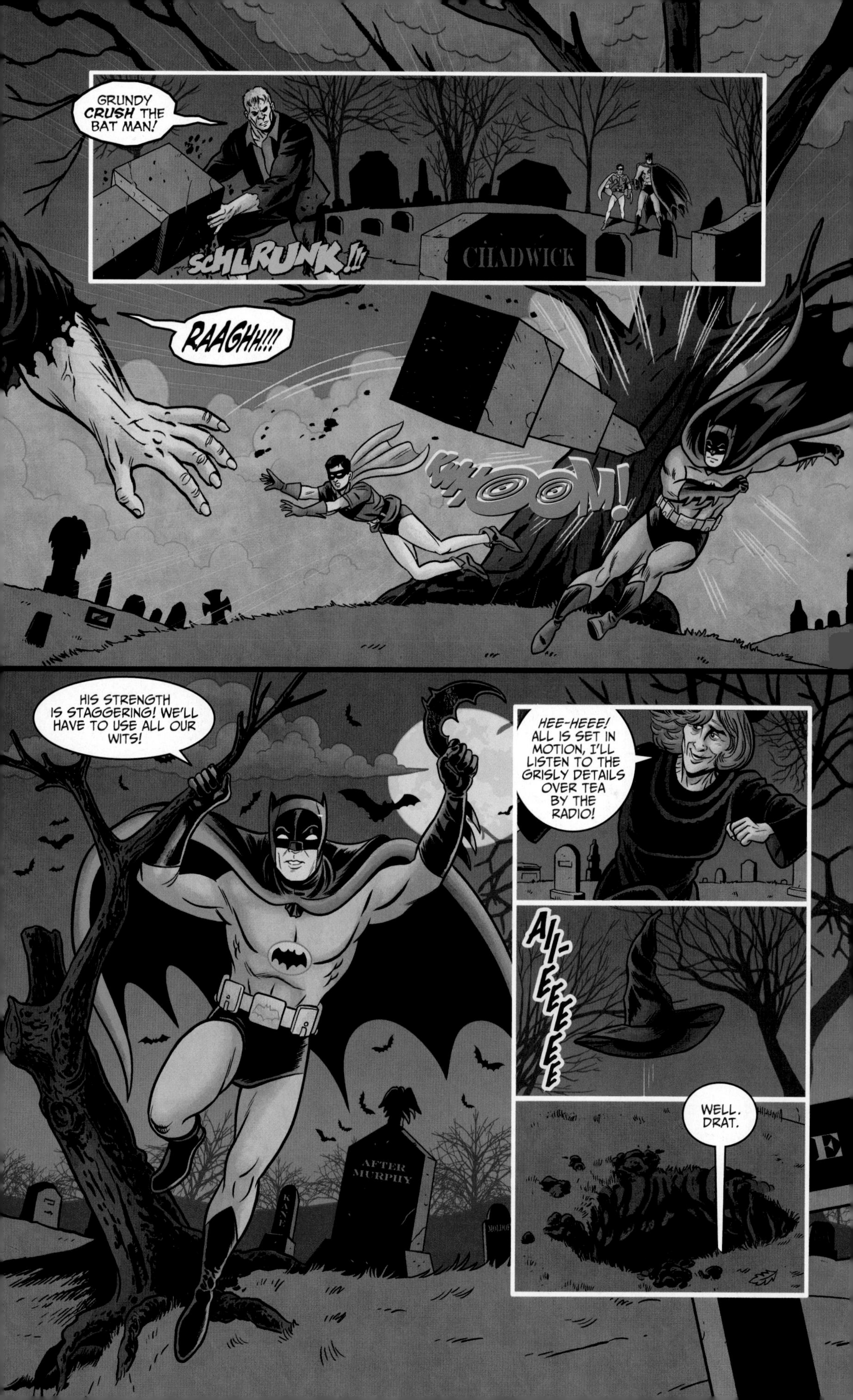

GRUNDY CRUSH THE BAT MAN!
SCHLRUNK!!!
CHADWICK
RAAGHH!!!
KWHOOOM!
HIS STRENGTH IS STAGGERING! WE'LL HAVE TO USE ALL OUR WITS!
HEE-HEEE! ALL IS SET IN MOTION, I'LL LISTEN TO THE GRISLY DETAILS OVER TEA BY THE RADIO!
AIIEEEEEE
AFTER MURPHY
KANE
WELL. DRAT.

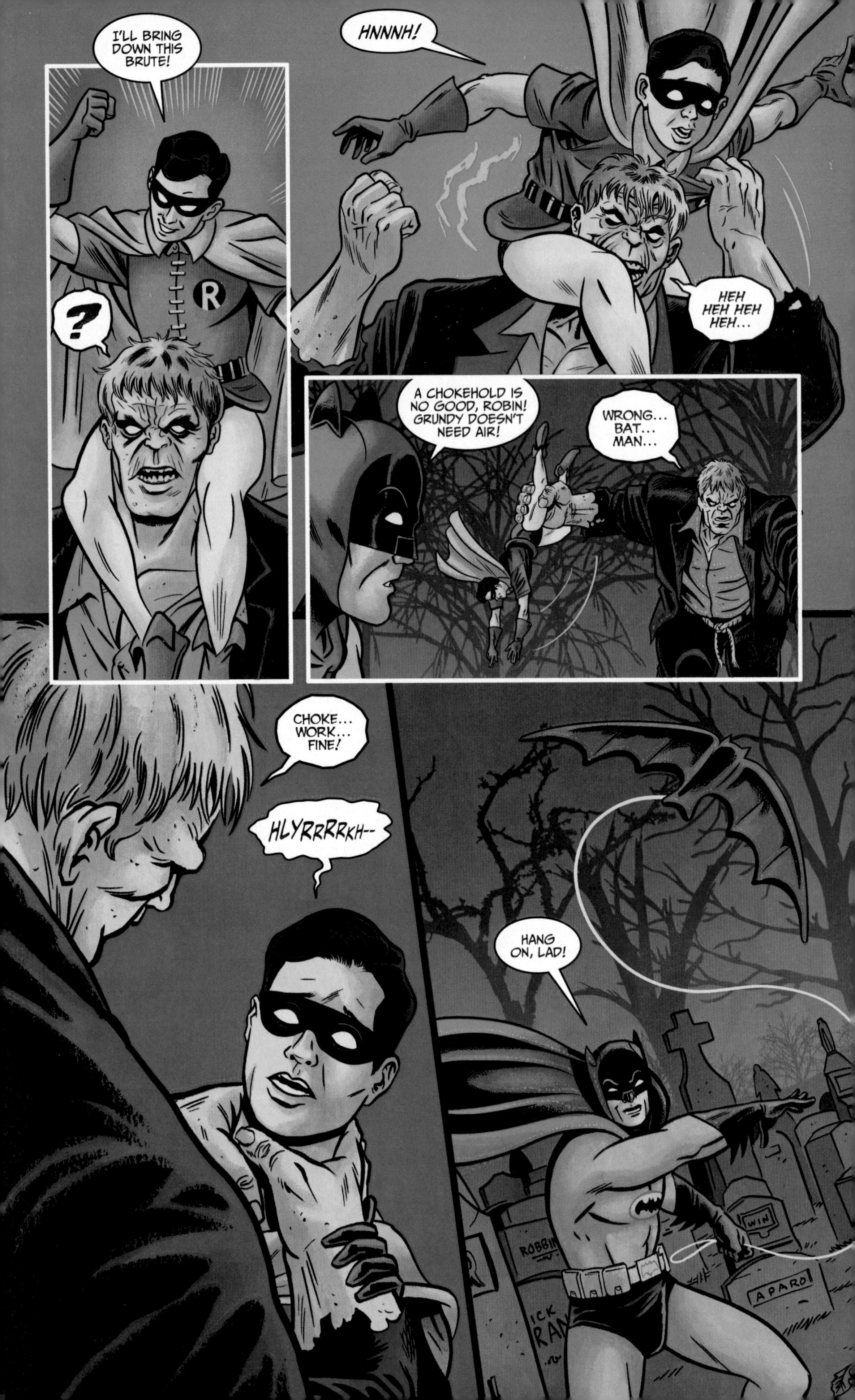

I'LL BRING DOWN THIS BRUTE!
?
HNNNH!
HEH HEH HEH HEH...
A CHOKEHOLD IS NO GOOD, ROBIN! GRUNDY DOESN'T NEED AIR!
WRONG... BAT... MAN...
CHOKE... WORK... FINE!
HLYRRRRKH--
HANG ON, LAD!
ROBBIN
WIN
APARO

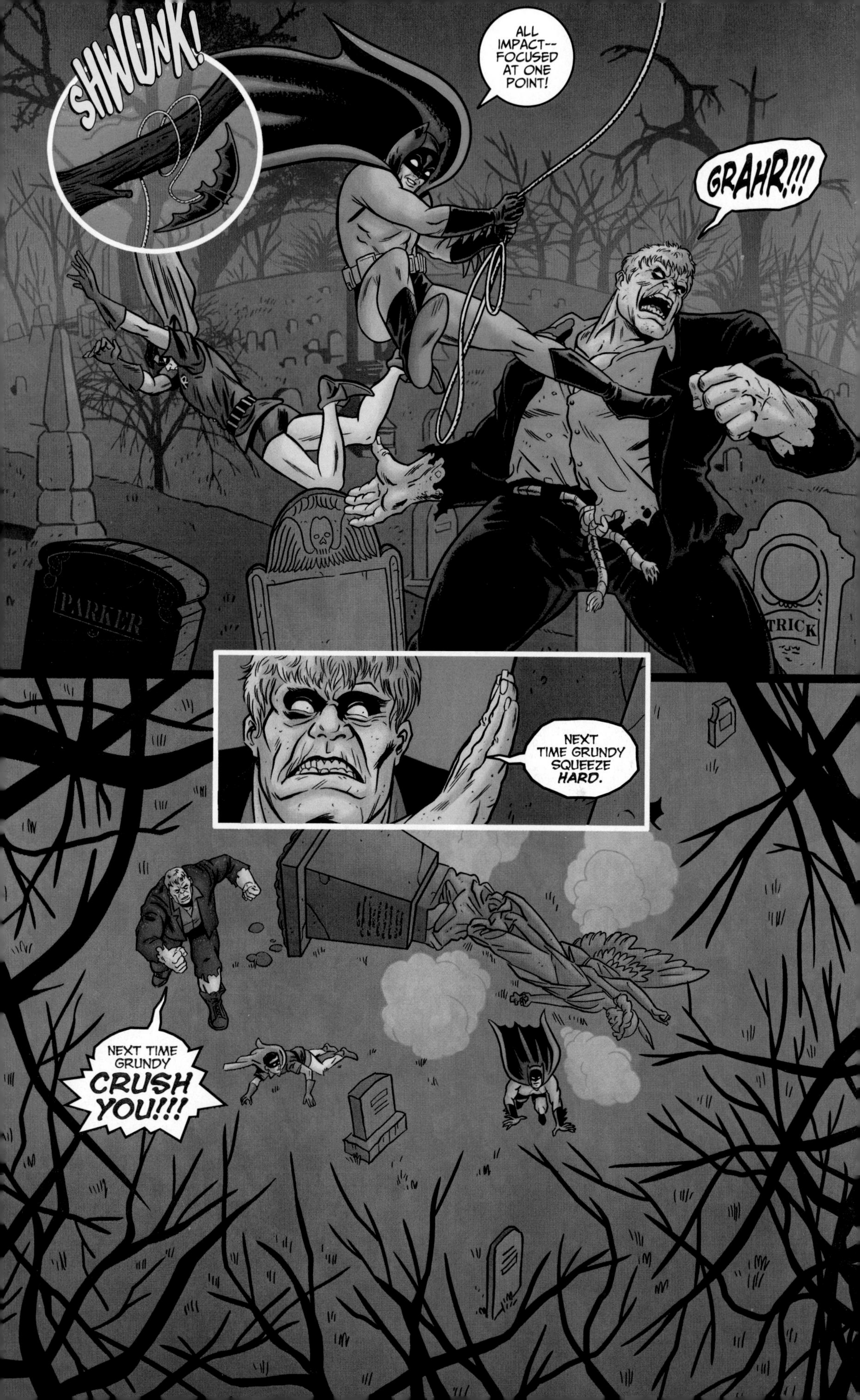
SHWUNK!
ALL IMPACT-- FOCUSED AT ONE POINT!
GRAHR!!!
PARKER
NEXT TIME GRUNDY SQUEEZE HARD.
NEXT TIME GRUNDY CRUSH YOU!!!

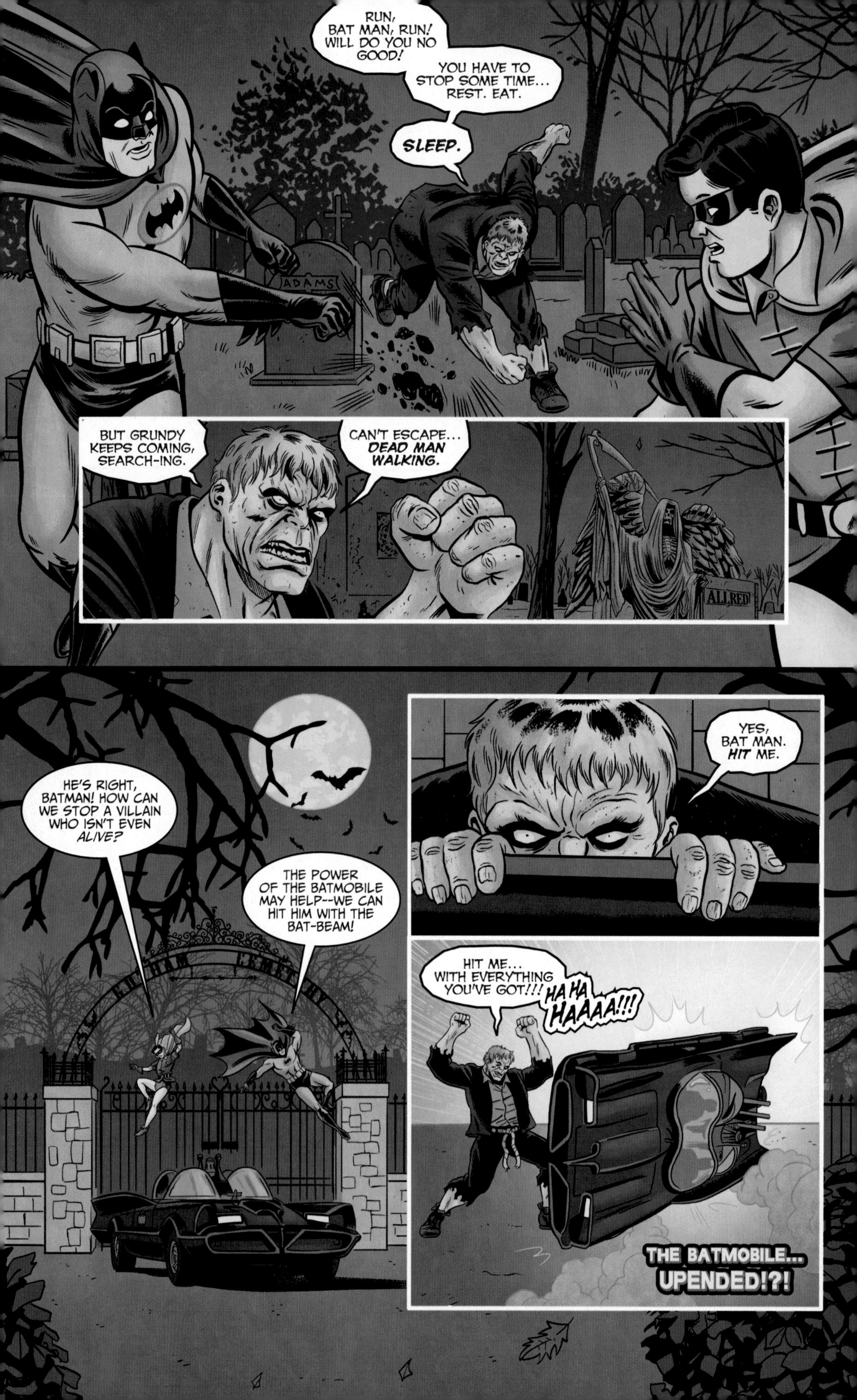

RUN, BAT MAN, RUN! WILL DO YOU NO GOOD!
YOU HAVE TO STOP SOME TIME... REST. EAT.
SLEEP.
ADAMS
BUT GRUNDY KEEPS COMING, SEARCH-ING.
CAN'T ESCAPE... DEAD MAN WALKING.
ALLRED
HE'S RIGHT, BATMAN! HOW CAN WE STOP A VILLAIN WHO ISN'T EVEN ALIVE?
THE POWER OF THE BATMOBILE MAY HELP--WE CAN HIT HIM WITH THE BAT-BEAM!
YES, BAT MAN. HIT ME.
HIT ME... WITH EVERYTHING YOU'VE GOT!!!
HA HA HAAAA!!!
THE BATMOBILE... UPENDED!?!

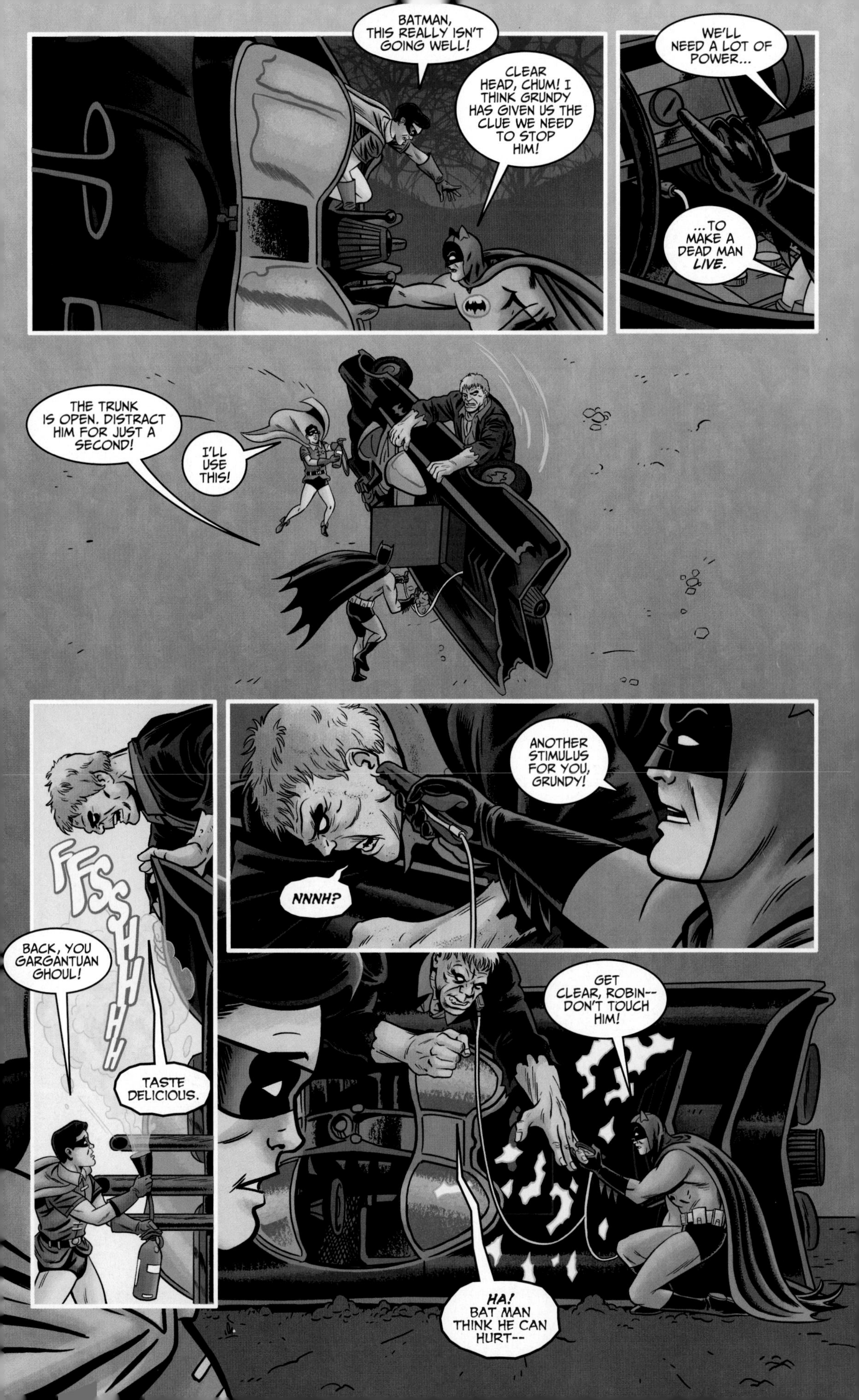
BATMAN, THIS REALLY ISN'T GOING WELL!
CLEAR HEAD, CHUM! I THINK GRUNDY HAS GIVEN US THE CLUE WE NEED TO STOP HIM!
WE'LL NEED A LOT OF POWER...
...TO MAKE A DEAD MAN *LIVE.*
THE TRUNK IS OPEN. DISTRACT HIM FOR JUST A SECOND!
I'LL USE THIS!
FFSSHHHHH
ANOTHER STIMULUS FOR YOU, GRUNDY!
*NNNH?*
BACK, YOU GARGANTUAN GHOUL!
TASTE DELICIOUS.
GET CLEAR, ROBIN-- DON'T TOUCH HIM!
*HA!* BAT MAN THINK HE CAN HURT--

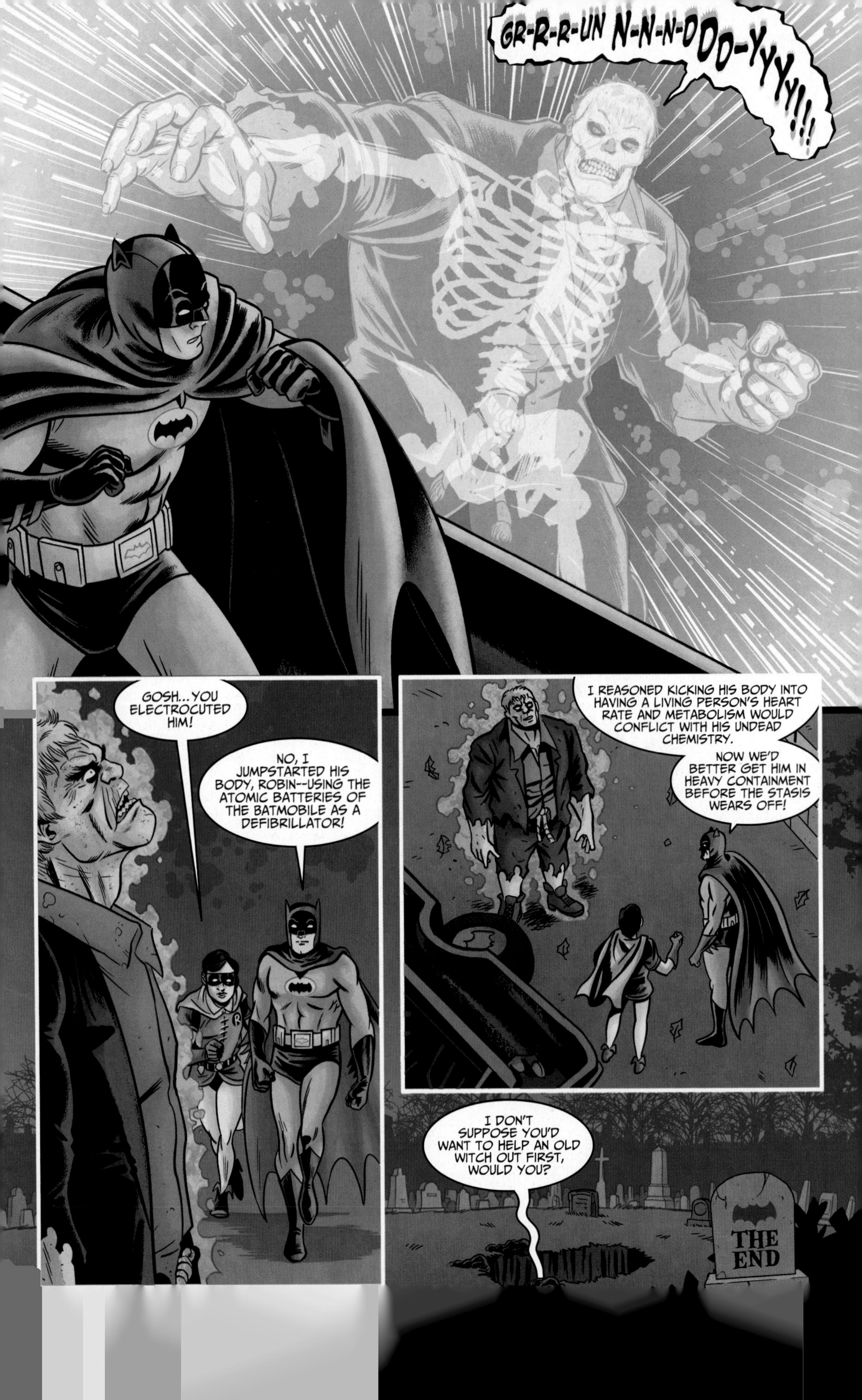
GR-R-R-UN N-N-N-DDD-YYY!!!
GOSH...YOU ELECTROCUTED HIM!
NO, I JUMPSTARTED HIS BODY, ROBIN--USING THE ATOMIC BATTERIES OF THE BATMOBILE AS A DEFIBRILLATOR!
I REASONED KICKING HIS BODY INTO HAVING A LIVING PERSON'S HEART RATE AND METABOLISM WOULD CONFLICT WITH HIS UNDEAD CHEMISTRY.
NOW WE'D BETTER GET HIM IN HEAVY CONTAINMENT BEFORE THE STASIS WEARS OFF!
I DON'T SUPPOSE YOU'D WANT TO HELP AN OLD WITCH OUT FIRST, WOULD YOU?
THE END

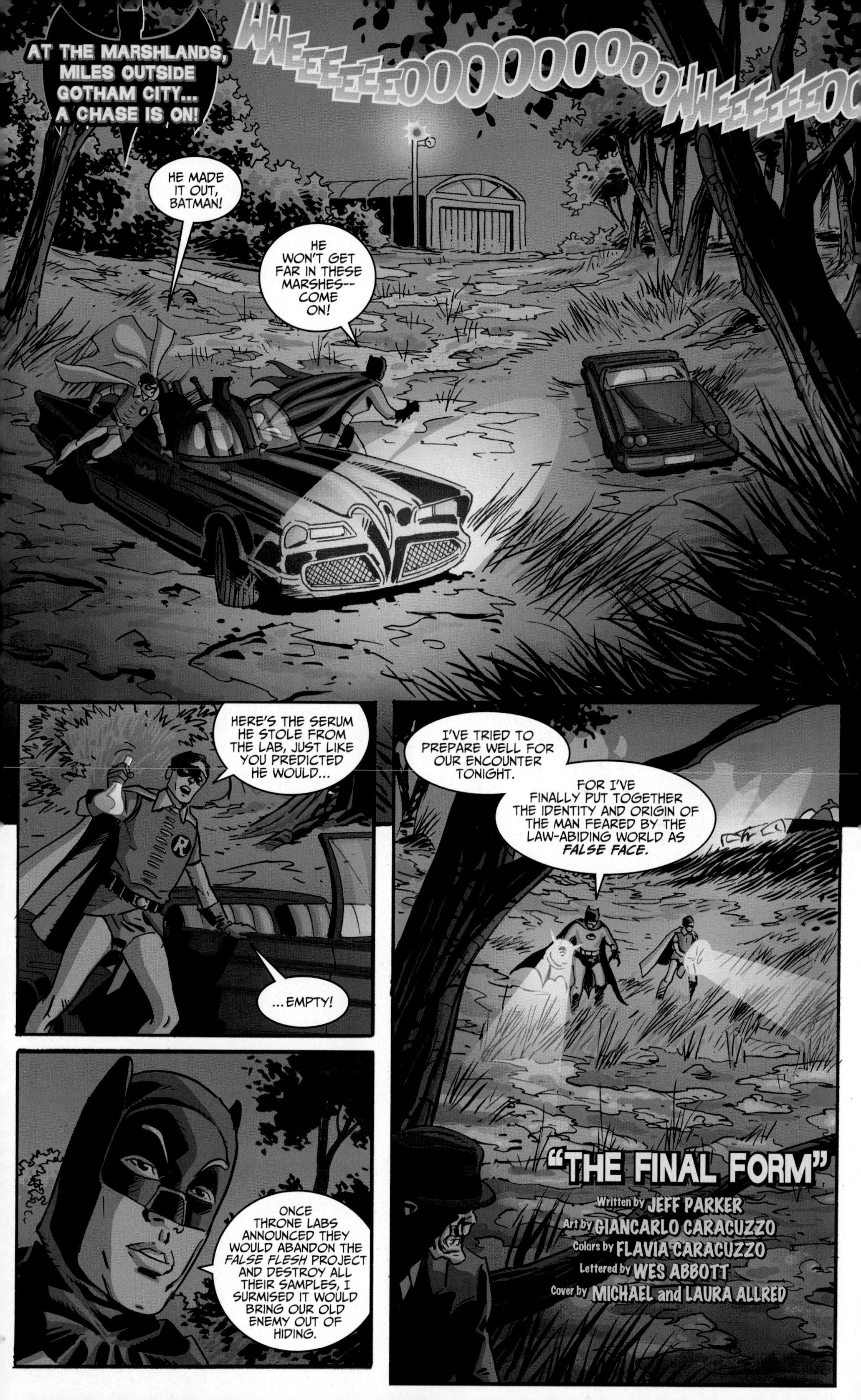
AT THE MARSHLANDS, MILES OUTSIDE GOTHAM CITY... A CHASE IS ON!
WWEEEEEOOOOOOOOOOWWEEEEEEOO
HE MADE IT OUT, BATMAN!
HE WON'T GET FAR IN THESE MARSHES-- COME ON!
HERE'S THE SERUM HE STOLE FROM THE LAB, JUST LIKE YOU PREDICTED HE WOULD...
...EMPTY!
ONCE THRONE LABS ANNOUNCED THEY WOULD ABANDON THE FALSE FLESH PROJECT AND DESTROY ALL THEIR SAMPLES, I SURMISED IT WOULD BRING OUR OLD ENEMY OUT OF HIDING.
I'VE TRIED TO PREPARE WELL FOR OUR ENCOUNTER TONIGHT.
FOR I'VE FINALLY PUT TOGETHER THE IDENTITY AND ORIGIN OF THE MAN FEARED BY THE LAW-ABIDING WORLD AS FALSE FACE.
"THE FINAL FORM"
Written by JEFF PARKER
Art by GIANCARLO CARACUZZO
Colors by FLAVIA CARACUZZO
Lettered by WES ABBOTT
Cover by MICHAEL and LAURA ALLRED

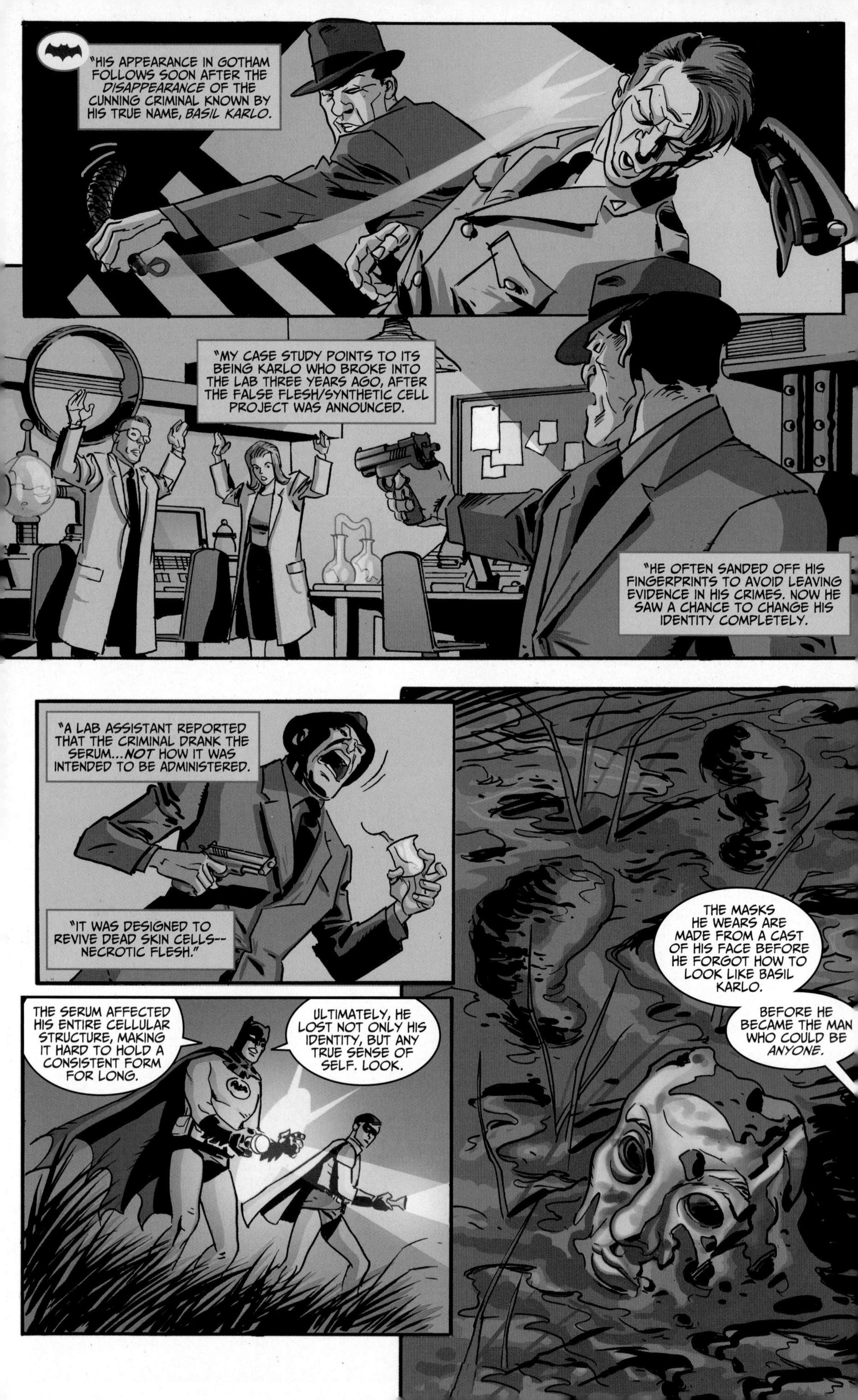
"HIS APPEARANCE IN GOTHAM FOLLOWS SOON AFTER THE *DISAPPEARANCE* OF THE CUNNING CRIMINAL KNOWN BY HIS TRUE NAME, *BASIL KARLO*.
"MY CASE STUDY POINTS TO ITS BEING KARLO WHO BROKE INTO THE LAB THREE YEARS AGO, AFTER THE FALSE FLESH/SYNTHETIC CELL PROJECT WAS ANNOUNCED.
"HE OFTEN SANDED OFF HIS FINGERPRINTS TO AVOID LEAVING EVIDENCE IN HIS CRIMES. NOW HE SAW A CHANCE TO CHANGE HIS IDENTITY COMPLETELY.
"A LAB ASSISTANT REPORTED THAT THE CRIMINAL DRANK THE SERUM...*NOT* HOW IT WAS INTENDED TO BE ADMINISTERED.
"IT WAS DESIGNED TO REVIVE DEAD SKIN CELLS--NECROTIC FLESH."
THE SERUM AFFECTED HIS ENTIRE CELLULAR STRUCTURE, MAKING IT HARD TO HOLD A CONSISTENT FORM FOR LONG.
ULTIMATELY, HE LOST NOT ONLY HIS IDENTITY, BUT ANY TRUE SENSE OF SELF. LOOK.
THE MASKS HE WEARS ARE MADE FROM A CAST OF HIS FACE BEFORE HE FORGOT HOW TO LOOK LIKE BASIL KARLO.
BEFORE HE BECAME THE MAN WHO COULD BE *ANYONE*.

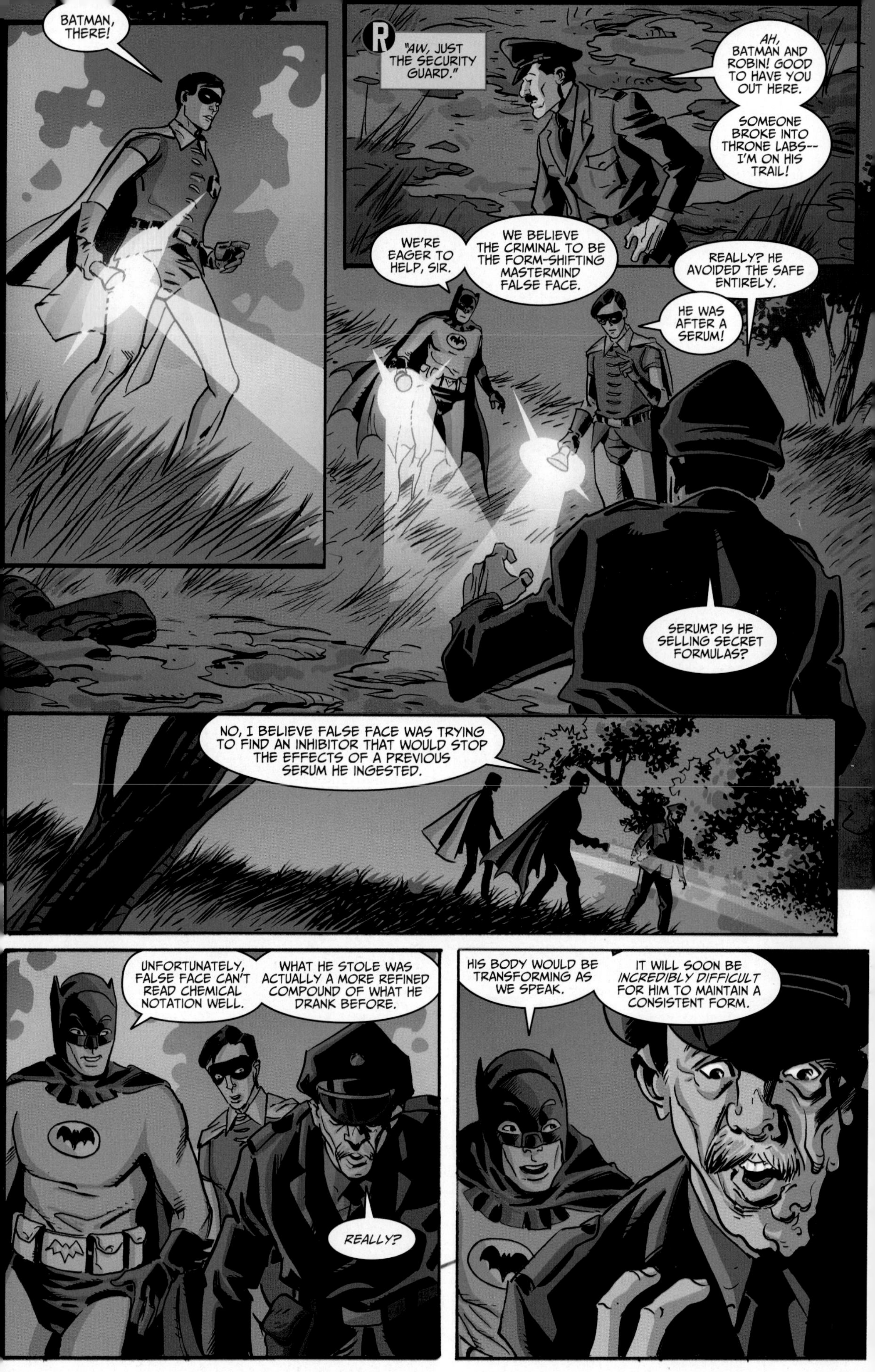
BATMAN, THERE!
"AW, JUST THE SECURITY GUARD."
AH, BATMAN AND ROBIN! GOOD TO HAVE YOU OUT HERE.
SOMEONE BROKE INTO THRONE LABS-- I'M ON HIS TRAIL!
WE'RE EAGER TO HELP, SIR.
WE BELIEVE THE CRIMINAL TO BE THE FORM-SHIFTING MASTERMIND FALSE FACE.
REALLY? HE AVOIDED THE SAFE ENTIRELY.
HE WAS AFTER A SERUM!
SERUM? IS HE SELLING SECRET FORMULAS?
NO, I BELIEVE FALSE FACE WAS TRYING TO FIND AN INHIBITOR THAT WOULD STOP THE EFFECTS OF A PREVIOUS SERUM HE INGESTED.
UNFORTUNATELY, FALSE FACE CAN'T READ CHEMICAL NOTATION WELL.
WHAT HE STOLE WAS ACTUALLY A MORE REFINED COMPOUND OF WHAT HE DRANK BEFORE.
REALLY?
HIS BODY WOULD BE TRANSFORMING AS WE SPEAK.
IT WILL SOON BE INCREDIBLY DIFFICULT FOR HIM TO MAINTAIN A CONSISTENT FORM.

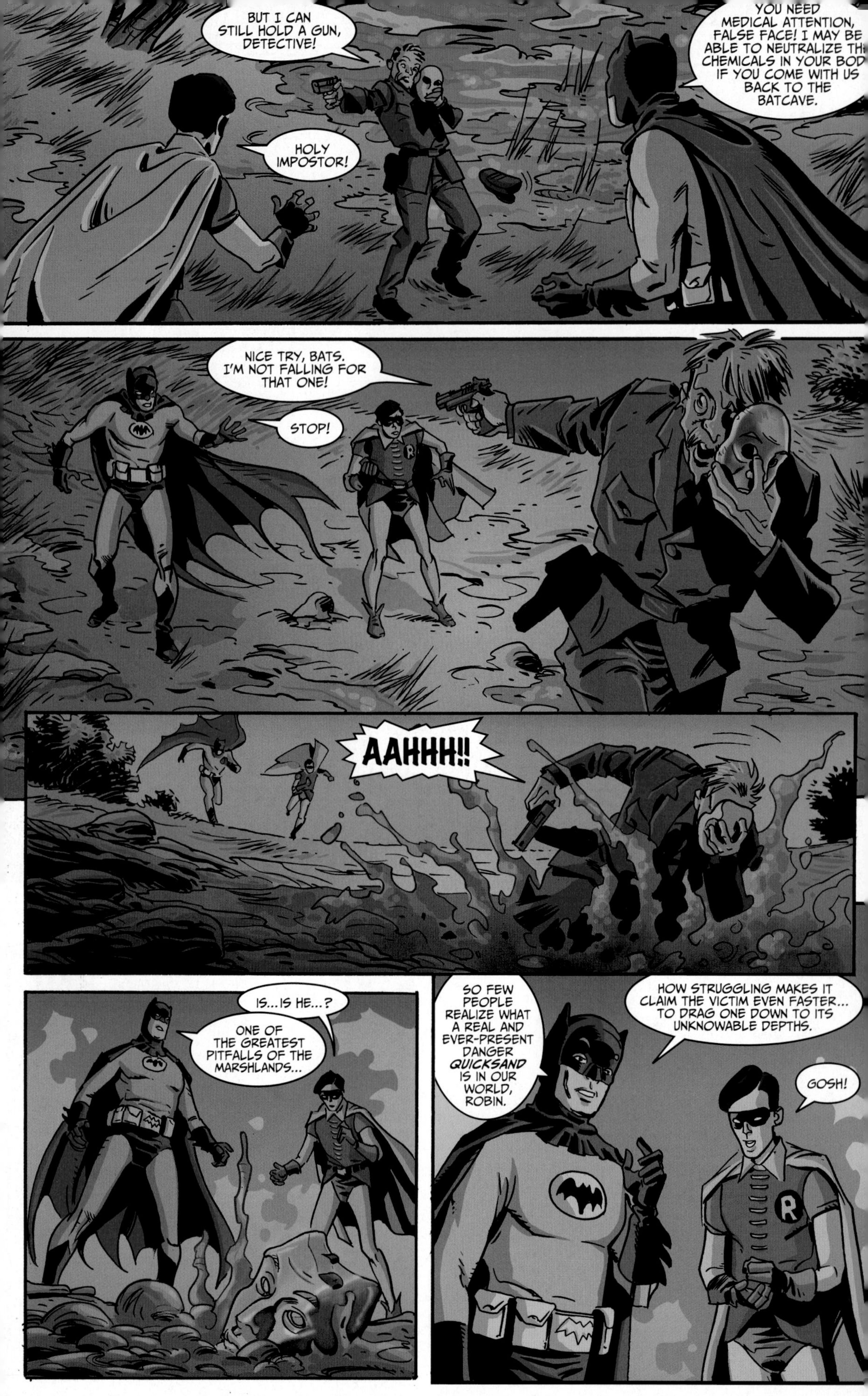
BUT I CAN STILL HOLD A GUN, DETECTIVE!
HOLY IMPOSTOR!
YOU NEED MEDICAL ATTENTION, FALSE FACE! I MAY BE ABLE TO NEUTRALIZE TH CHEMICALS IN YOUR BOD IF YOU COME WITH US BACK TO THE BATCAVE.
NICE TRY, BATS. I'M NOT FALLING FOR THAT ONE!
STOP!
AAHHH!!
IS...IS HE...?
ONE OF THE GREATEST PITFALLS OF THE MARSHLANDS...
SO FEW PEOPLE REALIZE WHAT A REAL AND EVER-PRESENT DANGER *QUICKSAND* IS IN OUR WORLD, ROBIN.
HOW STRUGGLING MAKES IT CLAIM THE VICTIM EVEN FASTER... TO DRAG ONE DOWN TO ITS UNKNOWABLE DEPTHS.
GOSH!

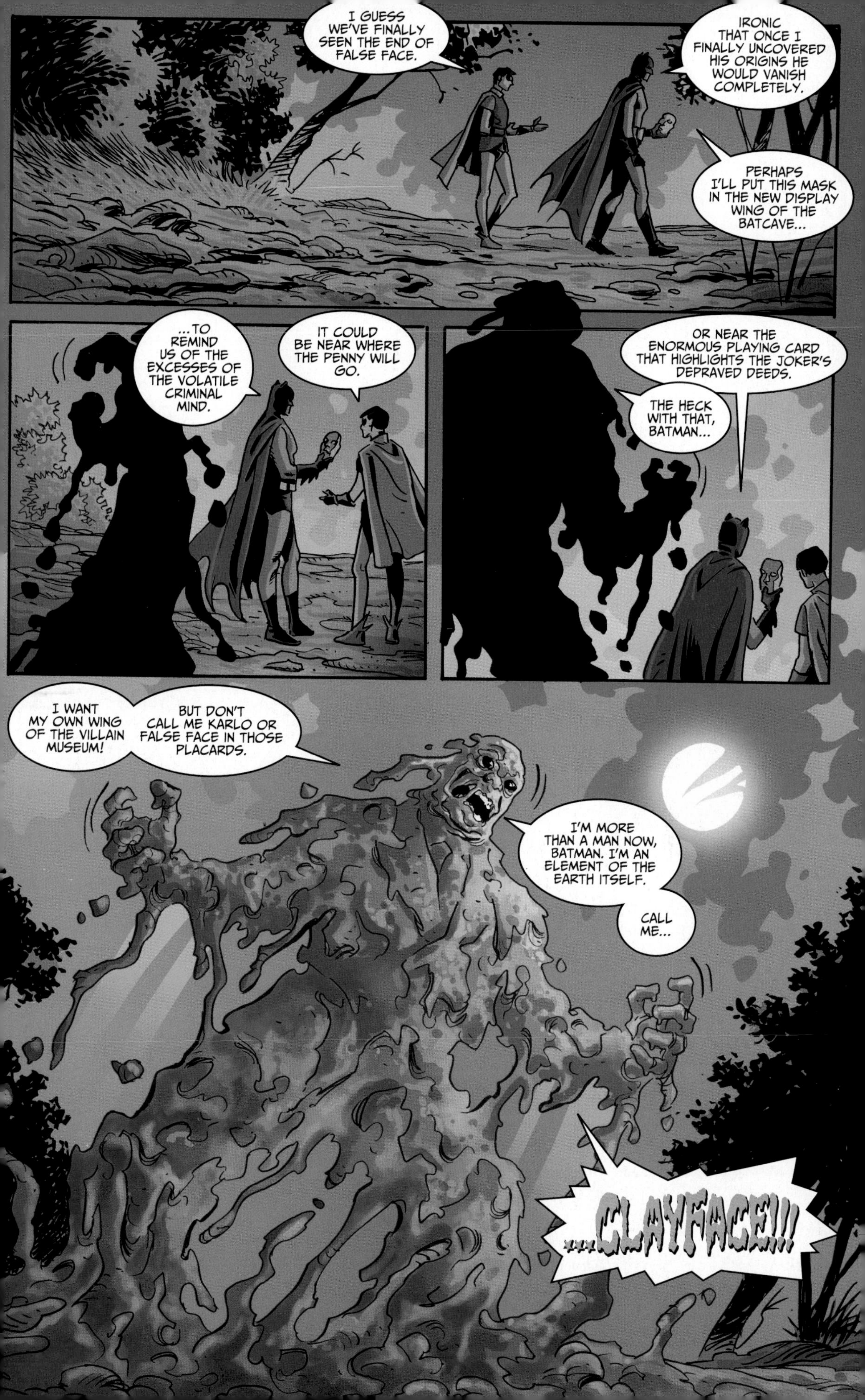

I GUESS WE'VE FINALLY SEEN THE END OF FALSE FACE.
IRONIC THAT ONCE I FINALLY UNCOVERED HIS ORIGINS HE WOULD VANISH COMPLETELY.
PERHAPS I'LL PUT THIS MASK IN THE NEW DISPLAY WING OF THE BATCAVE...
...TO REMIND US OF THE EXCESSES OF THE VOLATILE CRIMINAL MIND.
IT COULD BE NEAR WHERE THE PENNY WILL GO.
OR NEAR THE ENORMOUS PLAYING CARD THAT HIGHLIGHTS THE JOKER'S DEPRAVED DEEDS.
THE HECK WITH THAT, BATMAN...
I WANT MY OWN WING OF THE VILLAIN MUSEUM!
BUT DON'T CALL ME KARLO OR FALSE FACE IN THOSE PLACARDS.
I'M MORE THAN A MAN NOW, BATMAN. I'M AN ELEMENT OF THE EARTH ITSELF.
CALL ME...
...CLAYFACE!!!

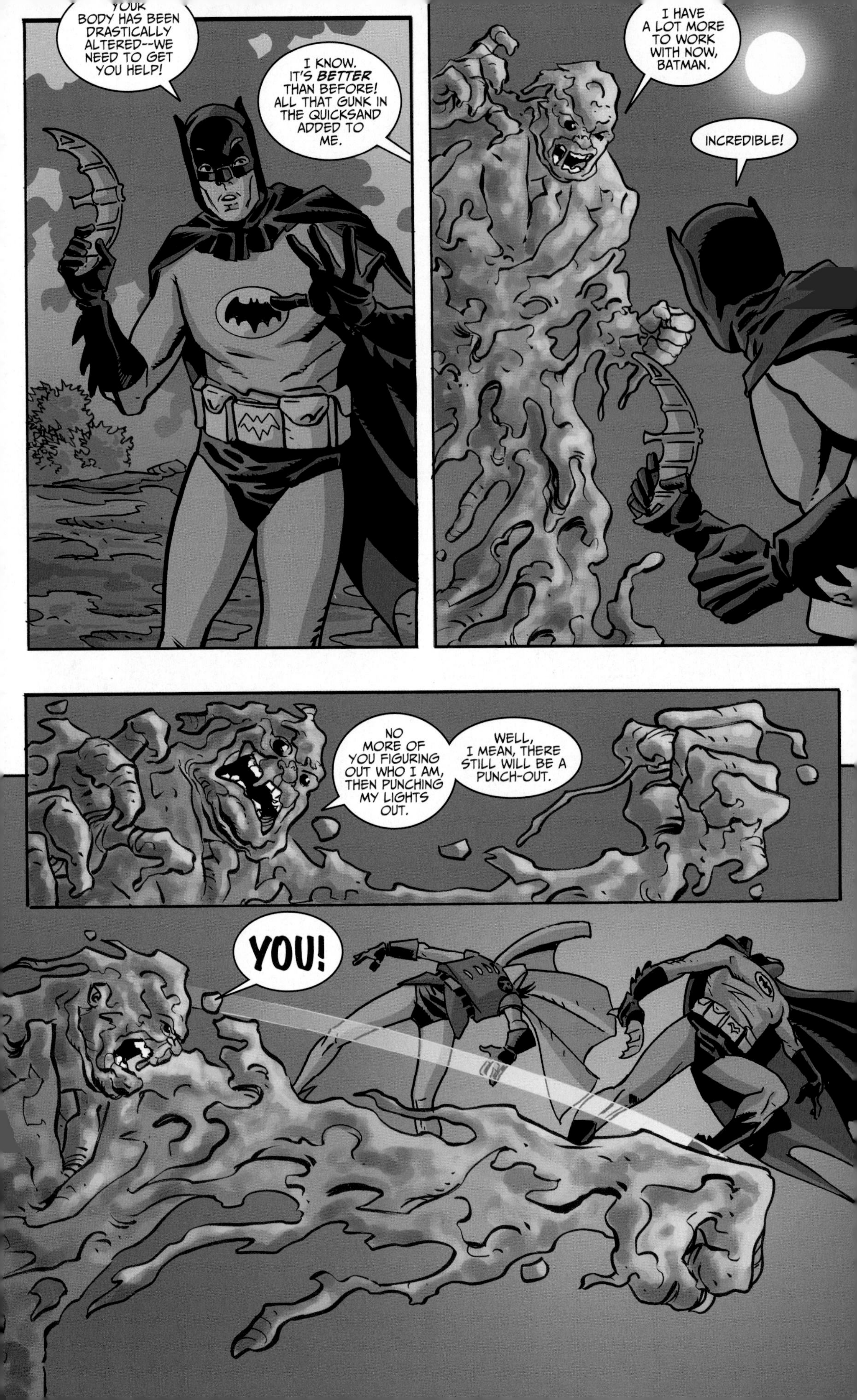
YOUR BODY HAS BEEN DRASTICALLY ALTERED--WE NEED TO GET YOU HELP!
I KNOW. IT'S **BETTER** THAN BEFORE! ALL THAT GUNK IN THE QUICKSAND ADDED TO ME.
I HAVE A LOT MORE TO WORK WITH NOW, BATMAN.
INCREDIBLE!
NO MORE OF YOU FIGURING OUT WHO I AM, THEN PUNCHING MY LIGHTS OUT.
WELL, I MEAN, THERE STILL WILL BE A PUNCH-OUT.
YOU!

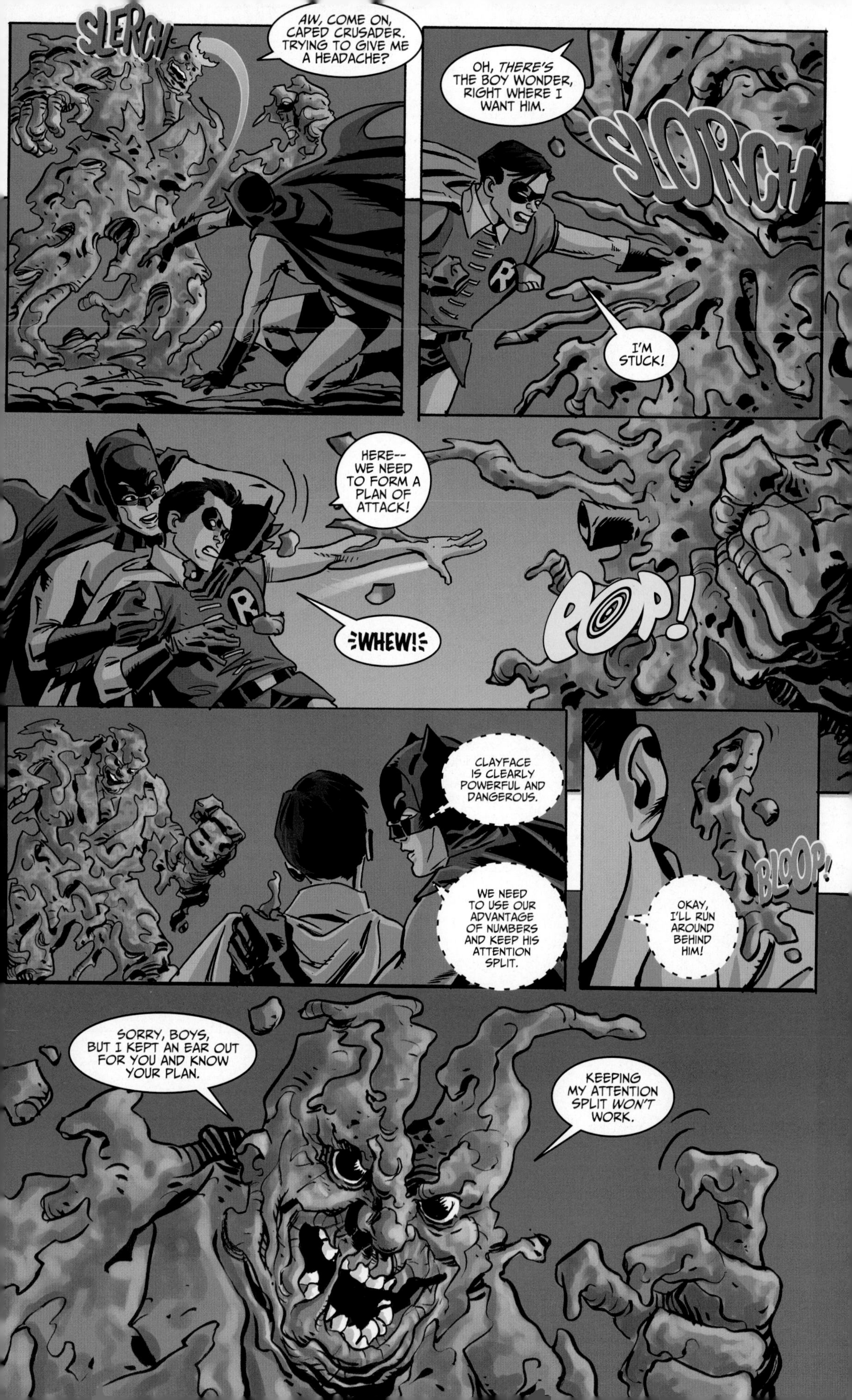
SLERCH
AW, COME ON, CAPED CRUSADER. TRYING TO GIVE ME A HEADACHE?
OH, *THERE'S* THE BOY WONDER, RIGHT WHERE I WANT HIM.
SLORCH
I'M STUCK!
HERE-- WE NEED TO FORM A PLAN OF ATTACK!
WHEW!
POP!
CLAYFACE IS CLEARLY POWERFUL AND DANGEROUS.
WE NEED TO USE OUR ADVANTAGE OF NUMBERS AND KEEP HIS ATTENTION SPLIT.
BLOOP!
OKAY, I'LL RUN AROUND BEHIND HIM!
SORRY, BOYS, BUT I KEPT AN EAR OUT FOR YOU AND KNOW YOUR PLAN.
KEEPING MY ATTENTION SPLIT *WON'T* WORK.

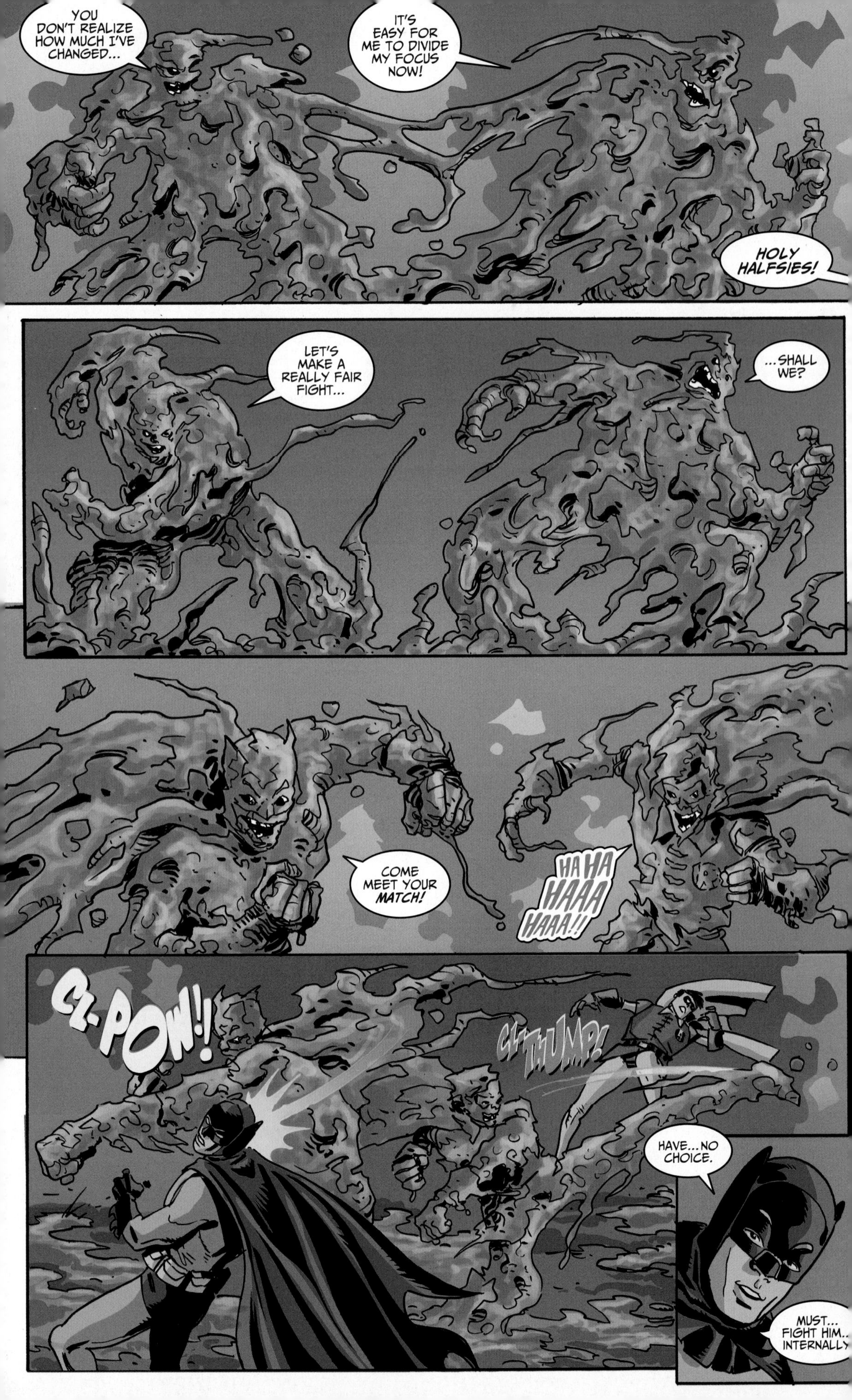
YOU DON'T REALIZE HOW MUCH I'VE CHANGED...
IT'S EASY FOR ME TO DIVIDE MY FOCUS NOW!
HOLY HALFSIES!
LET'S MAKE A REALLY FAIR FIGHT...
...SHALL WE?
COME MEET YOUR MATCH!
HA HA HAAA HAAA!!
CL-POW!!
CL-THUMP!
HAVE...NO CHOICE.
MUST... FIGHT HIM... INTERNALLY

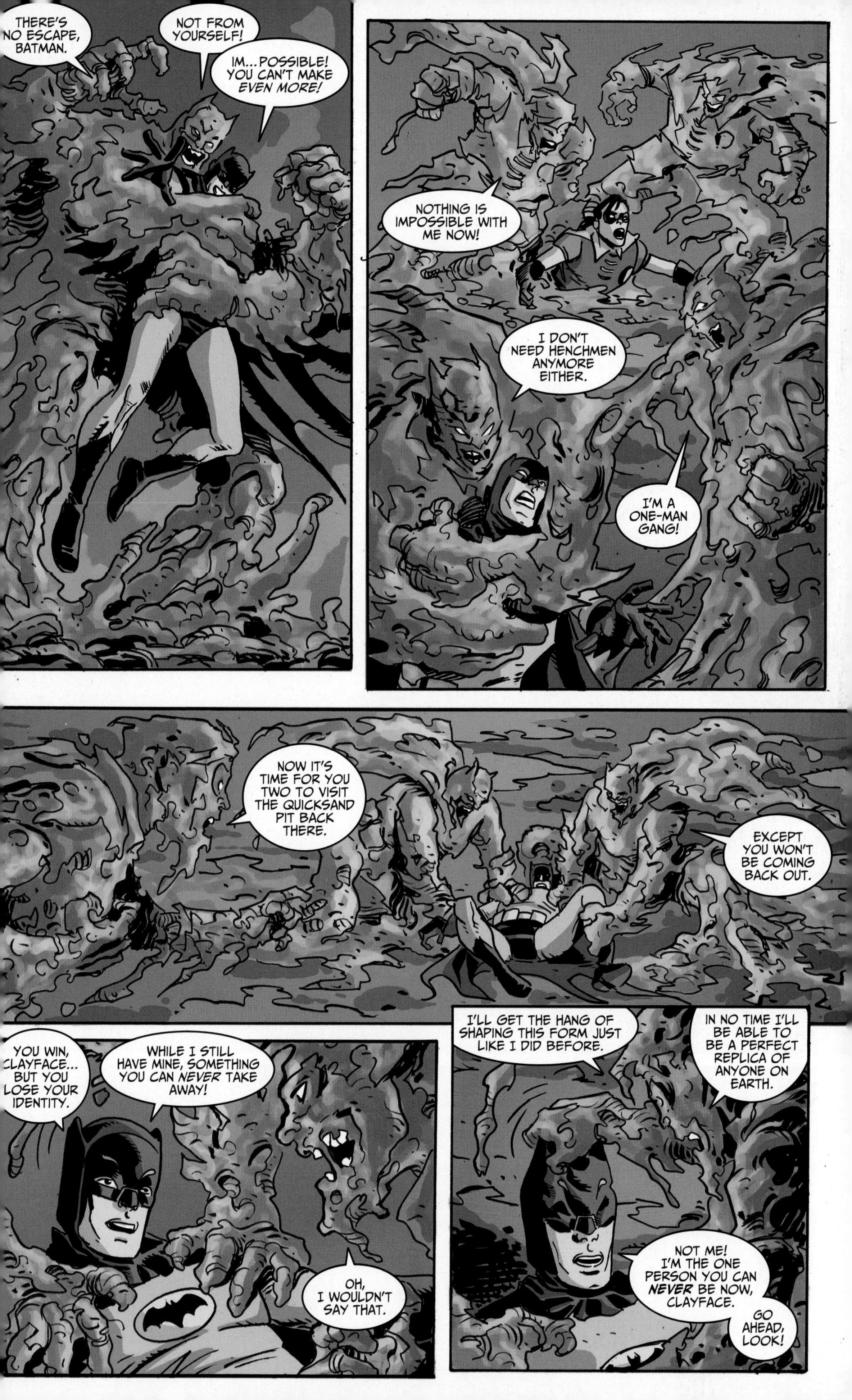
THERE'S NO ESCAPE, BATMAN.
NOT FROM YOURSELF!
IM...POSSIBLE! YOU CAN'T MAKE EVEN MORE!
NOTHING IS IMPOSSIBLE WITH ME NOW!
I DON'T NEED HENCHMEN ANYMORE EITHER.
I'M A ONE-MAN GANG!
NOW IT'S TIME FOR YOU TWO TO VISIT THE QUICKSAND PIT BACK THERE.
EXCEPT YOU WON'T BE COMING BACK OUT.
YOU WIN, CLAYFACE... BUT YOU LOSE YOUR IDENTITY.
WHILE I STILL HAVE MINE, SOMETHING YOU CAN NEVER TAKE AWAY!
OH, I WOULDN'T SAY THAT.
I'LL GET THE HANG OF SHAPING THIS FORM JUST LIKE I DID BEFORE.
IN NO TIME I'LL BE ABLE TO BE A PERFECT REPLICA OF ANYONE ON EARTH.
NOT ME! I'M THE ONE PERSON YOU CAN NEVER BE NOW, CLAYFACE.
GO AHEAD, LOOK!

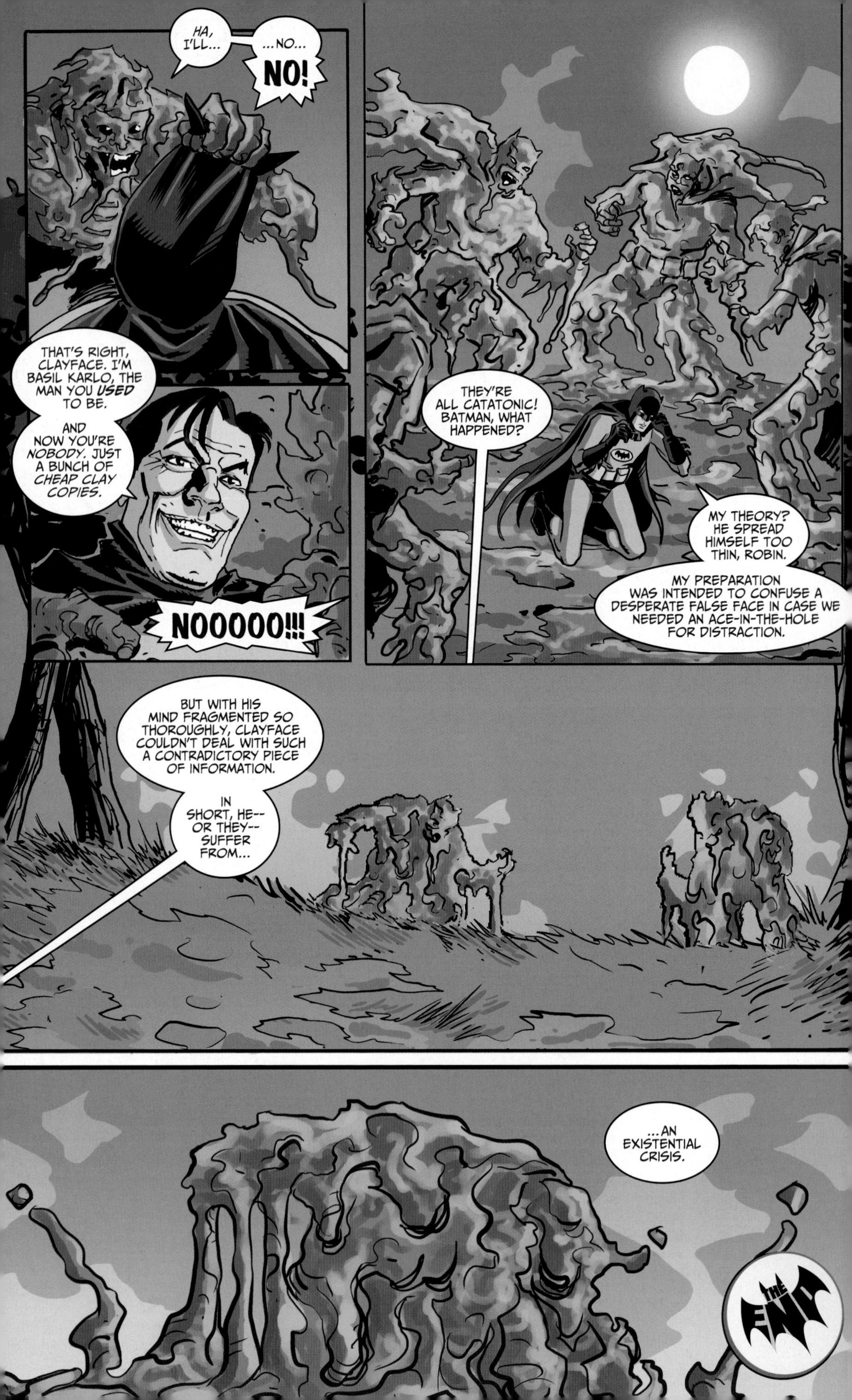
HA, I'LL...
...NO...
NO!
THAT'S RIGHT, CLAYFACE. I'M BASIL KARLO, THE MAN YOU *USED* TO BE.
AND NOW YOU'RE *NOBODY*. JUST A BUNCH OF *CHEAP CLAY COPIES*.
NOOOOO!!!
THEY'RE ALL CATATONIC! BATMAN, WHAT HAPPENED?
MY THEORY? HE SPREAD HIMSELF TOO THIN, ROBIN.
MY PREPARATION WAS INTENDED TO CONFUSE A DESPERATE FALSE FACE IN CASE WE NEEDED AN ACE-IN-THE-HOLE FOR DISTRACTION.
BUT WITH HIS MIND FRAGMENTED SO THOROUGHLY, CLAYFACE COULDN'T DEAL WITH SUCH A CONTRADICTORY PIECE OF INFORMATION.
IN SHORT, HE-- OR THEY-- SUFFER FROM...
...AN EXISTENTIAL CRISIS.
THE END

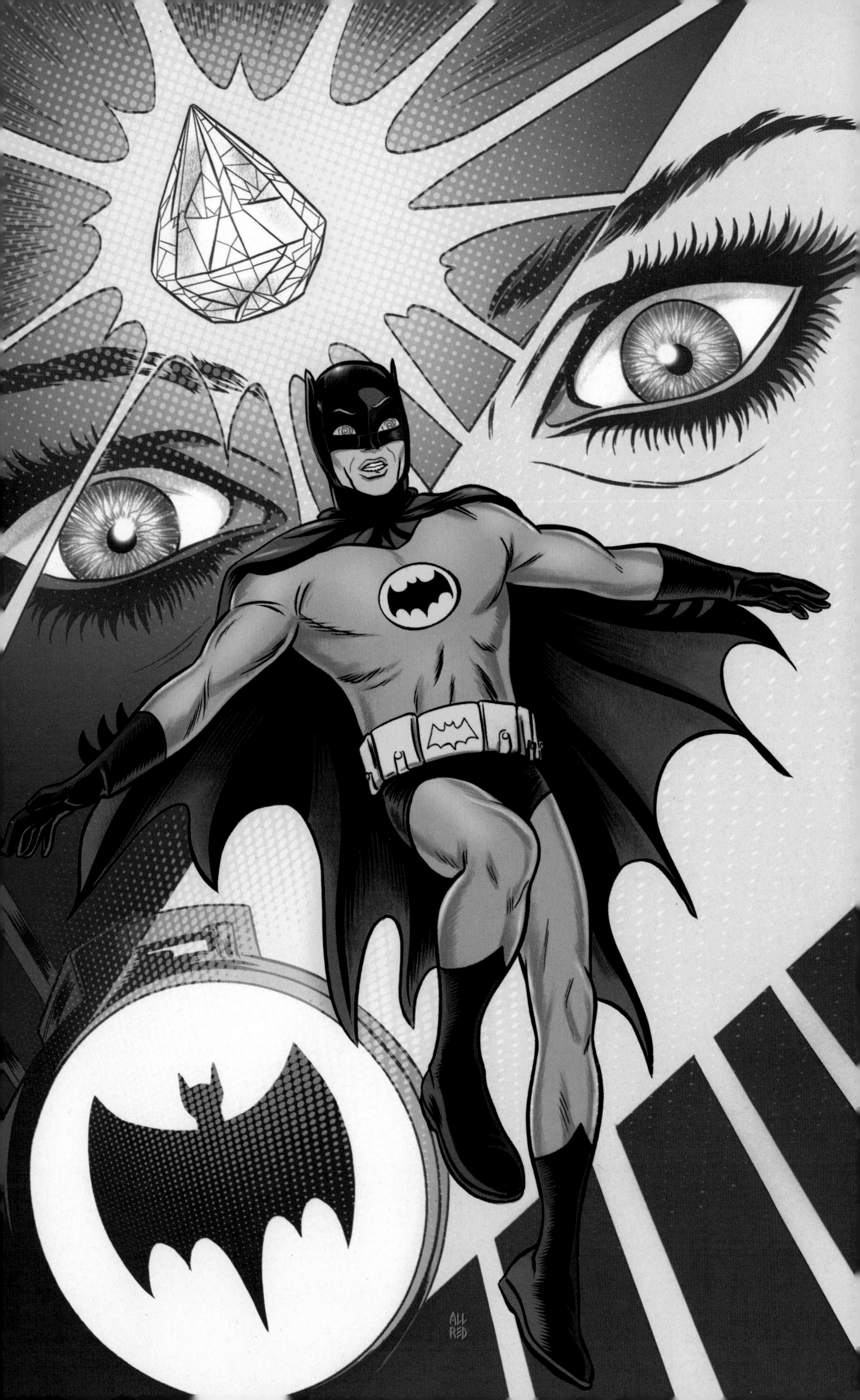
ALL
RED

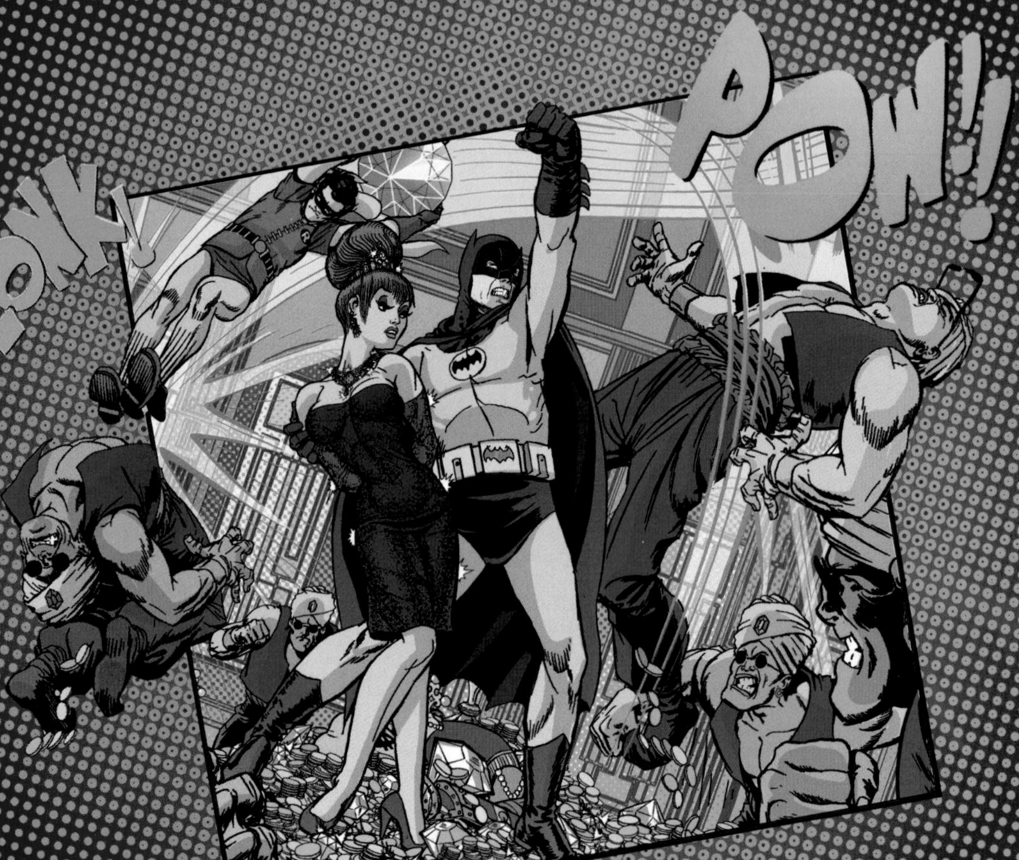
ZLONK!
POW!!

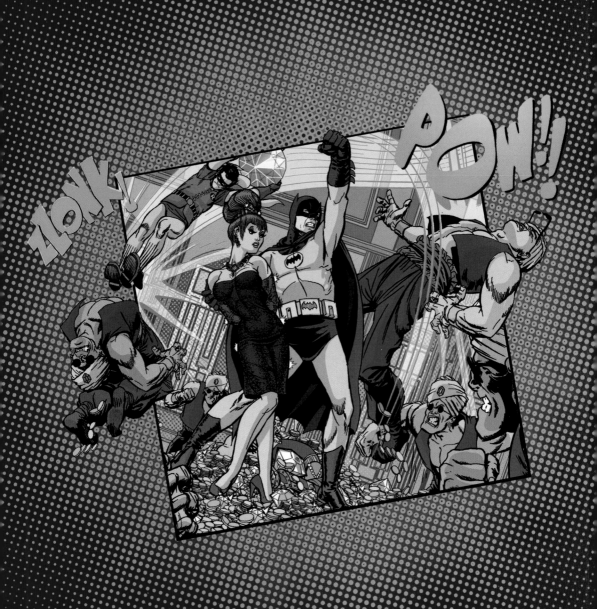

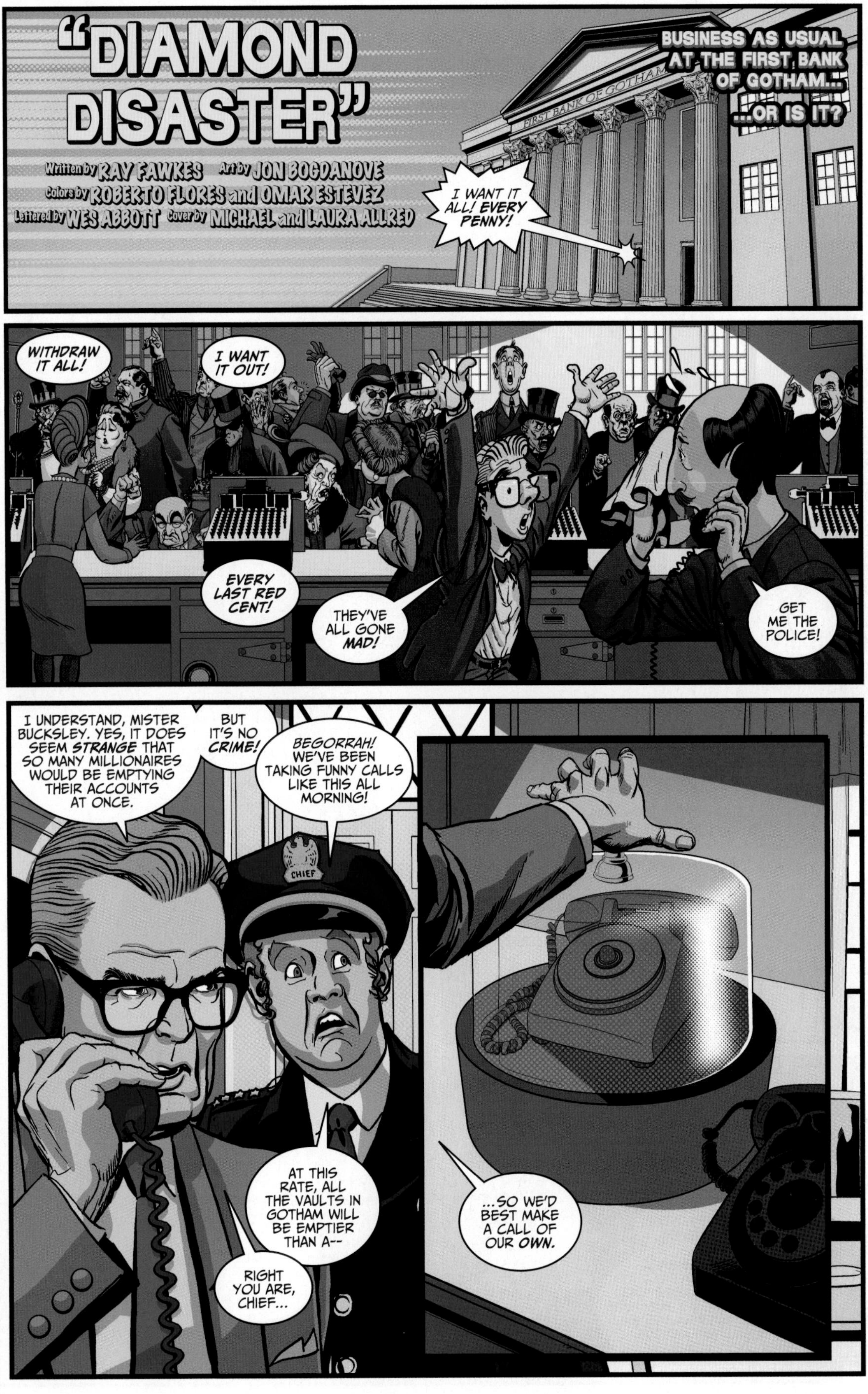
"DIAMOND DISASTER"
Written by RAY FAWKES Art by JON BOGDANOVE
Colors by ROBERTO FLORES and OMAR ESTEVEZ
Lettered by WES ABBOTT Cover by MICHAEL and LAURA ALLRED
BUSINESS AS USUAL AT THE FIRST BANK OF GOTHAM... ...OR IS IT?
FIRST BANK OF GOTHAM
I WANT IT ALL! EVERY PENNY!
WITHDRAW IT ALL!
I WANT IT OUT!
EVERY LAST RED CENT!
THEY'VE ALL GONE MAD!
GET ME THE POLICE!
I UNDERSTAND, MISTER BUCKSLEY. YES, IT DOES SEEM STRANGE THAT SO MANY MILLIONAIRES WOULD BE EMPTYING THEIR ACCOUNTS AT ONCE.
BUT IT'S NO CRIME!
BEGORRAH! WE'VE BEEN TAKING FUNNY CALLS LIKE THIS ALL MORNING!
CHIEF
AT THIS RATE, ALL THE VAULTS IN GOTHAM WILL BE EMPTIER THAN A--
RIGHT YOU ARE, CHIEF...
...SO WE'D BEST MAKE A CALL OF OUR OWN.

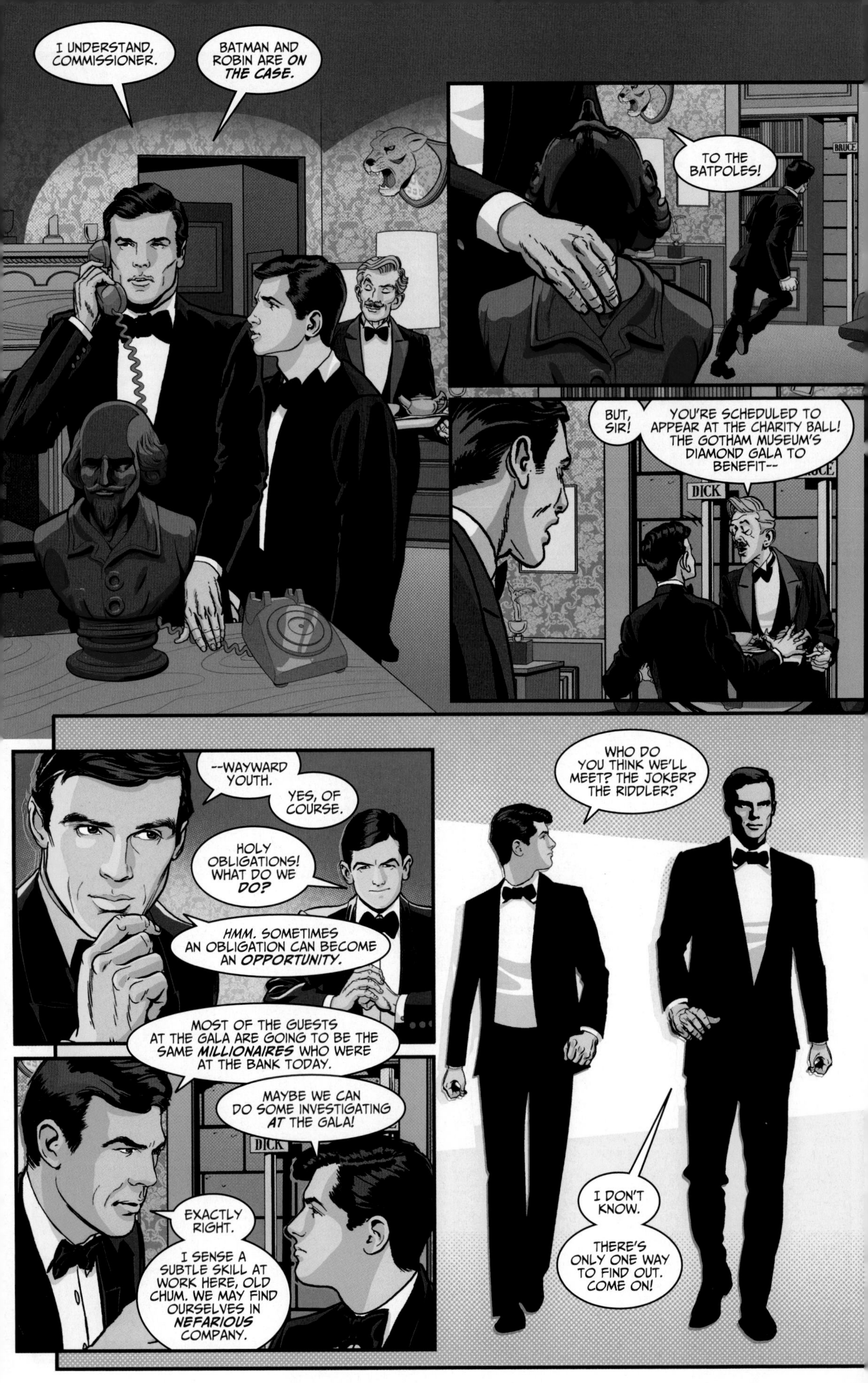

I UNDERSTAND, COMMISSIONER.
BATMAN AND ROBIN ARE *ON THE CASE.*
TO THE BATPOLES!
BRUCE
BUT, SIR!
YOU'RE SCHEDULED TO APPEAR AT THE CHARITY BALL! THE GOTHAM MUSEUM'S DIAMOND GALA TO BENEFIT--
DICK
--WAYWARD YOUTH.
YES, OF COURSE.
HOLY OBLIGATIONS! WHAT DO WE *DO?*
*HMM.* SOMETIMES AN OBLIGATION CAN BECOME AN *OPPORTUNITY.*
MOST OF THE GUESTS AT THE GALA ARE GOING TO BE THE SAME *MILLIONAIRES* WHO WERE AT THE BANK TODAY.
MAYBE WE CAN DO SOME INVESTIGATING *AT* THE GALA!
DICK
EXACTLY RIGHT.
I SENSE A SUBTLE SKILL AT WORK HERE, OLD CHUM. WE MAY FIND OURSELVES IN *NEFARIOUS* COMPANY.
WHO DO YOU THINK WE'LL MEET? THE JOKER? THE RIDDLER?
I DON'T KNOW.
THERE'S ONLY ONE WAY TO FIND OUT. COME ON!

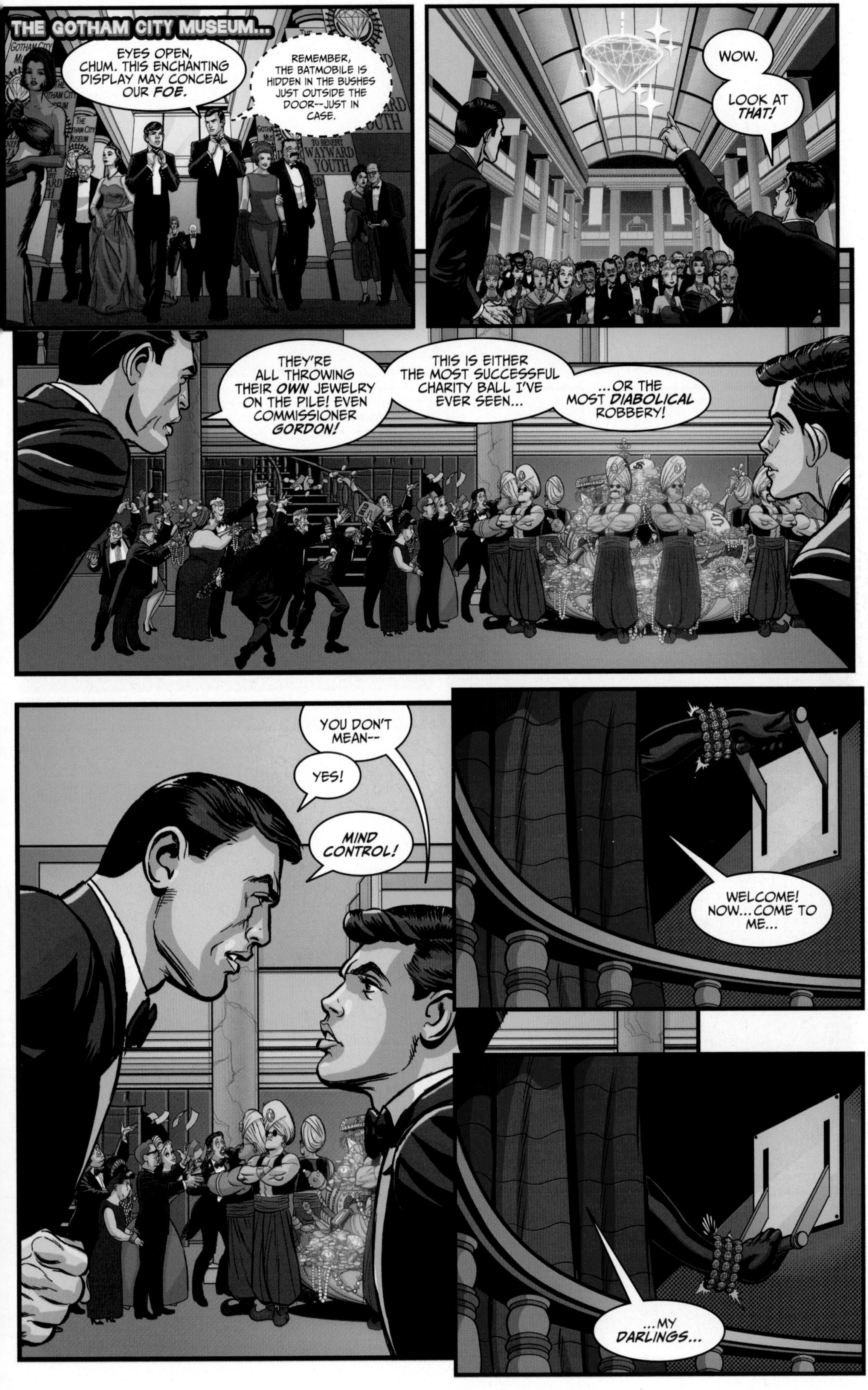
THE GOTHAM CITY MUSEUM...
EYES OPEN, CHUM. THIS ENCHANTING DISPLAY MAY CONCEAL OUR FOE.
REMEMBER, THE BATMOBILE IS HIDDEN IN THE BUSHES JUST OUTSIDE THE DOOR--JUST IN CASE.
TO BENEFIT WAYWARD YOUTH
WOW.
LOOK AT THAT!
THEY'RE ALL THROWING THEIR OWN JEWELRY ON THE PILE! EVEN COMMISSIONER GORDON!
THIS IS EITHER THE MOST SUCCESSFUL CHARITY BALL I'VE EVER SEEN...
...OR THE MOST DIABOLICAL ROBBERY!
YOU DON'T MEAN--
YES!
MIND CONTROL!
WELCOME! NOW...COME TO ME...
...MY DARLINGS...

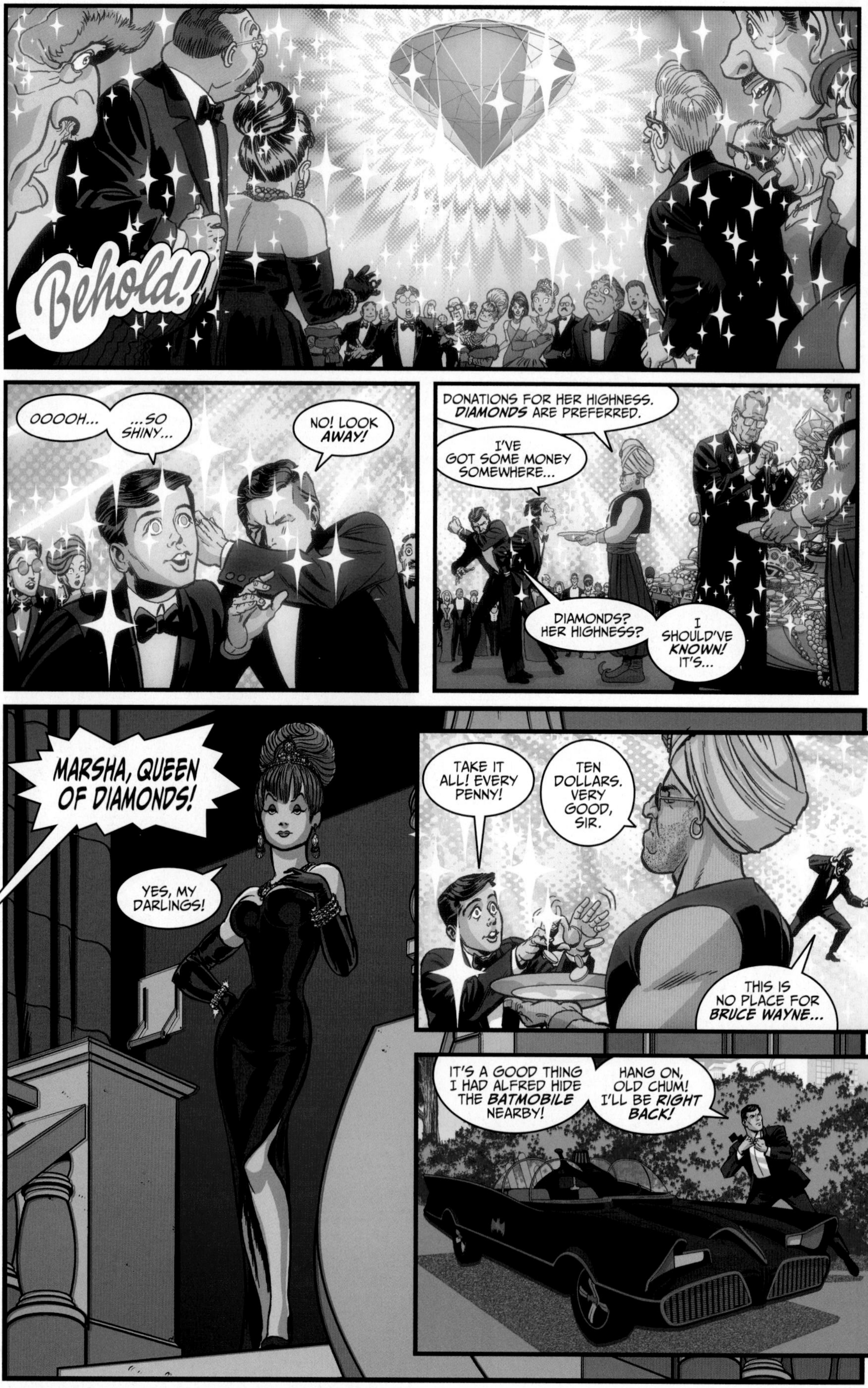
Behold!
OOOOH...
...SO SHINY...
NO! LOOK AWAY!
DONATIONS FOR HER HIGHNESS. DIAMONDS ARE PREFERRED.
I'VE GOT SOME MONEY SOMEWHERE...
DIAMONDS? HER HIGHNESS?
I SHOULD'VE KNOWN! IT'S...
MARSHA, QUEEN OF DIAMONDS!
YES, MY DARLINGS!
TAKE IT ALL! EVERY PENNY!
TEN DOLLARS. VERY GOOD, SIR.
THIS IS NO PLACE FOR BRUCE WAYNE...
IT'S A GOOD THING I HAD ALFRED HIDE THE BATMOBILE NEARBY!
HANG ON, OLD CHUM! I'LL BE RIGHT BACK!

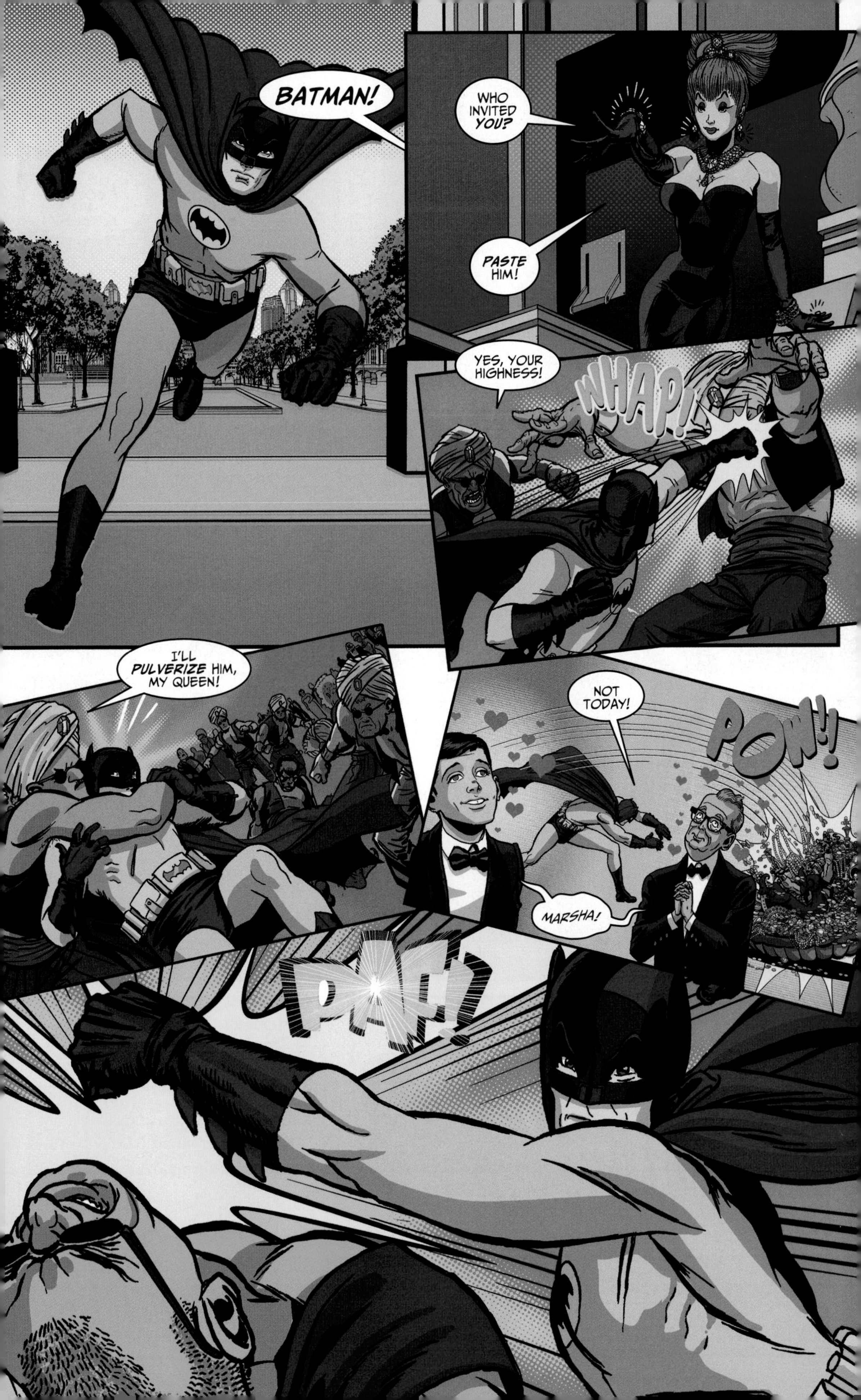

BATMAN!
WHO INVITED YOU?
PASTE HIM!
YES, YOUR HIGHNESS!
WHAP!
I'LL PULVERIZE HIM, MY QUEEN!
NOT TODAY!
POW!!
MARSHA!
PAF!

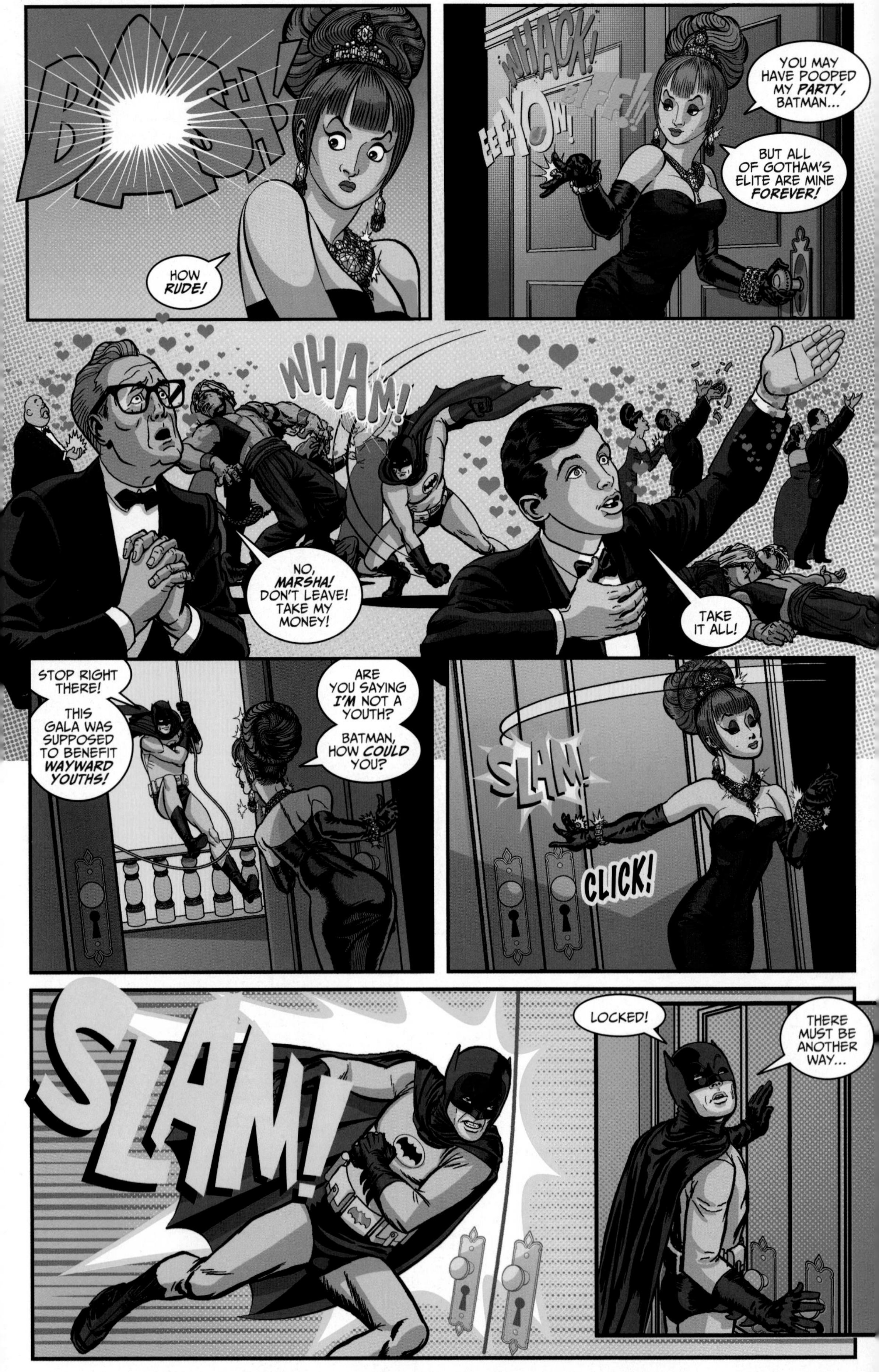
BLASH!
HOW RUDE!
WHACK!
EEEYOW!
BIFF!!
YOU MAY HAVE POOPED MY PARTY, BATMAN...
BUT ALL OF GOTHAM'S ELITE ARE MINE FOREVER!
WHAM!
NO, MARSHA! DON'T LEAVE! TAKE MY MONEY!
TAKE IT ALL!
STOP RIGHT THERE!
THIS GALA WAS SUPPOSED TO BENEFIT WAYWARD YOUTHS!
ARE YOU SAYING I'M NOT A YOUTH?
BATMAN, HOW COULD YOU?
SLAM!
CLICK!
SLAM!
LOCKED!
THERE MUST BE ANOTHER WAY...

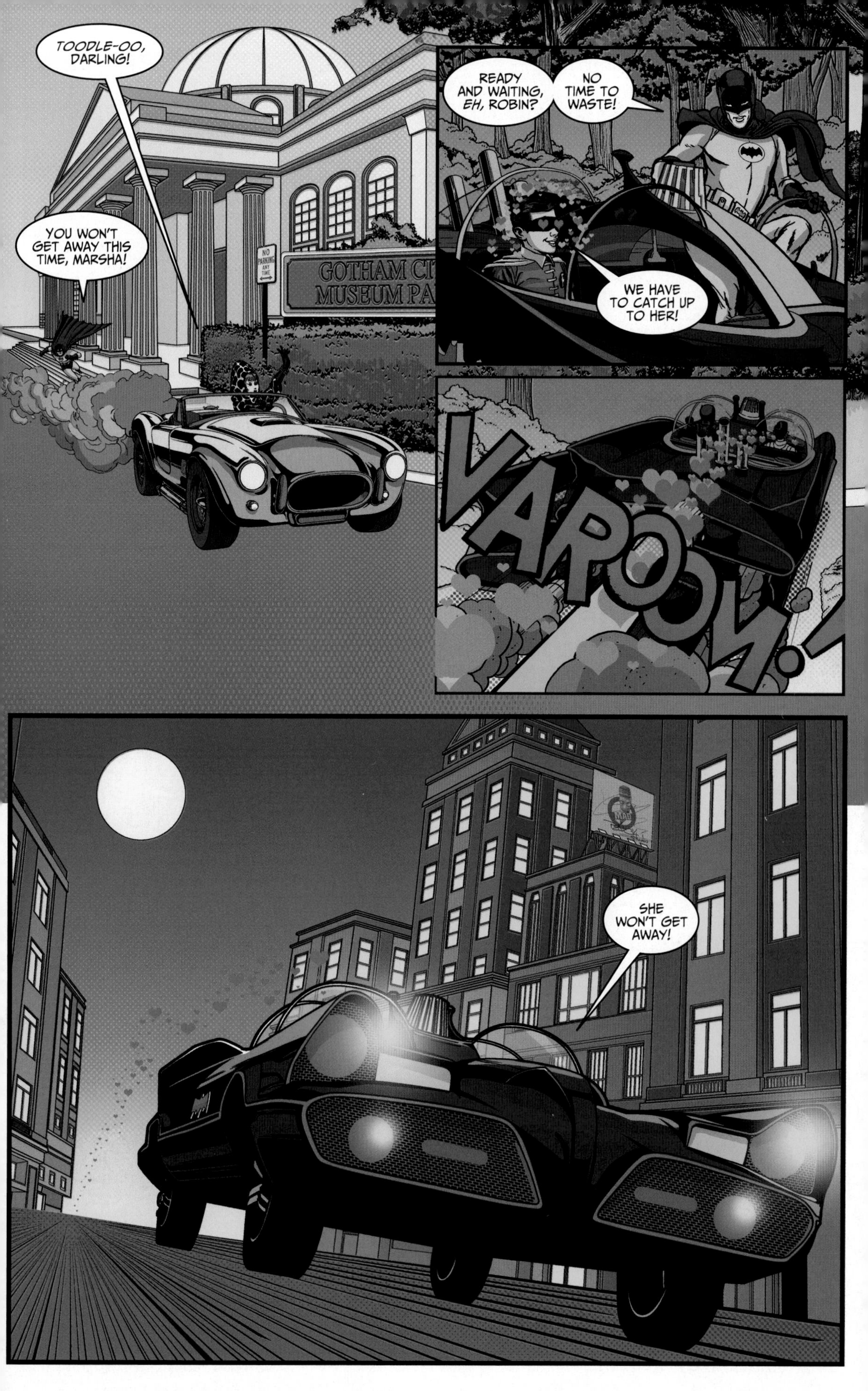
TOODLE-OO, DARLING!
YOU WON'T GET AWAY THIS TIME, MARSHA!
NO PARKING ANY TIME
READY AND WAITING, EH, ROBIN?
NO TIME TO WASTE!
WE HAVE TO CATCH UP TO HER!
VAROOM!
SHE WON'T GET AWAY!

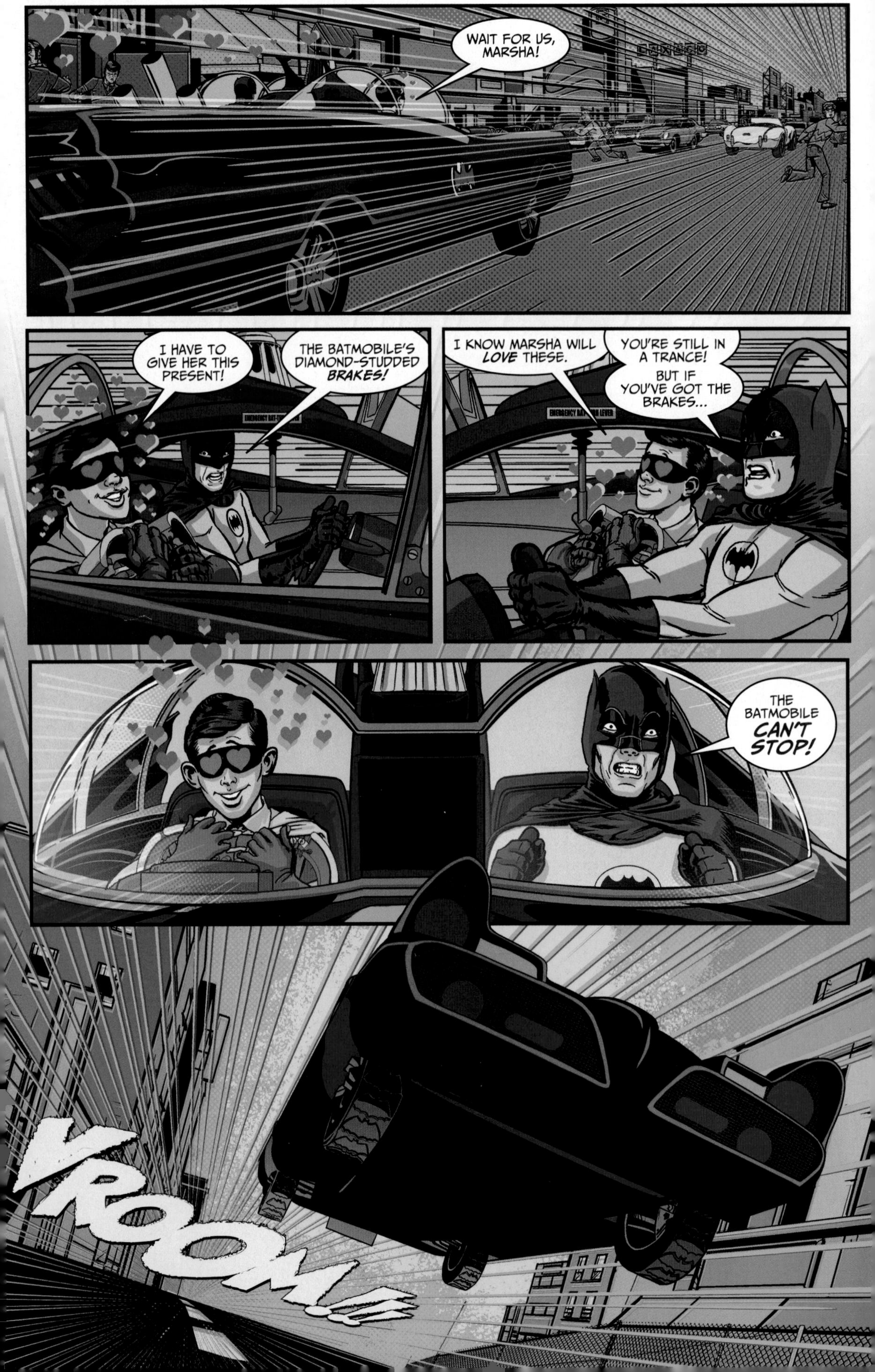
WAIT FOR US, MARSHA!
I HAVE TO GIVE HER THIS PRESENT!
THE BATMOBILE'S DIAMOND-STUDDED BRAKES!
I KNOW MARSHA WILL LOVE THESE.
YOU'RE STILL IN A TRANCE!
BUT IF YOU'VE GOT THE BRAKES...
THE BATMOBILE CAN'T STOP!
VROOM!!!

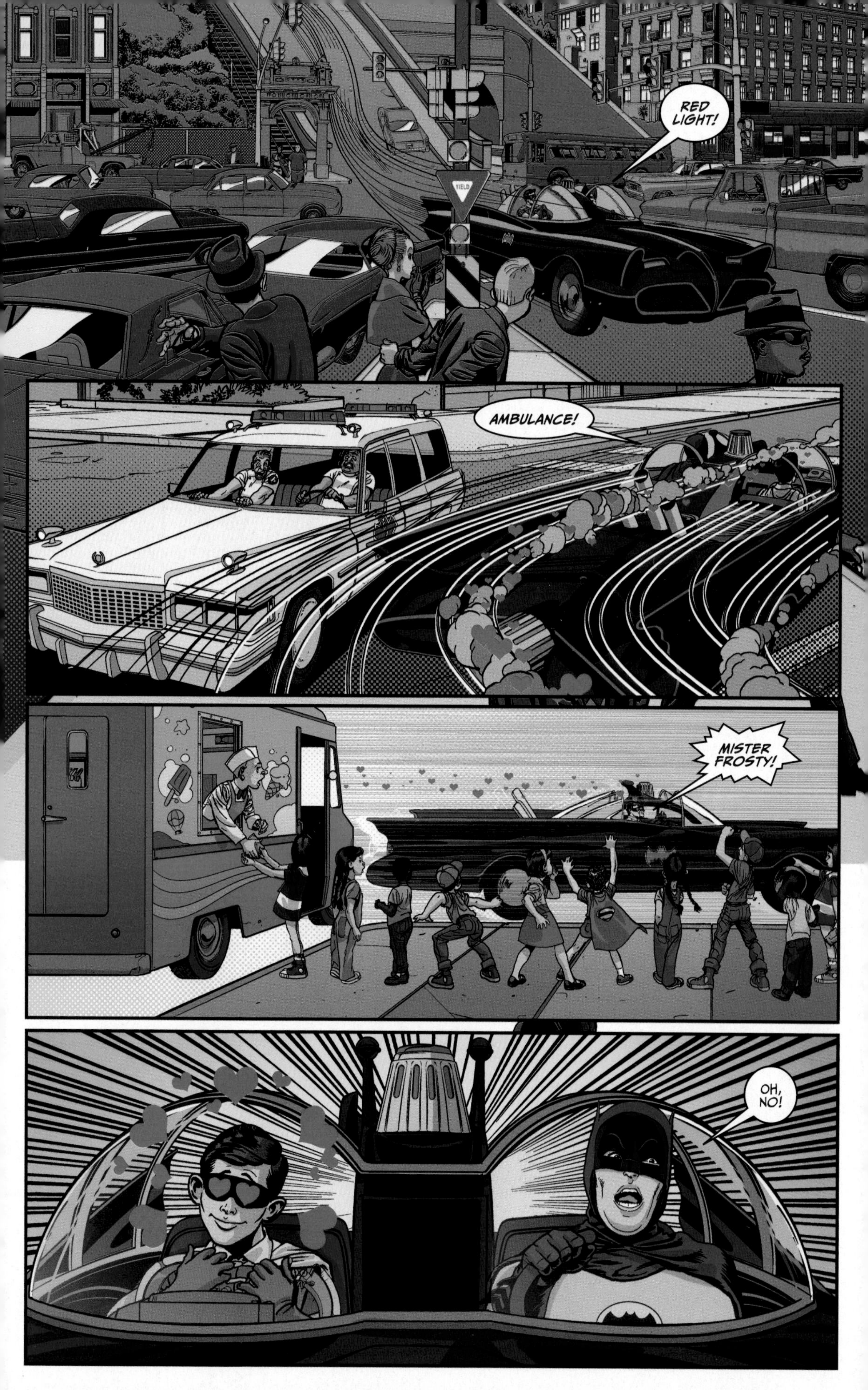
RED LIGHT!
YIELD
AMBULANCE!
MISTER FROSTY!
OH, NO!

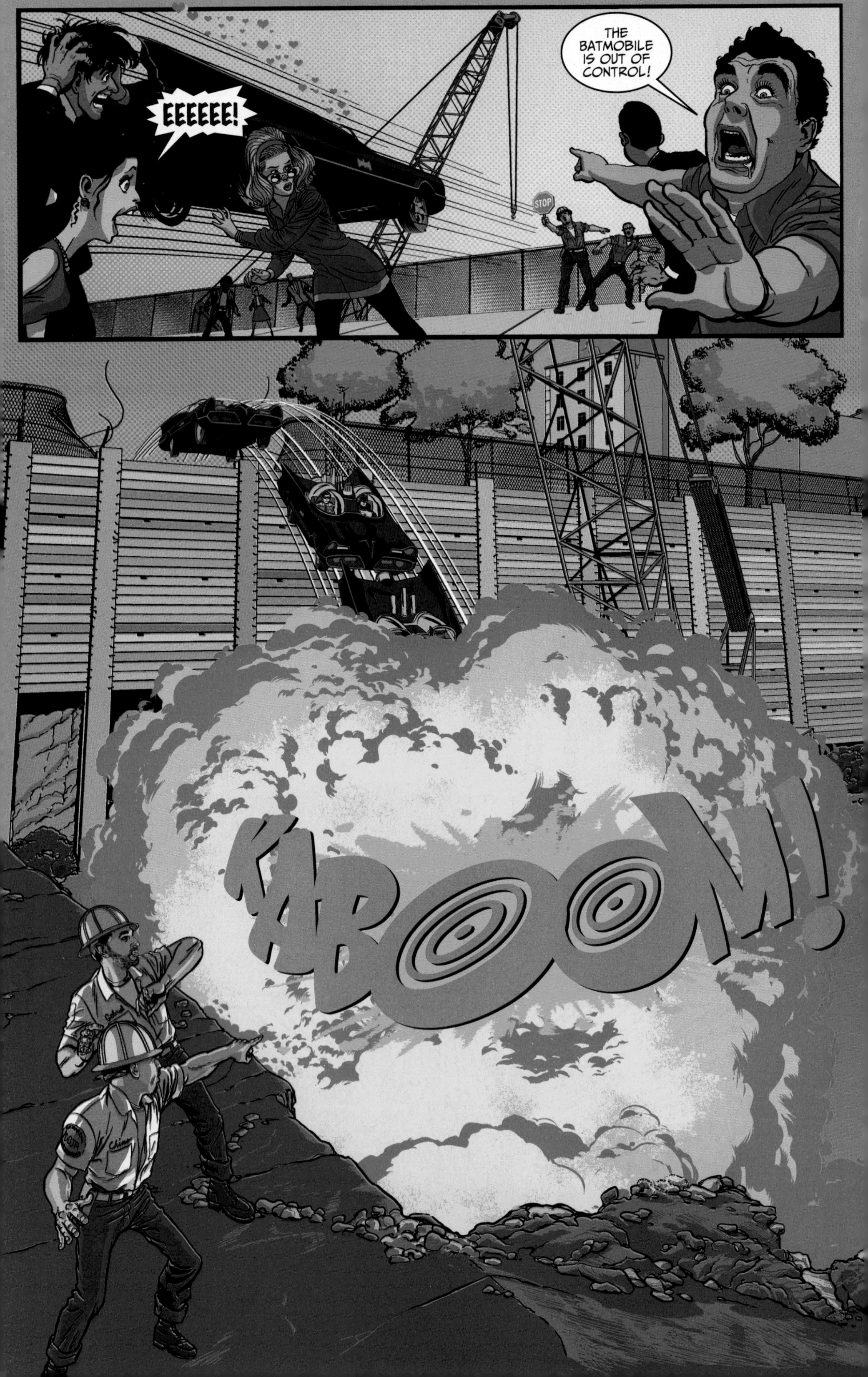
EEEEEE!
THE BATMOBILE IS OUT OF CONTROL!
STOP
KABOOM!

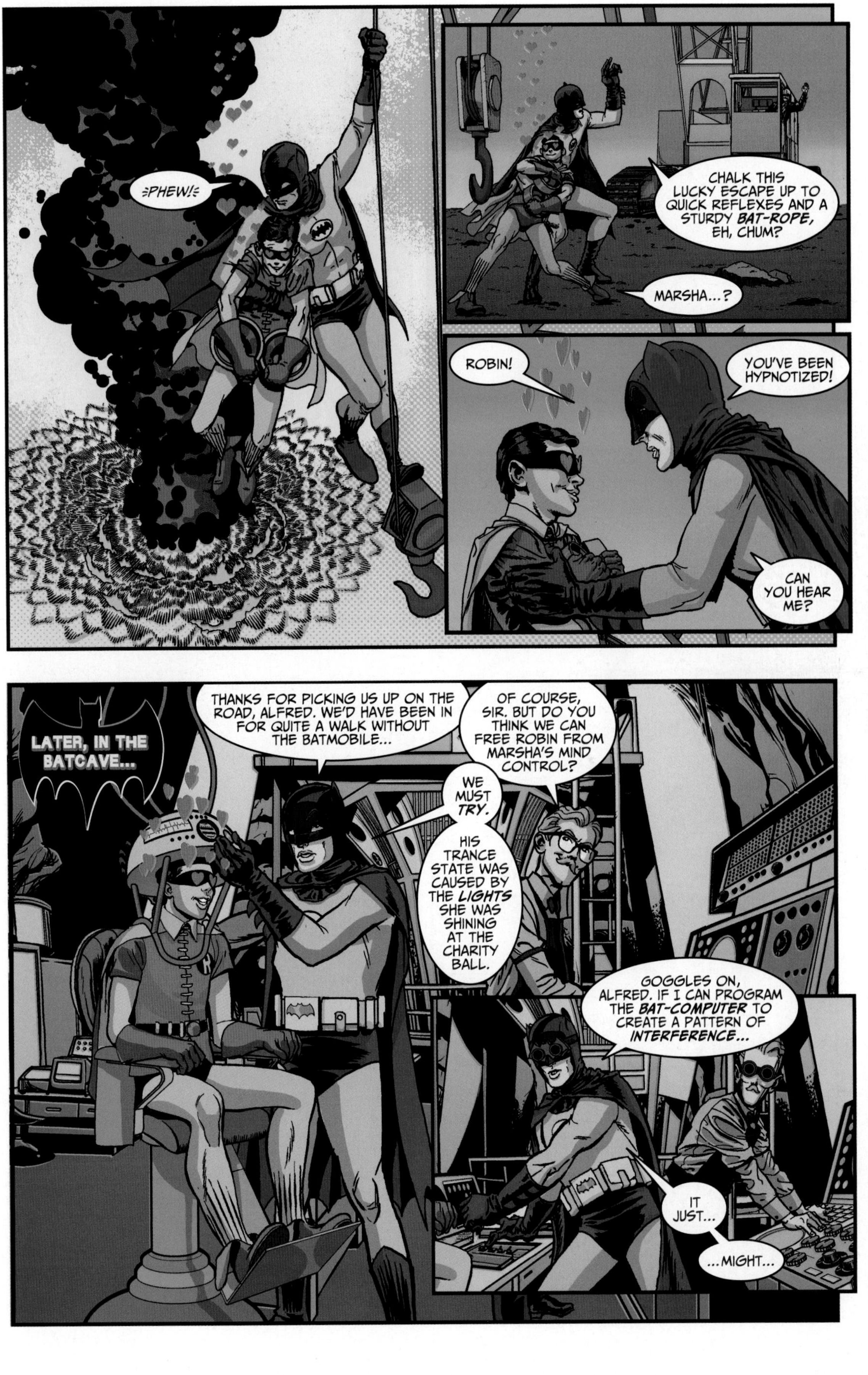
PHEW!
CHALK THIS LUCKY ESCAPE UP TO QUICK REFLEXES AND A STURDY BAT-ROPE, EH, CHUM?
MARSHA...?
ROBIN!
YOU'VE BEEN HYPNOTIZED!
CAN YOU HEAR ME?
LATER, IN THE BATCAVE...
THANKS FOR PICKING US UP ON THE ROAD, ALFRED. WE'D HAVE BEEN IN FOR QUITE A WALK WITHOUT THE BATMOBILE...
OF COURSE, SIR. BUT DO YOU THINK WE CAN FREE ROBIN FROM MARSHA'S MIND CONTROL?
WE MUST TRY.
HIS TRANCE STATE WAS CAUSED BY THE LIGHTS SHE WAS SHINING AT THE CHARITY BALL.
GOGGLES ON, ALFRED. IF I CAN PROGRAM THE BAT-COMPUTER TO CREATE A PATTERN OF INTERFERENCE...
IT JUST...
...MIGHT...

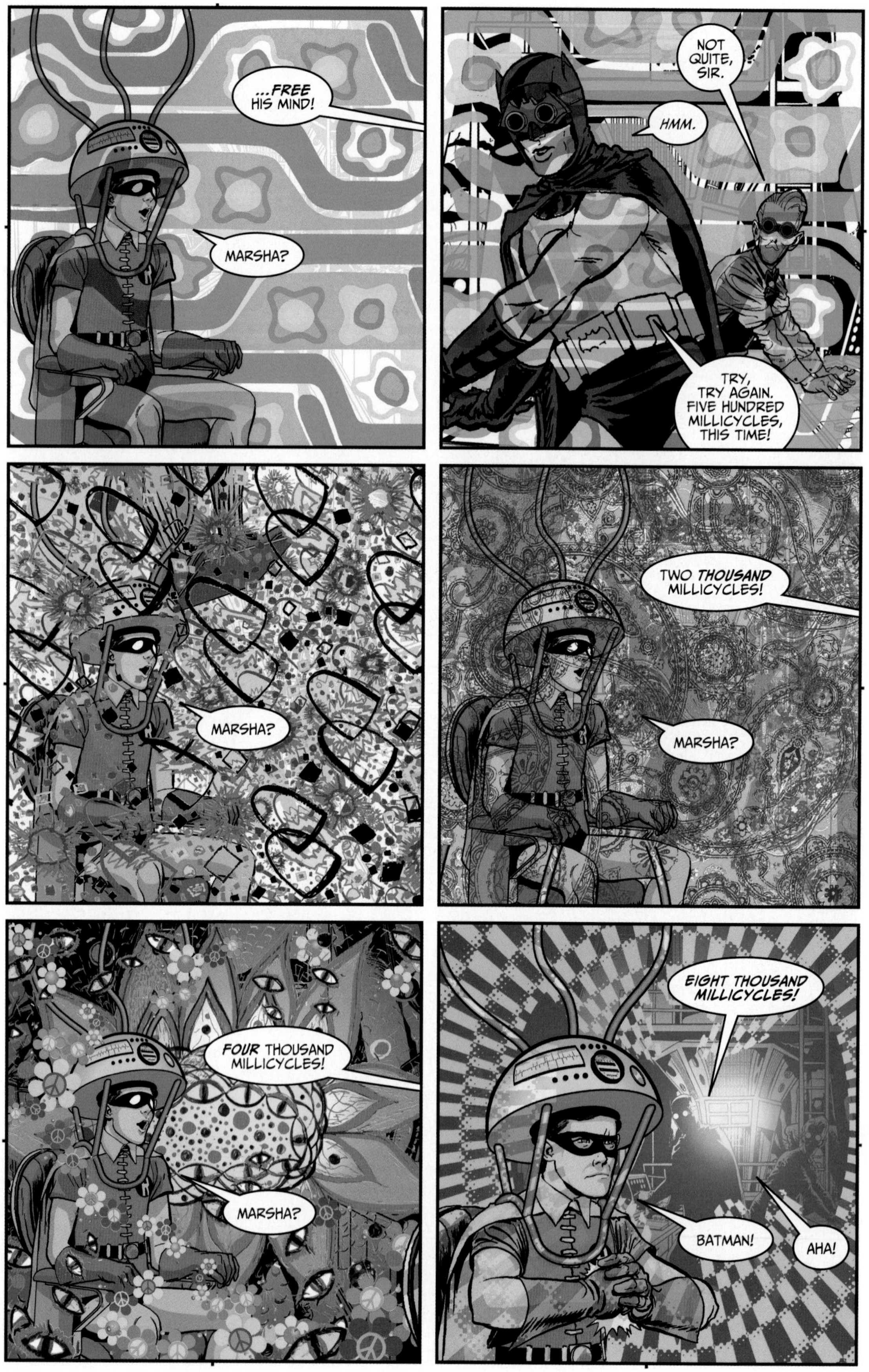
...FREE HIS MIND!
MARSHA?
NOT QUITE, SIR.
HMM.
TRY, TRY AGAIN. FIVE HUNDRED MILLICYCLES, THIS TIME!
MARSHA?
TWO THOUSAND MILLICYCLES!
MARSHA?
FOUR THOUSAND MILLICYCLES!
MARSHA?
EIGHT THOUSAND MILLICYCLES!
BATMAN!
AHA!

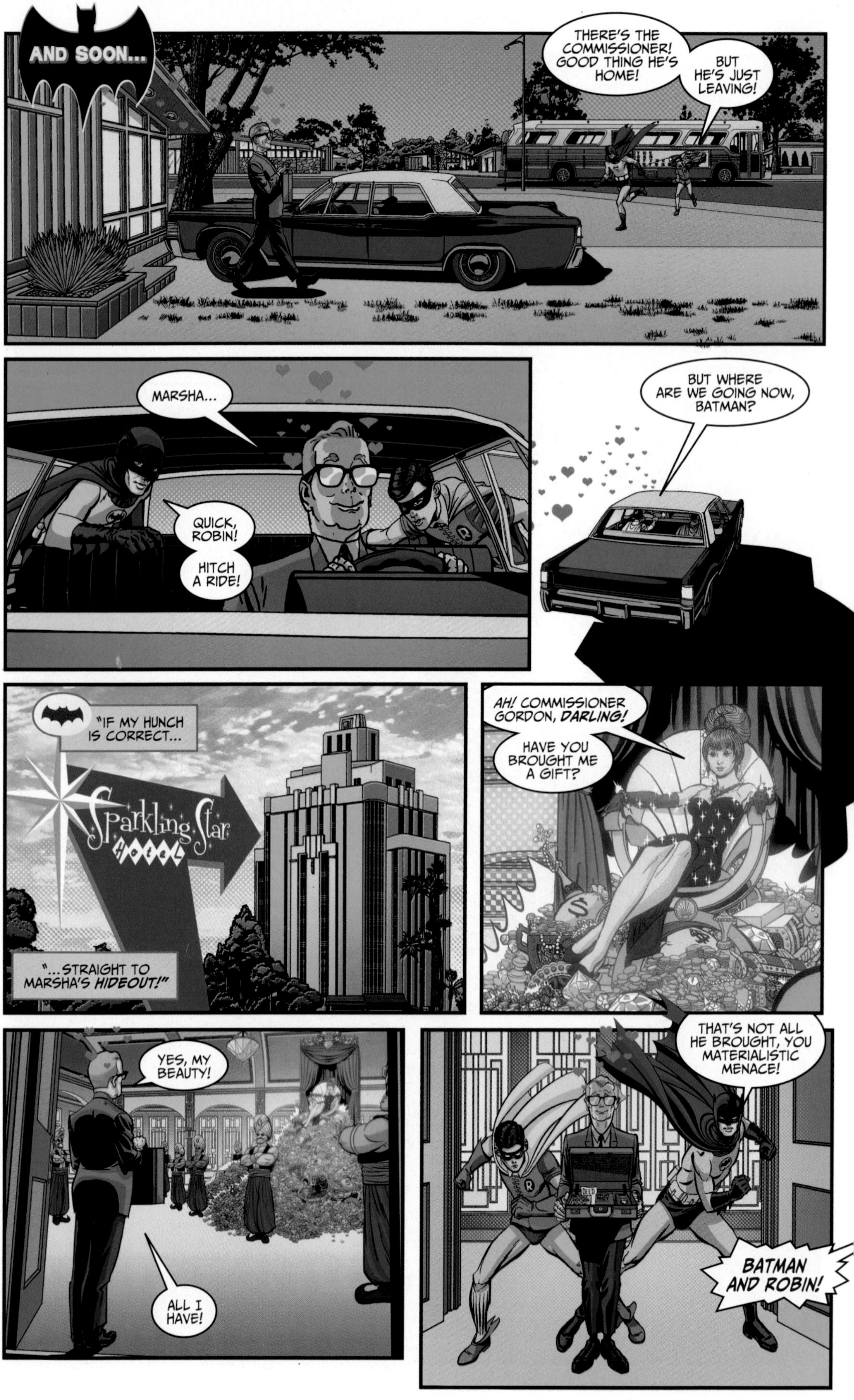
AND SOON...
THERE'S THE COMMISSIONER! GOOD THING HE'S HOME!
BUT HE'S JUST LEAVING!
MARSHA...
QUICK, ROBIN!
HITCH A RIDE!
BUT WHERE ARE WE GOING NOW, BATMAN?
"IF MY HUNCH IS CORRECT...
Sparkling Star Hotel
"...STRAIGHT TO MARSHA'S HIDEOUT!"
AH! COMMISSIONER GORDON, DARLING!
HAVE YOU BROUGHT ME A GIFT?
YES, MY BEAUTY!
ALL I HAVE!
THAT'S NOT ALL HE BROUGHT, YOU MATERIALISTIC MENACE!
BATMAN AND ROBIN!

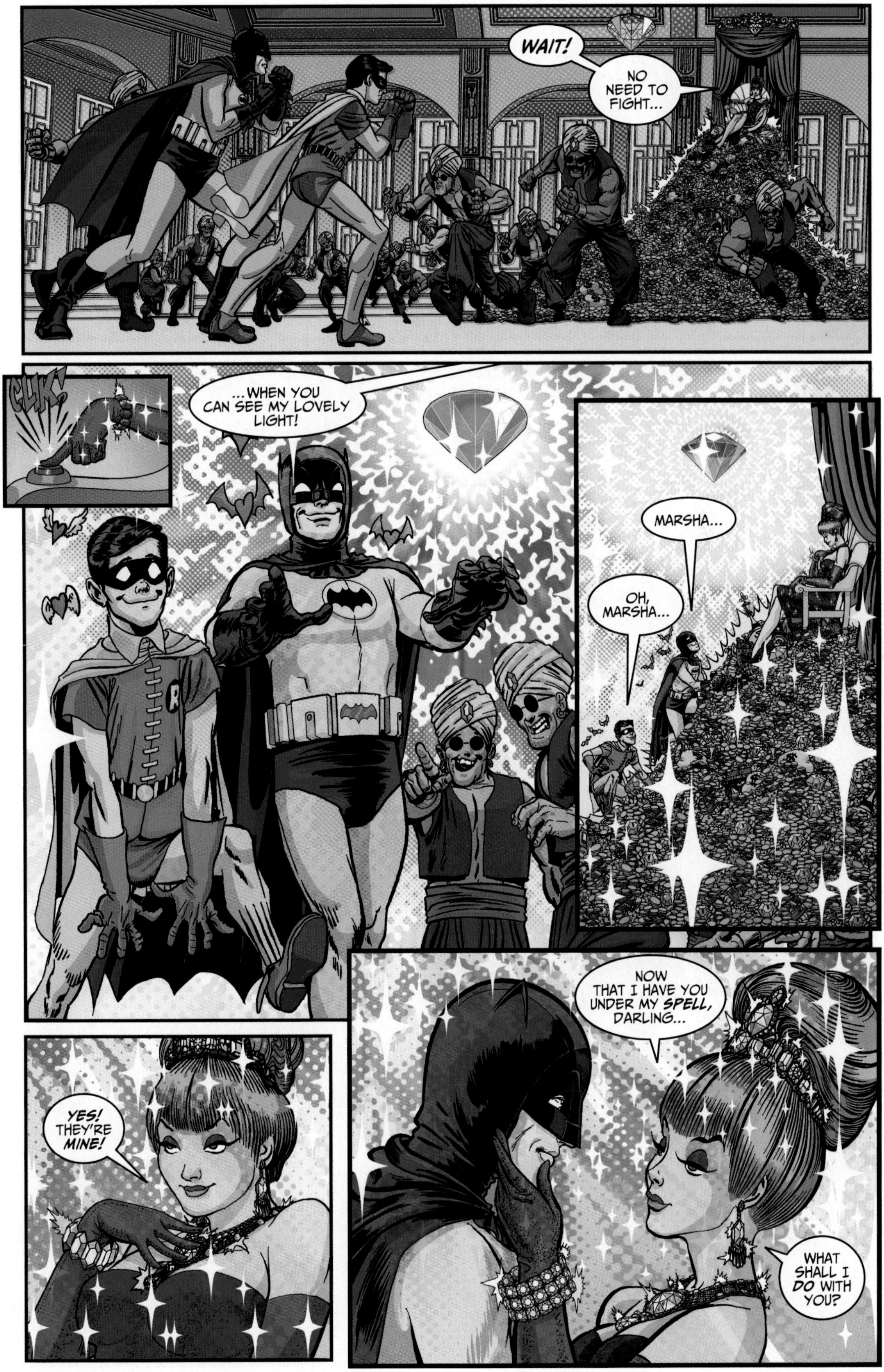
WAIT!
NO NEED TO FIGHT...
CLIK!
...WHEN YOU CAN SEE MY LOVELY LIGHT!
MARSHA...
OH, MARSHA...
YES! THEY'RE MINE!
NOW THAT I HAVE YOU UNDER MY SPELL, DARLING...
WHAT SHALL I DO WITH YOU?

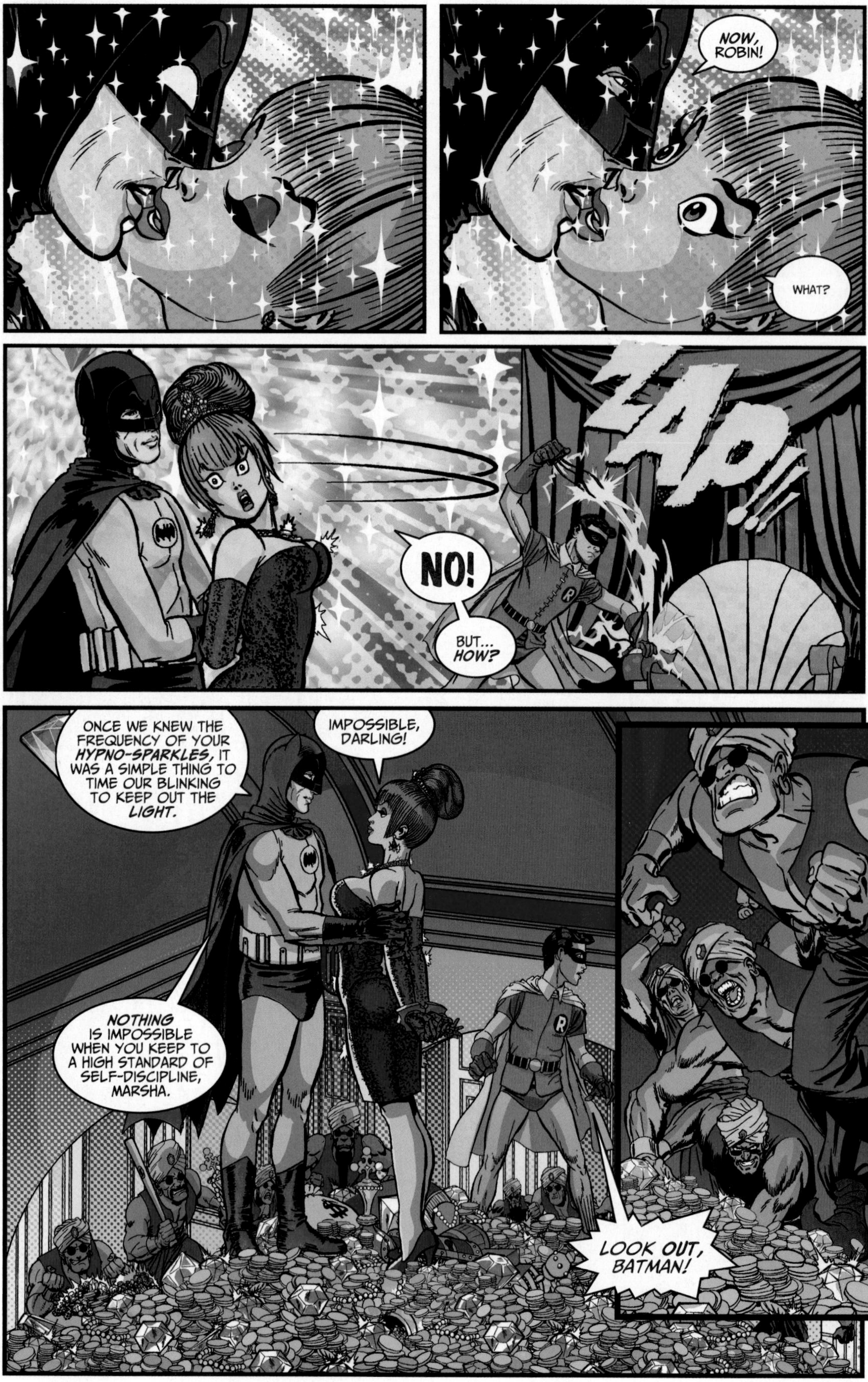
NOW, ROBIN!
WHAT?
ZAP!!!
NO!
BUT... HOW?
ONCE WE KNEW THE FREQUENCY OF YOUR HYPNO-SPARKLES, IT WAS A SIMPLE THING TO TIME OUR BLINKING TO KEEP OUT THE LIGHT.
IMPOSSIBLE, DARLING!
NOTHING IS IMPOSSIBLE WHEN YOU KEEP TO A HIGH STANDARD OF SELF-DISCIPLINE, MARSHA.
LOOK OUT, BATMAN!

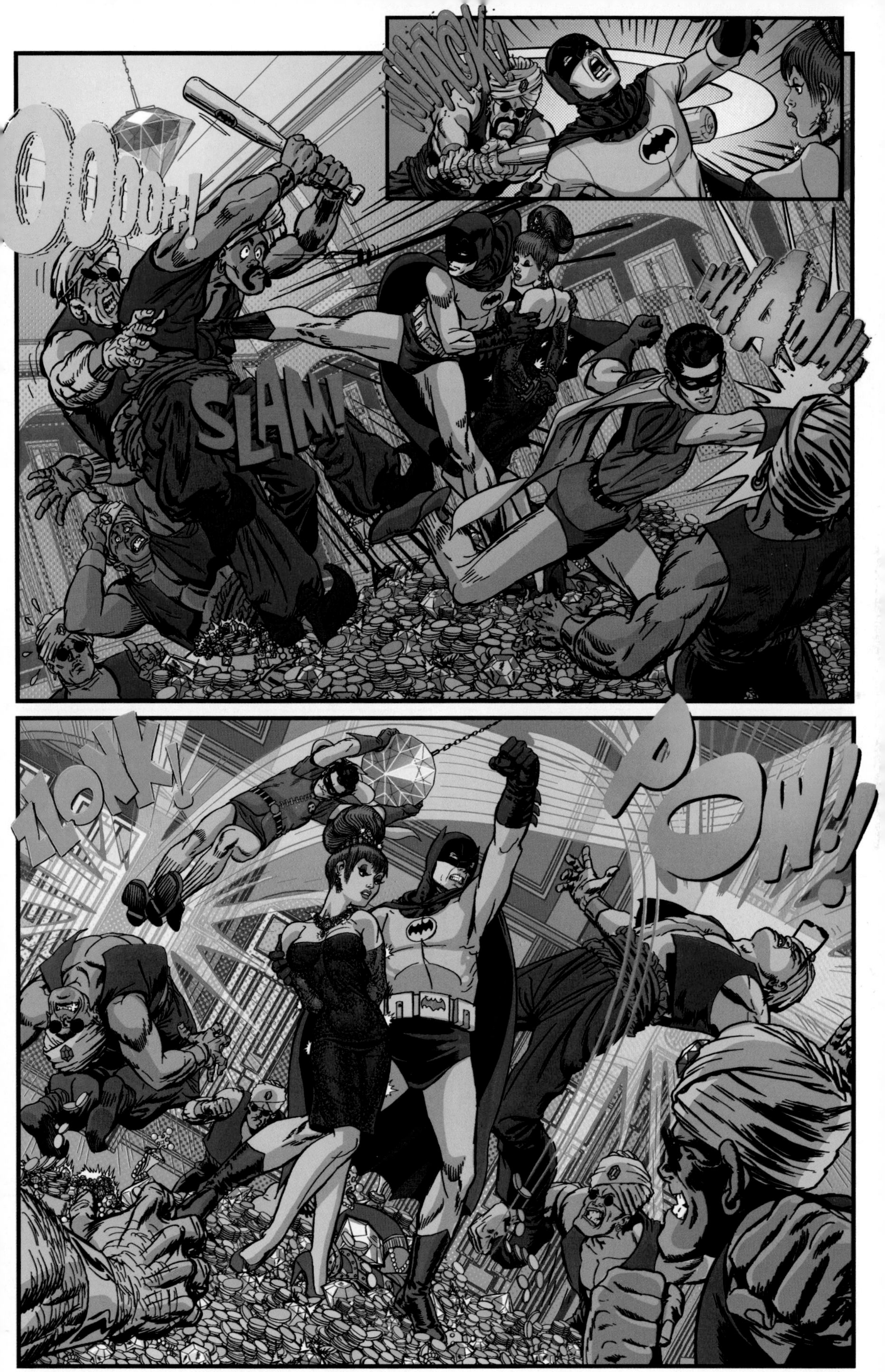
OOOOOFF!
WHACK!
SLAM!
WHAM!
ZOWK!
POW!!

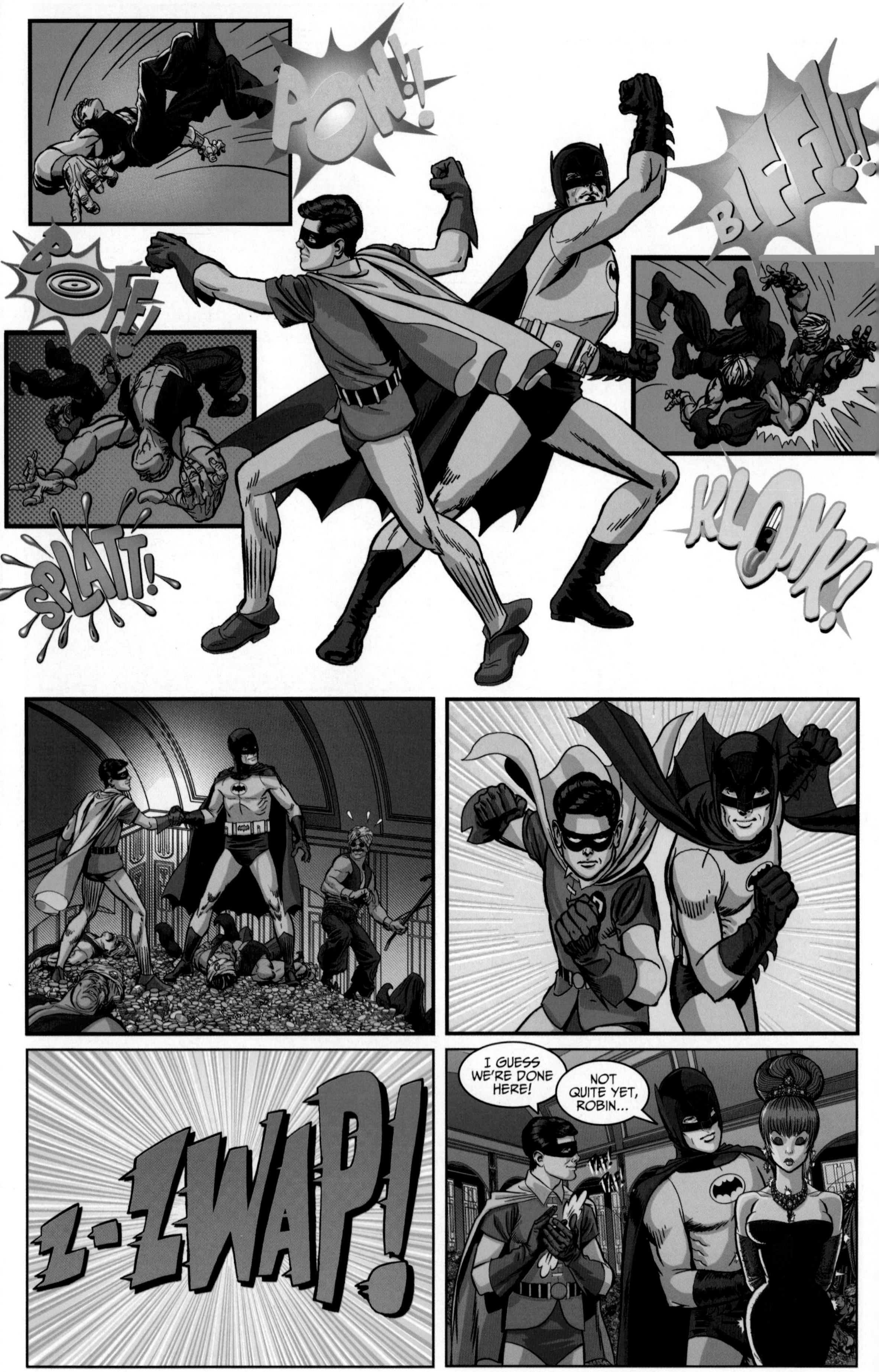
POW!!
BIFF!!
BOFF!
SPLATT!
KLONK!!
Z-ZWAP!
I GUESS WE'RE DONE HERE!
NOT QUITE YET, ROBIN...
PAF!
PAF!

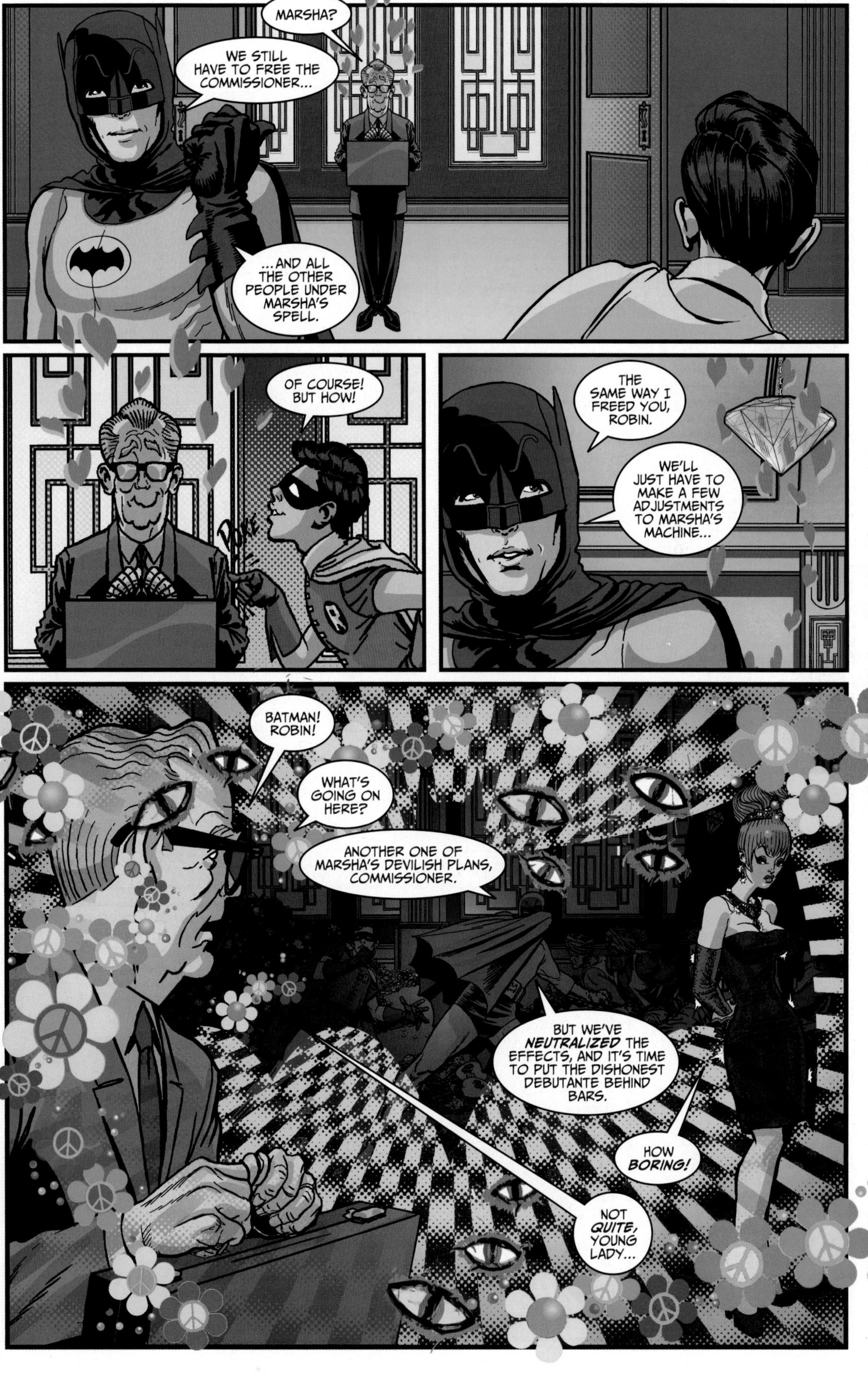
MARSHA?
WE STILL HAVE TO FREE THE COMMISSIONER...
...AND ALL THE OTHER PEOPLE UNDER MARSHA'S SPELL.
OF COURSE! BUT HOW!
THE SAME WAY I FREED YOU, ROBIN.
WE'LL JUST HAVE TO MAKE A FEW ADJUSTMENTS TO MARSHA'S MACHINE...
BATMAN! ROBIN!
WHAT'S GOING ON HERE?
ANOTHER ONE OF MARSHA'S DEVILISH PLANS, COMMISSIONER.
BUT WE'VE *NEUTRALIZED* THE EFFECTS, AND IT'S TIME TO PUT THE DISHONEST DEBUTANTE BEHIND BARS.
HOW *BORING!*
NOT *QUITE,* YOUNG LADY...

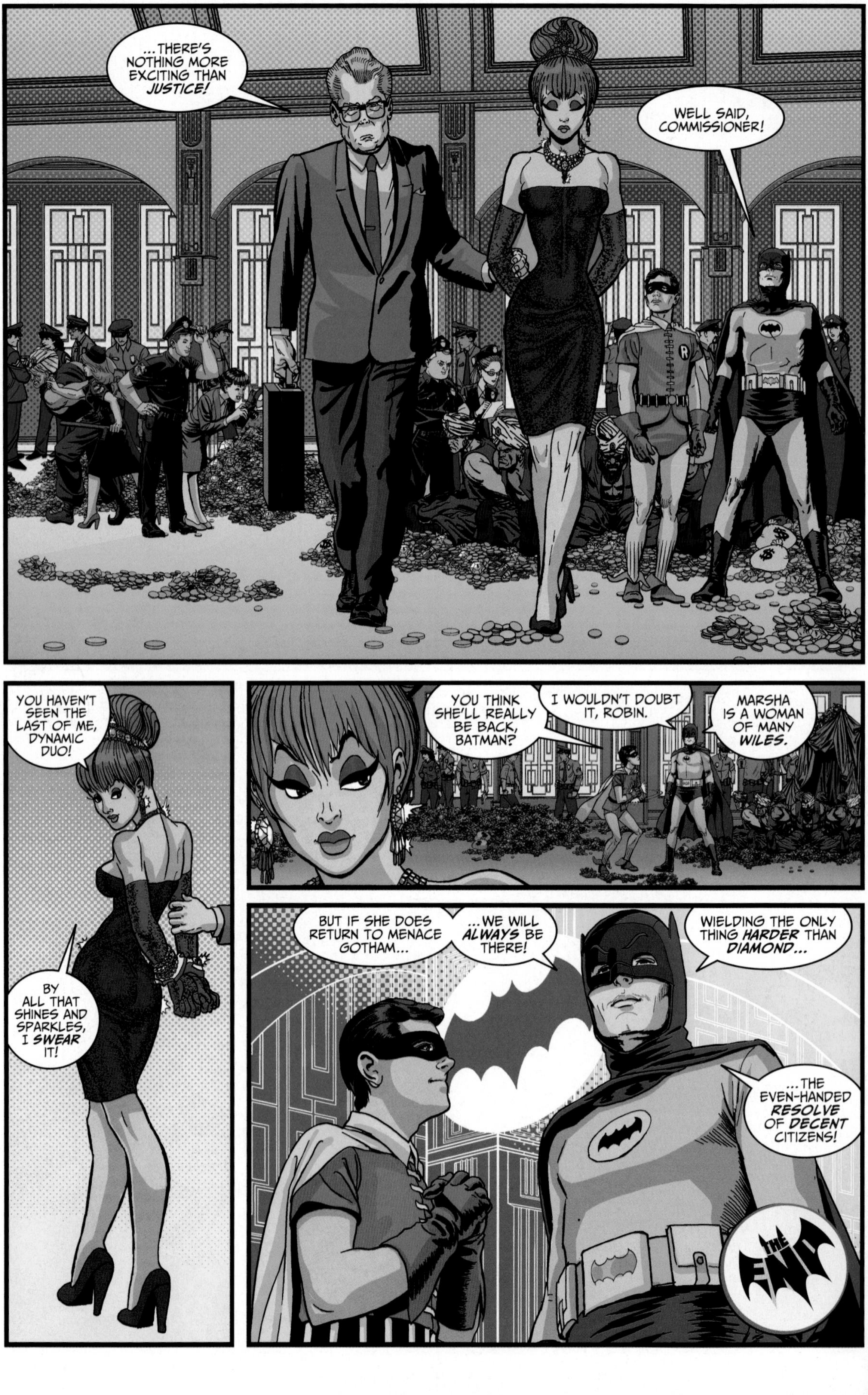
...THERE'S NOTHING MORE EXCITING THAN JUSTICE!
WELL SAID, COMMISSIONER!
YOU HAVEN'T SEEN THE LAST OF ME, DYNAMIC DUO!
BY ALL THAT SHINES AND SPARKLES, I SWEAR IT!
YOU THINK SHE'LL REALLY BE BACK, BATMAN?
I WOULDN'T DOUBT IT, ROBIN.
MARSHA IS A WOMAN OF MANY WILES.
BUT IF SHE DOES RETURN TO MENACE GOTHAM...
...WE WILL ALWAYS BE THERE!
WIELDING THE ONLY THING HARDER THAN DIAMOND...
...THE EVEN-HANDED RESOLVE OF DECENT CITIZENS!
THE END

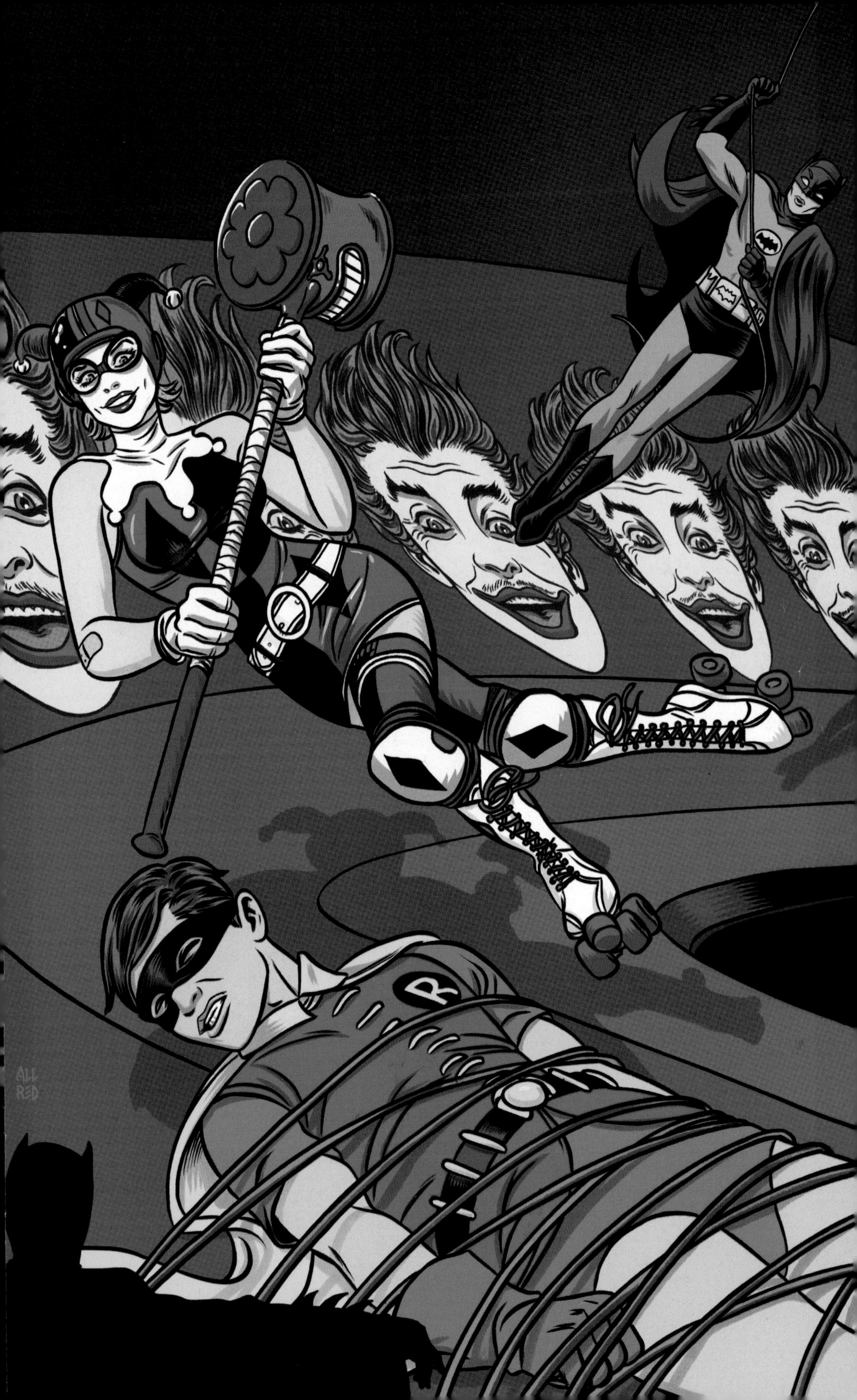
ALL
RED

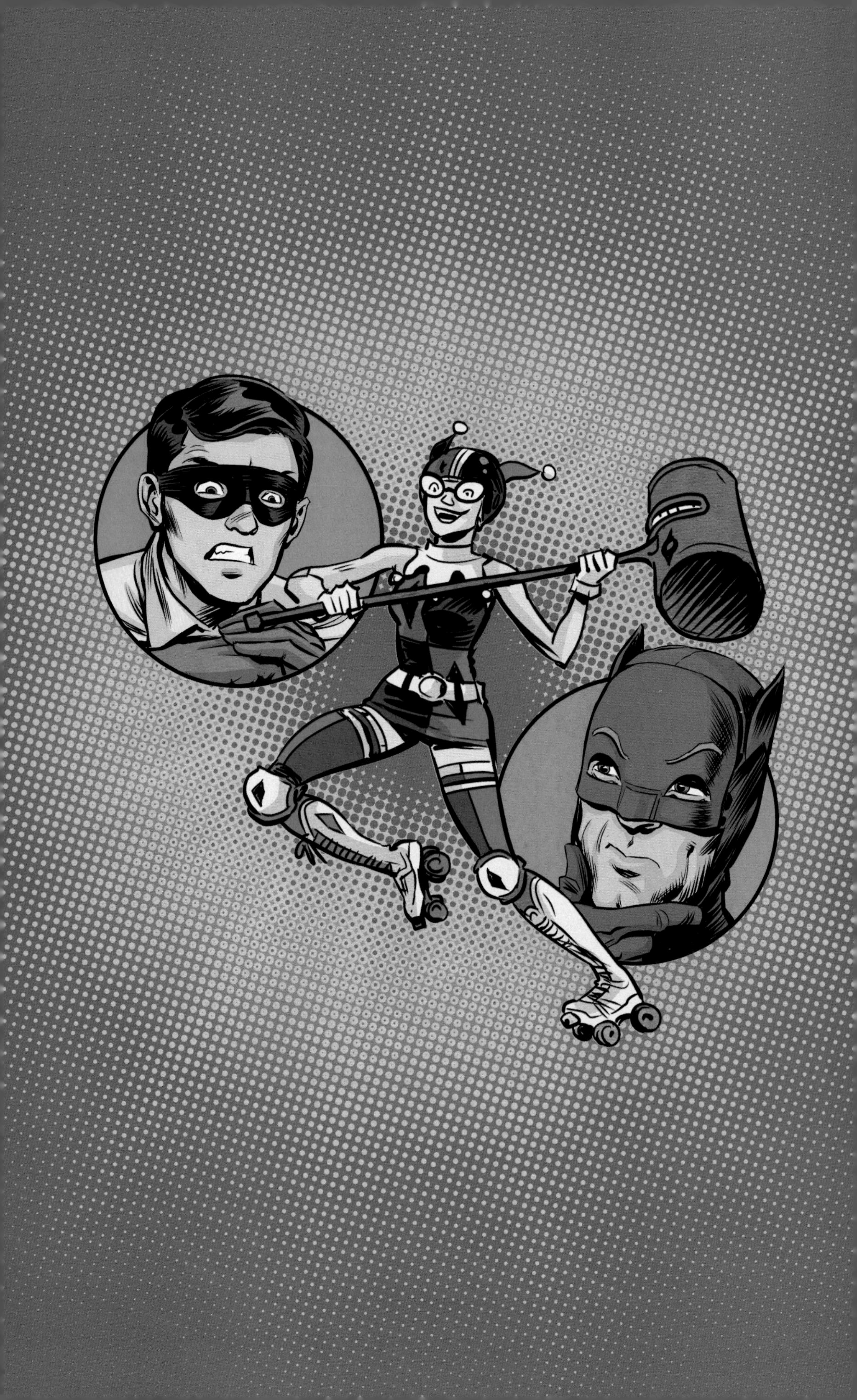

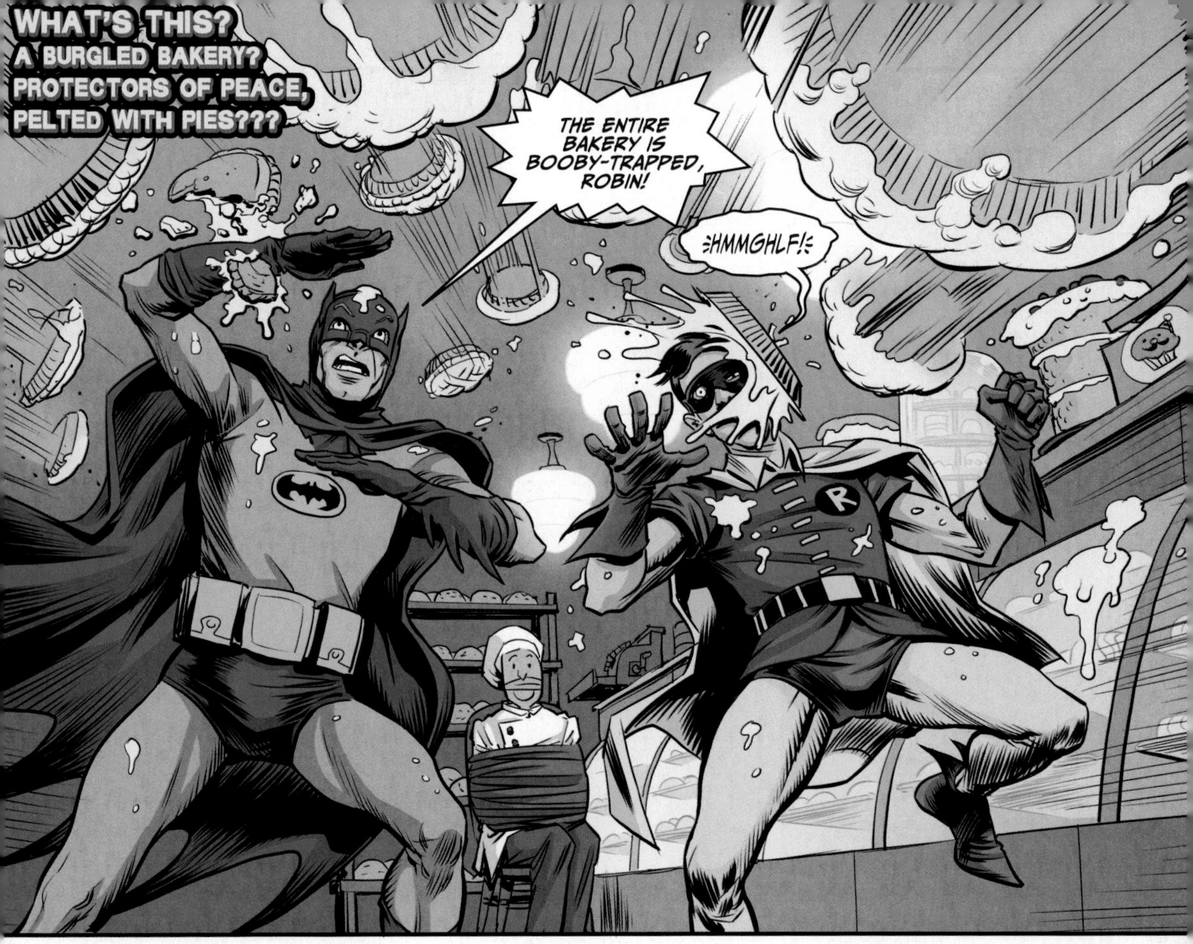
WHAT'S THIS? A BURGLED BAKERY? PROTECTORS OF PEACE, PELTED WITH PIES???
THE ENTIRE BAKERY IS BOOBY-TRAPPED, ROBIN!
HMMGHLF!

# "NIGHT OF THE HARLEQUIN"

Written by JEFF PARKER Art by LUKAS KETNER Colors by KELLY FITZPATRICK
Lettered by WES ABBOTT Cover by MICHAEL and LAURA ALLRED

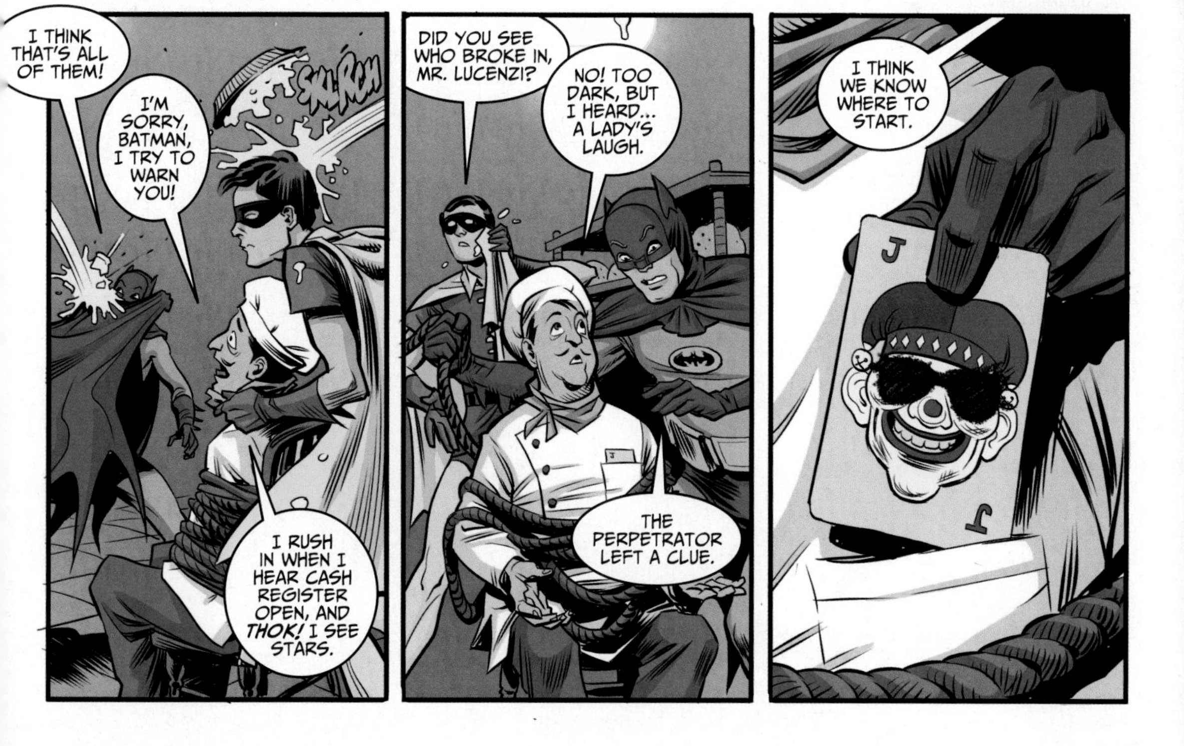
I THINK THAT'S ALL OF THEM!
SKLRCH
I'M SORRY, BATMAN, I TRY TO WARN YOU!
I RUSH IN WHEN I HEAR CASH REGISTER OPEN, AND THOK! I SEE STARS.
DID YOU SEE WHO BROKE IN, MR. LUCENZI?
NO! TOO DARK, BUT I HEARD... A LADY'S LAUGH.
THE PERPETRATOR LEFT A CLUE.
I THINK WE KNOW WHERE TO START.

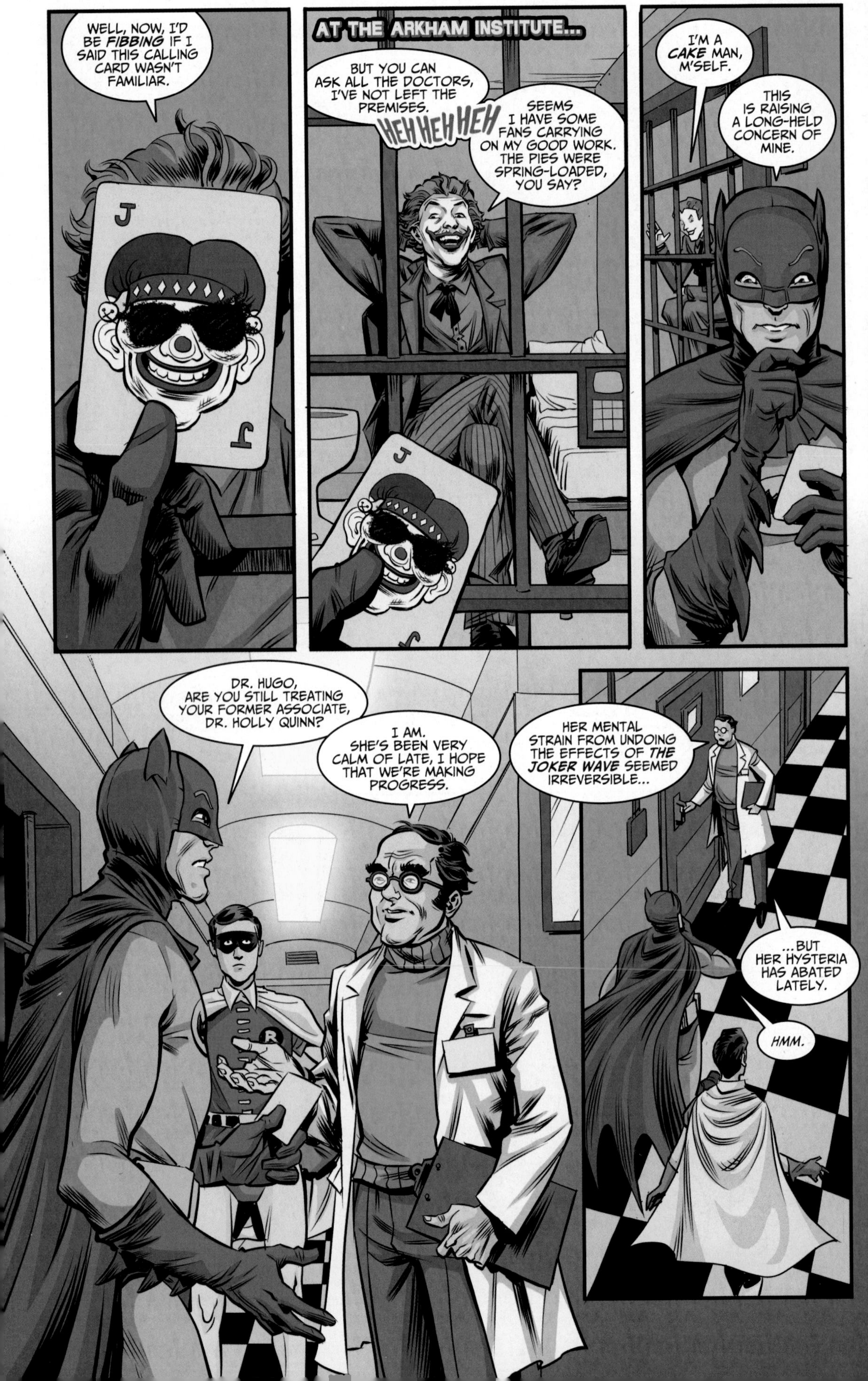
WELL, NOW, I'D BE *FIBBING* IF I SAID THIS CALLING CARD WASN'T FAMILIAR.
AT THE ARKHAM INSTITUTE...
BUT YOU CAN ASK ALL THE DOCTORS, I'VE NOT LEFT THE PREMISES.
HEH HEH HEH
SEEMS I HAVE SOME FANS CARRYING ON MY GOOD WORK. THE PIES WERE SPRING-LOADED, YOU SAY?
I'M A *CAKE* MAN, M'SELF.
THIS IS RAISING A LONG-HELD CONCERN OF MINE.
DR. HUGO, ARE YOU STILL TREATING YOUR FORMER ASSOCIATE, DR. HOLLY QUINN?
I AM. SHE'S BEEN VERY CALM OF LATE, I HOPE THAT WE'RE MAKING PROGRESS.
HER MENTAL STRAIN FROM UNDOING THE EFFECTS OF *THE JOKER WAVE* SEEMED IRREVERSIBLE...
...BUT HER HYSTERIA HAS ABATED LATELY.
*HMM.*

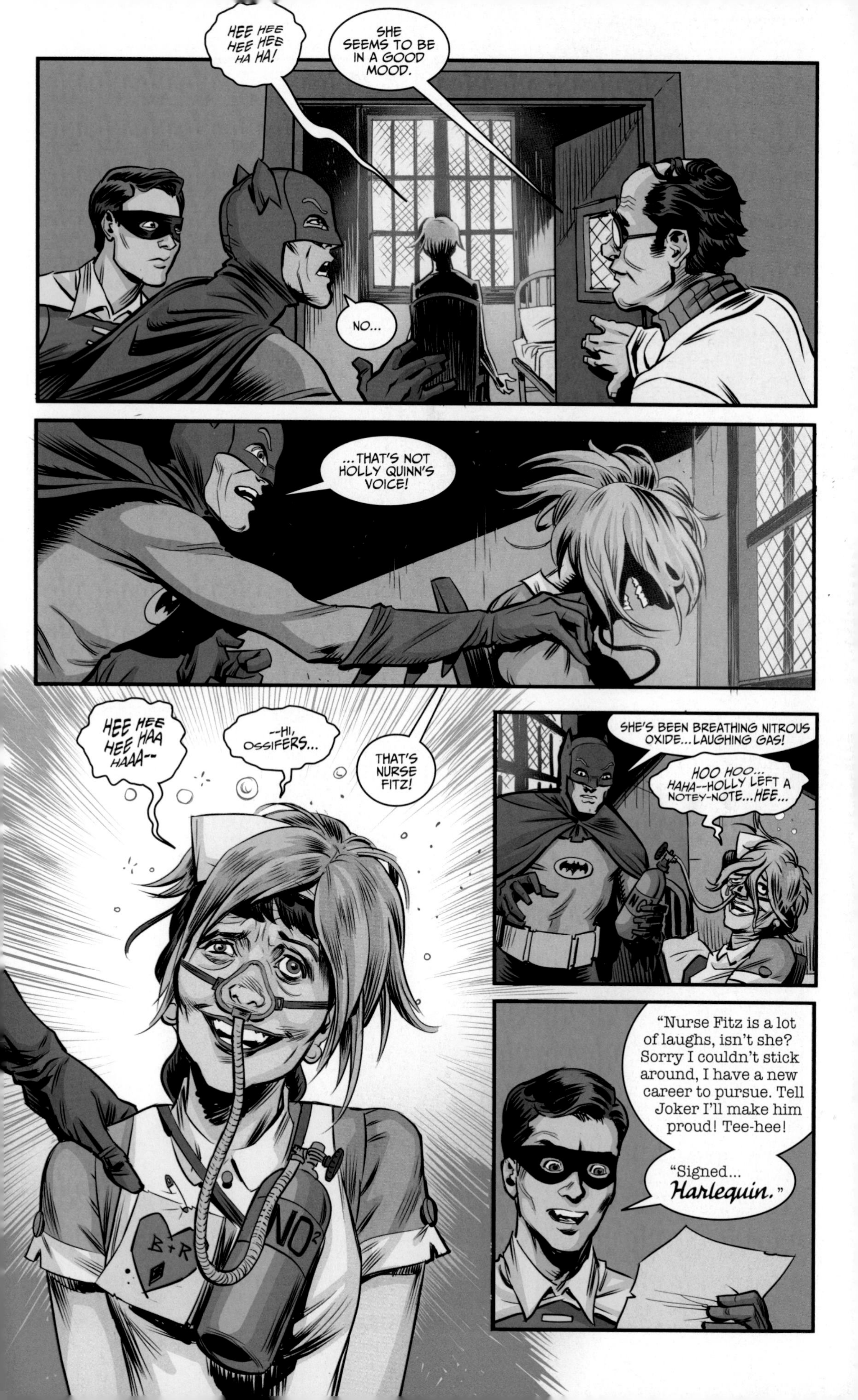
HEE HEE HEE HEE HA HA!
SHE SEEMS TO BE IN A GOOD MOOD.
NO...
...THAT'S NOT HOLLY QUINN'S VOICE!
HEE HEE HEE HAA HAAA--
--HI, OSSIFERS...
THAT'S NURSE FITZ!
SHE'S BEEN BREATHING NITROUS OXIDE... LAUGHING GAS!
HOO HOO... HAHA--HOLLY LEFT A NOTEY-NOTE...HEE...
"Nurse Fitz is a lot of laughs, isn't she? Sorry I couldn't stick around, I have a new career to pursue. Tell Joker I'll make him proud! Tee-hee!
"Signed... Harlequin."

IT'S WORSE THAN I FEARED. THAT POOR WOMAN'S MIND WAS PUSHED OVER THE EDGE.

SHE SACRIFICED HER SANITY SO THAT THE GOOD PEOPLE OF GOTHAM COULD KEEP THEIRS.

WITH HER YEARS OF STUDY AND DEPTH OF KNOWLEDGE, SHE MAY BE MORE DANGEROUS THAN THE JOKER EVER WAS!

YOU COULD HAVE WAITED TO SAY THAT OUTSIDE!

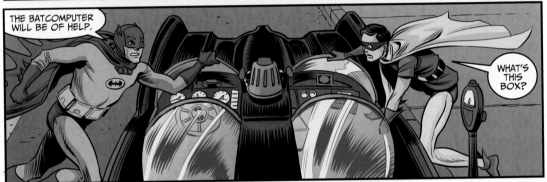

THE BATCOMPUTER WILL BE OF HELP.

WHAT'S THIS BOX?

THAT WASN'T THERE BEFORE!

UH...

BOING

SPROING

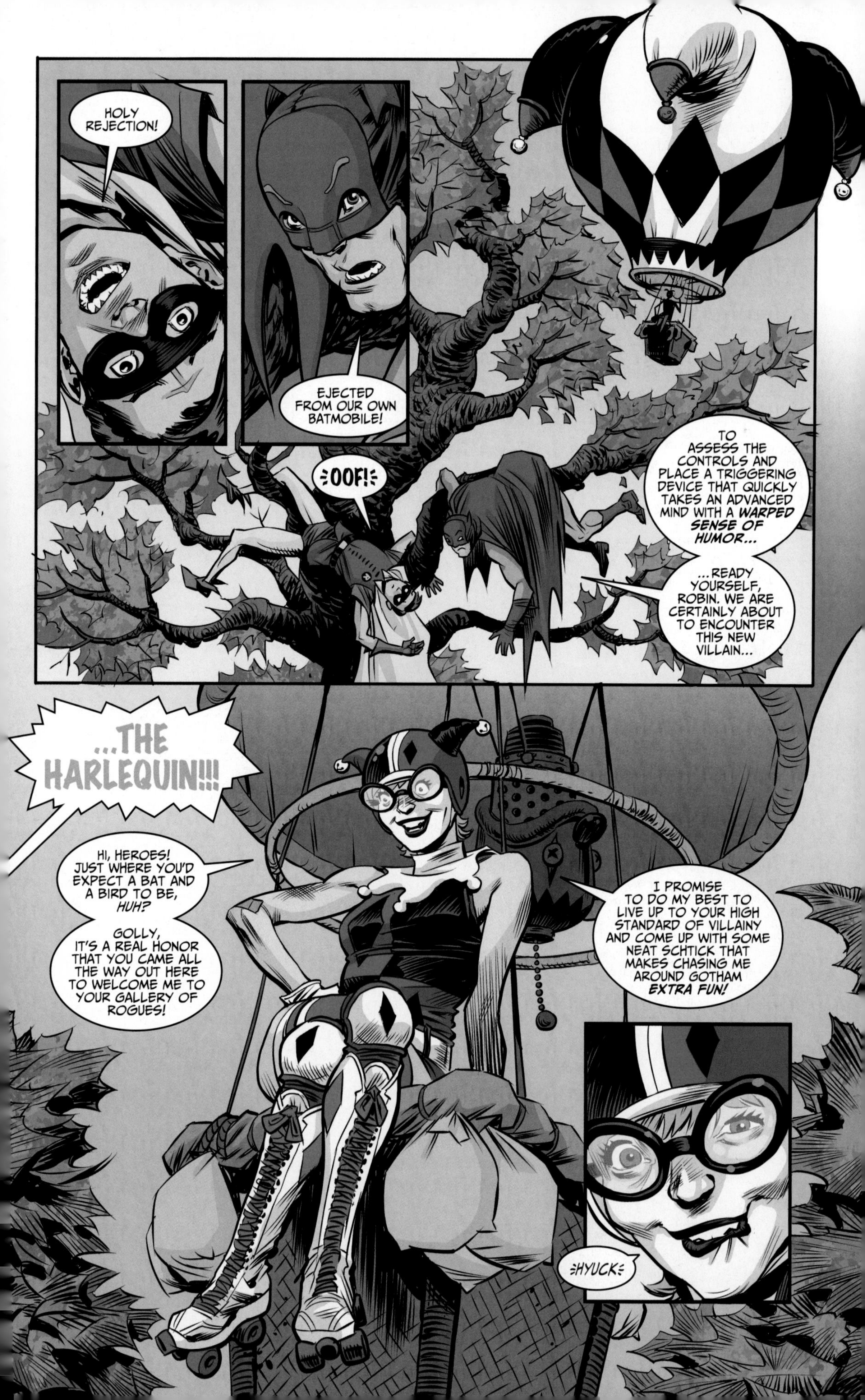

HOLY REJECTION!
EJECTED FROM OUR OWN BATMOBILE!
OOF!
TO ASSESS THE CONTROLS AND PLACE A TRIGGERING DEVICE THAT QUICKLY TAKES AN ADVANCED MIND WITH A WARPED SENSE OF HUMOR...
...READY YOURSELF, ROBIN. WE ARE CERTAINLY ABOUT TO ENCOUNTER THIS NEW VILLAIN...
...THE HARLEQUIN!!!
HI, HEROES! JUST WHERE YOU'D EXPECT A BAT AND A BIRD TO BE, HUH?
GOLLY, IT'S A REAL HONOR THAT YOU CAME ALL THE WAY OUT HERE TO WELCOME ME TO YOUR GALLERY OF ROGUES!
I PROMISE TO DO MY BEST TO LIVE UP TO YOUR HIGH STANDARD OF VILLAINY AND COME UP WITH SOME NEAT SCHTICK THAT MAKES CHASING ME AROUND GOTHAM EXTRA FUN!
HYUCK

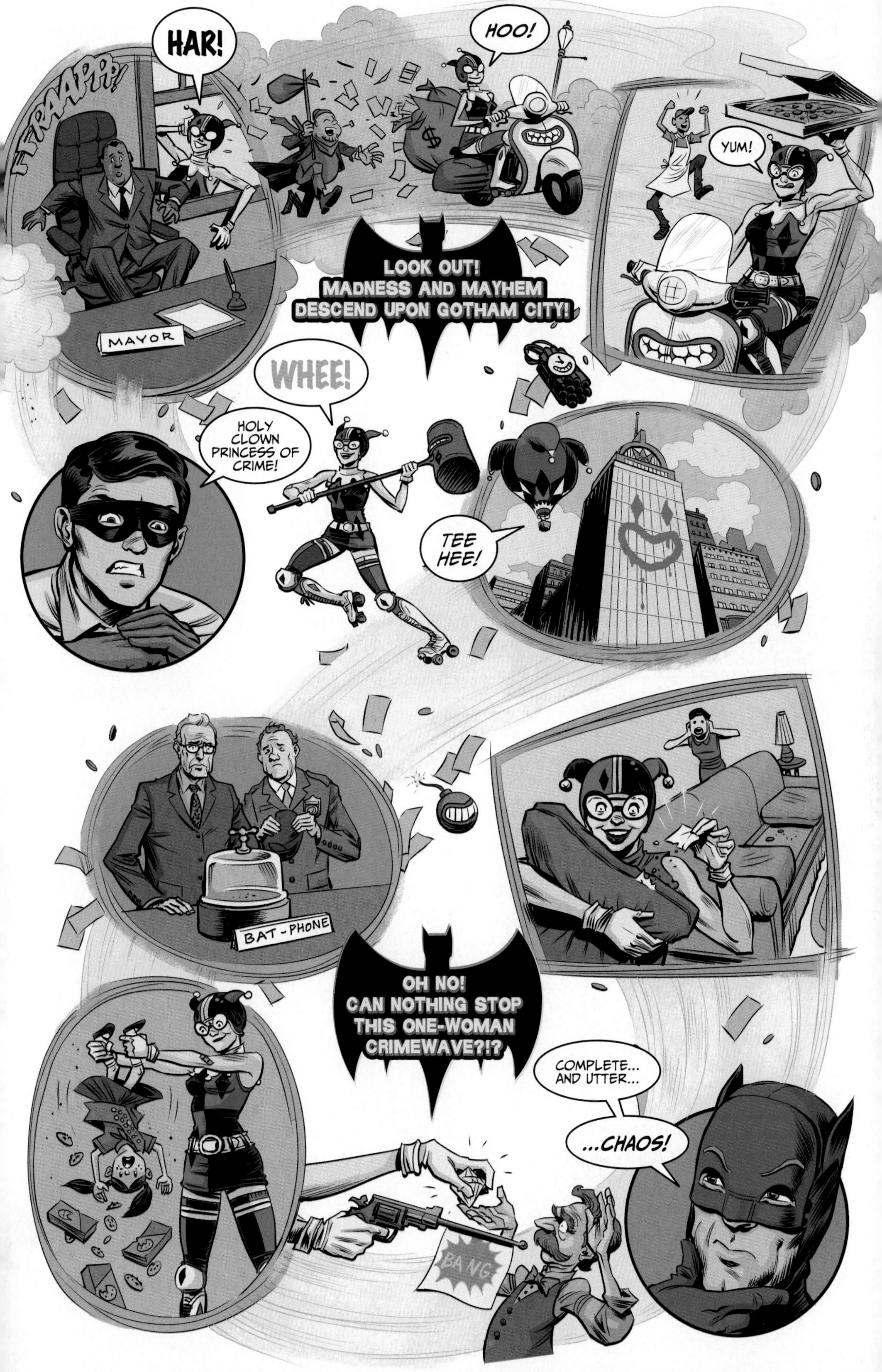
FFRAAPPP!
HAR!
HOO!
YUM!
MAYOR
LOOK OUT!
MADNESS AND MAYHEM
DESCEND UPON GOTHAM CITY!
WHEE!
HOLY CLOWN PRINCESS OF CRIME!
TEE HEE!
BAT-PHONE
OH NO!
CAN NOTHING STOP
THIS ONE-WOMAN
CRIMEWAVE?!?
COMPLETE... AND UTTER...
...CHAOS!
BANG

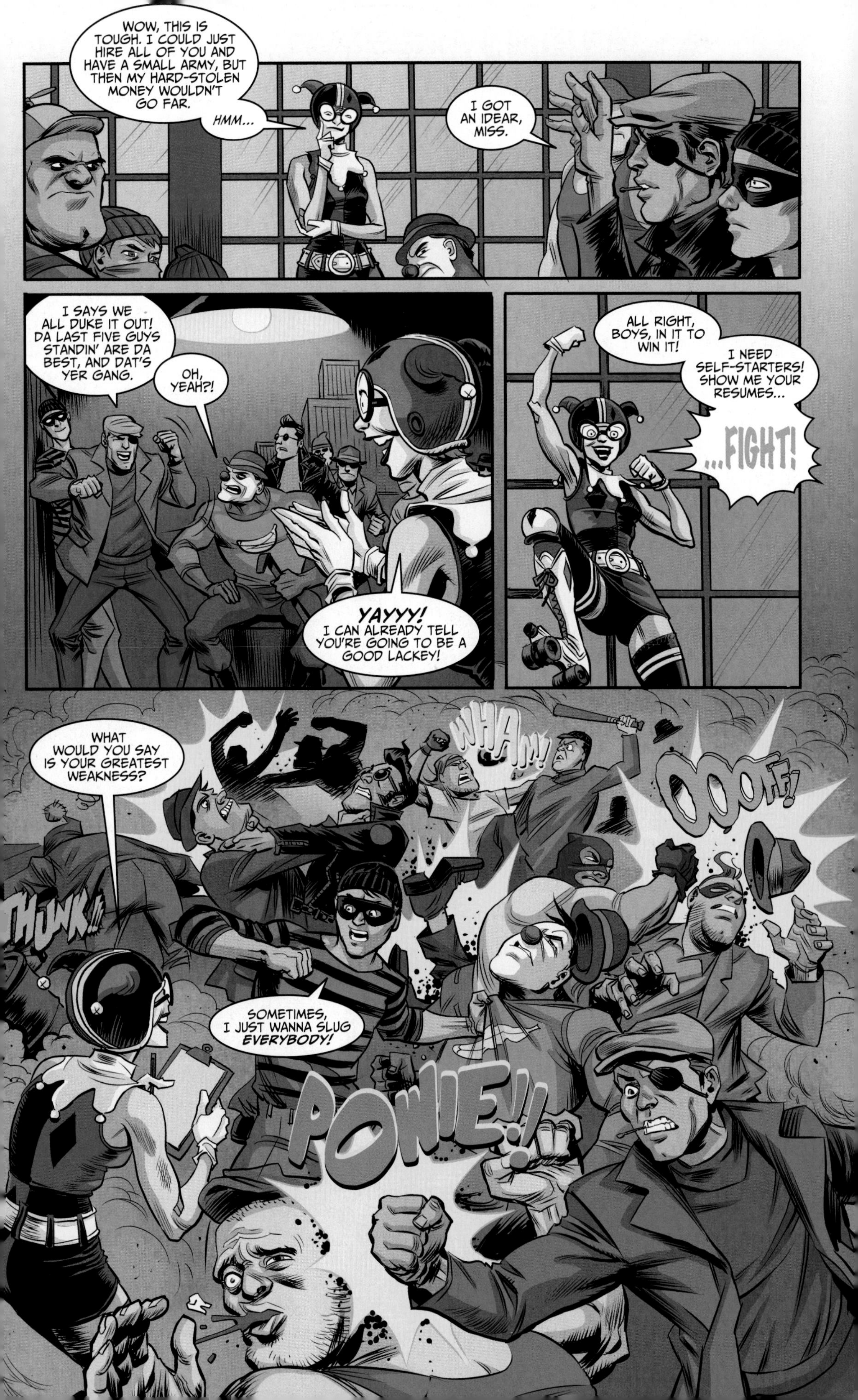
WOW, THIS IS TOUGH. I COULD JUST HIRE ALL OF YOU AND HAVE A SMALL ARMY, BUT THEN MY HARD-STOLEN MONEY WOULDN'T GO FAR.
HMM...
I GOT AN IDEAR, MISS.
I SAYS WE ALL DUKE IT OUT! DA LAST FIVE GUYS STANDIN' ARE DA BEST, AND DAT'S YER GANG.
OH, YEAH?!
YAYYY! I CAN ALREADY TELL YOU'RE GOING TO BE A GOOD LACKEY!
ALL RIGHT, BOYS, IN IT TO WIN IT!
I NEED SELF-STARTERS! SHOW ME YOUR RESUMES...
...FIGHT!
WHAT WOULD YOU SAY IS YOUR GREATEST WEAKNESS?
WHAM!
OOOFF!
THUNK!!
SOMETIMES, I JUST WANNA SLUG EVERYBODY!
POWIE!!

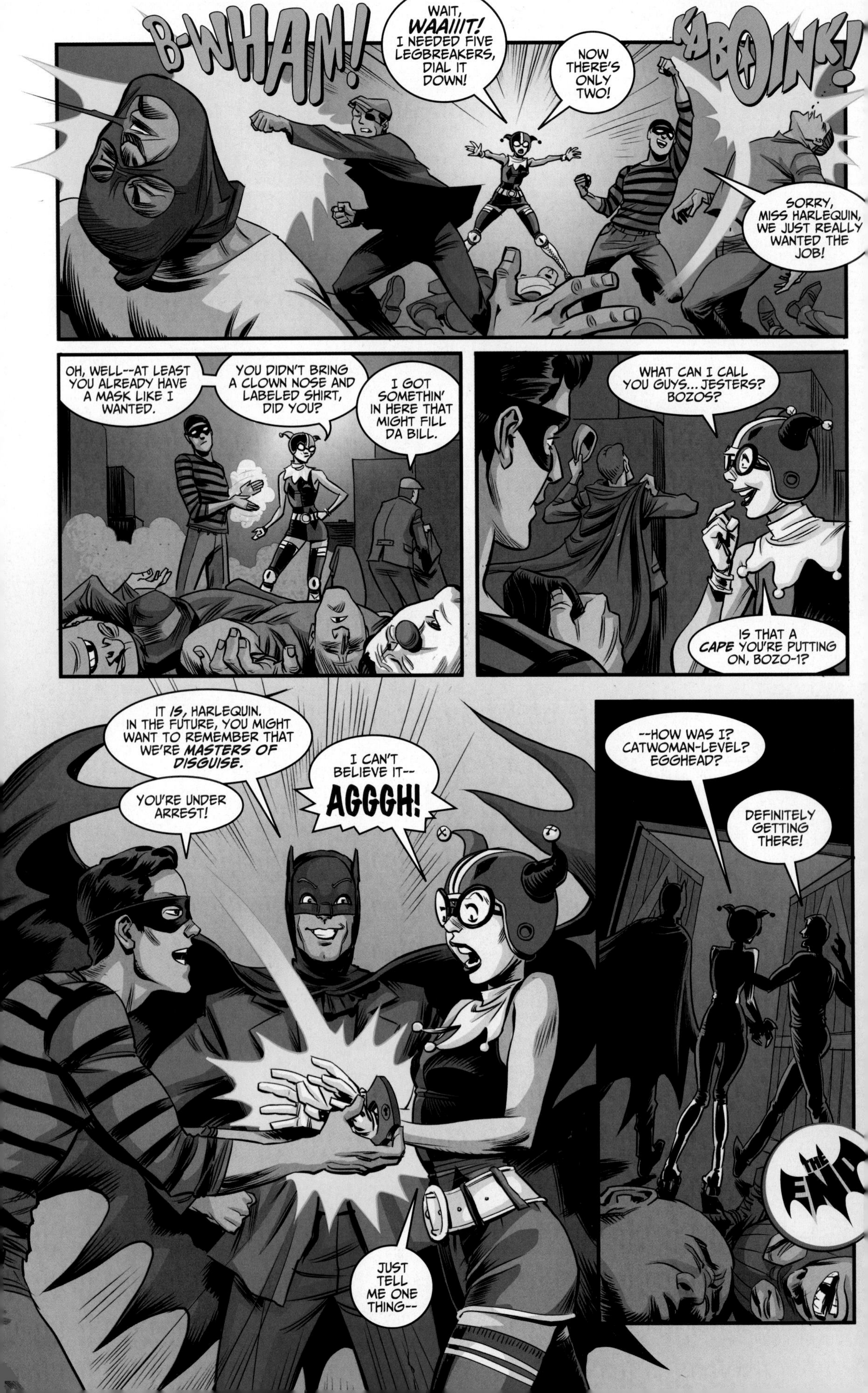
B-WHAM!
WAIT, WAAIIIT! I NEEDED FIVE LEGBREAKERS, DIAL IT DOWN!
NOW THERE'S ONLY TWO!
KABOINK!
SORRY, MISS HARLEQUIN, WE JUST REALLY WANTED THE JOB!
OH, WELL--AT LEAST YOU ALREADY HAVE A MASK LIKE I WANTED.
YOU DIDN'T BRING A CLOWN NOSE AND LABELED SHIRT, DID YOU?
I GOT SOMETHIN' IN HERE THAT MIGHT FILL DA BILL.
WHAT CAN I CALL YOU GUYS... JESTERS? BOZOS?
IS THAT A CAPE YOU'RE PUTTING ON, BOZO-1?
IT IS, HARLEQUIN. IN THE FUTURE, YOU MIGHT WANT TO REMEMBER THAT WE'RE MASTERS OF DISGUISE.
YOU'RE UNDER ARREST!
I CAN'T BELIEVE IT--
AGGGH!
JUST TELL ME ONE THING--
--HOW WAS I? CATWOMAN-LEVEL? EGGHEAD?
DEFINITELY GETTING THERE!
THE END

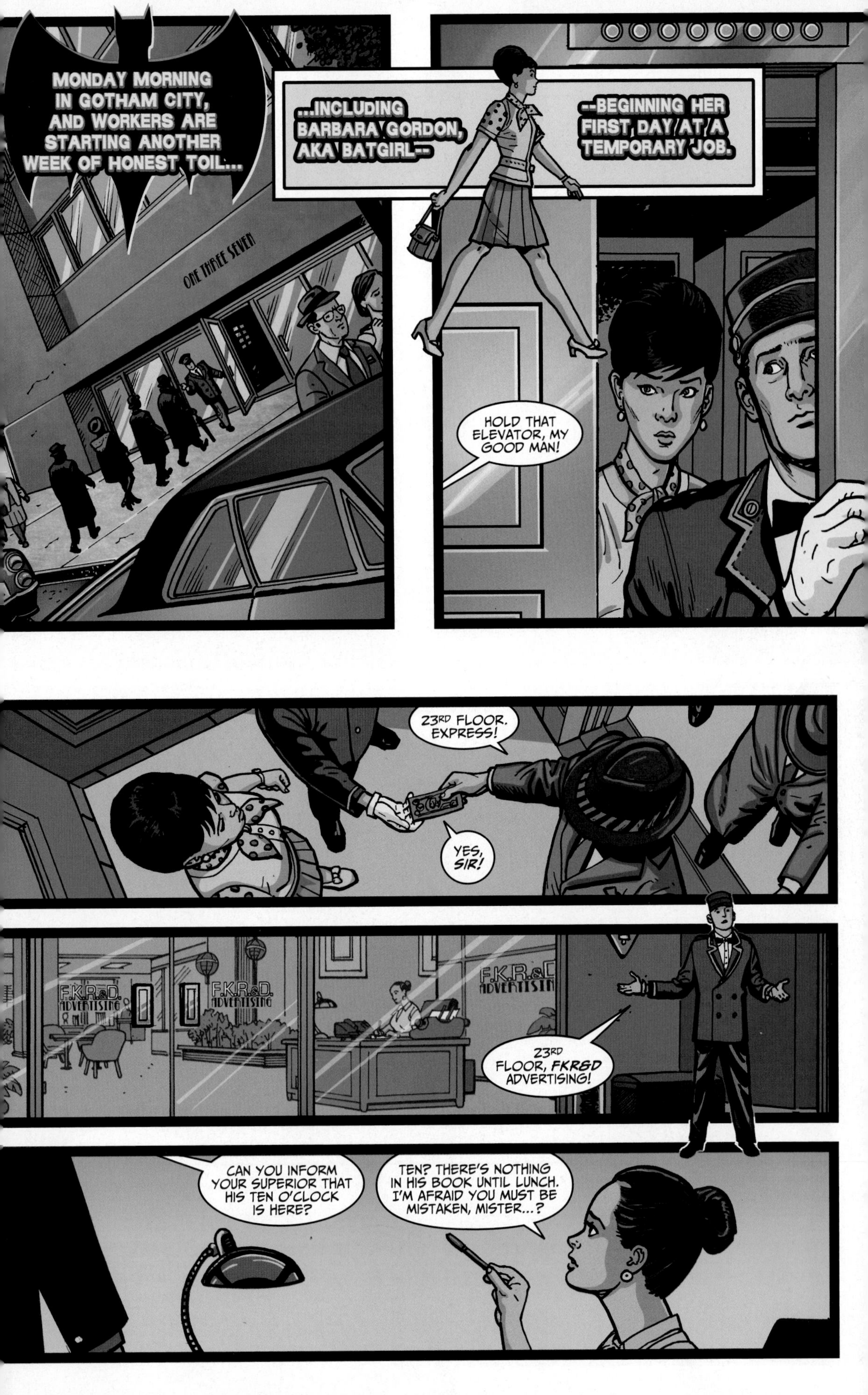
MONDAY MORNING IN GOTHAM CITY, AND WORKERS ARE STARTING ANOTHER WEEK OF HONEST TOIL...
ONE THREE SEVEN
...INCLUDING BARBARA GORDON, AKA BATGIRL--
--BEGINNING HER FIRST DAY AT A TEMPORARY JOB.
HOLD THAT ELEVATOR, MY GOOD MAN!
23RD FLOOR. EXPRESS!
YES, SIR!
F.K.R.&D. ADVERTISING
F.K.R.&D. ADVERTISING
23RD FLOOR, FKR&D ADVERTISING!
CAN YOU INFORM YOUR SUPERIOR THAT HIS TEN O'CLOCK IS HERE?
TEN? THERE'S NOTHING IN HIS BOOK UNTIL LUNCH. I'M AFRAID YOU MUST BE MISTAKEN, MISTER...?

WRITTEN BY **GABE** SORIA
ART BY **TY** TEMPLETON
COLORS BY **TONY** AVIÑA
LETTERED BY **WES** ABBOTT

BATMAN '66 PRESENTS
PENGUIN, CATWOMAN, JOKER, RIDDLER
AND BARBARA GORDON IN...

**BAD**MEN

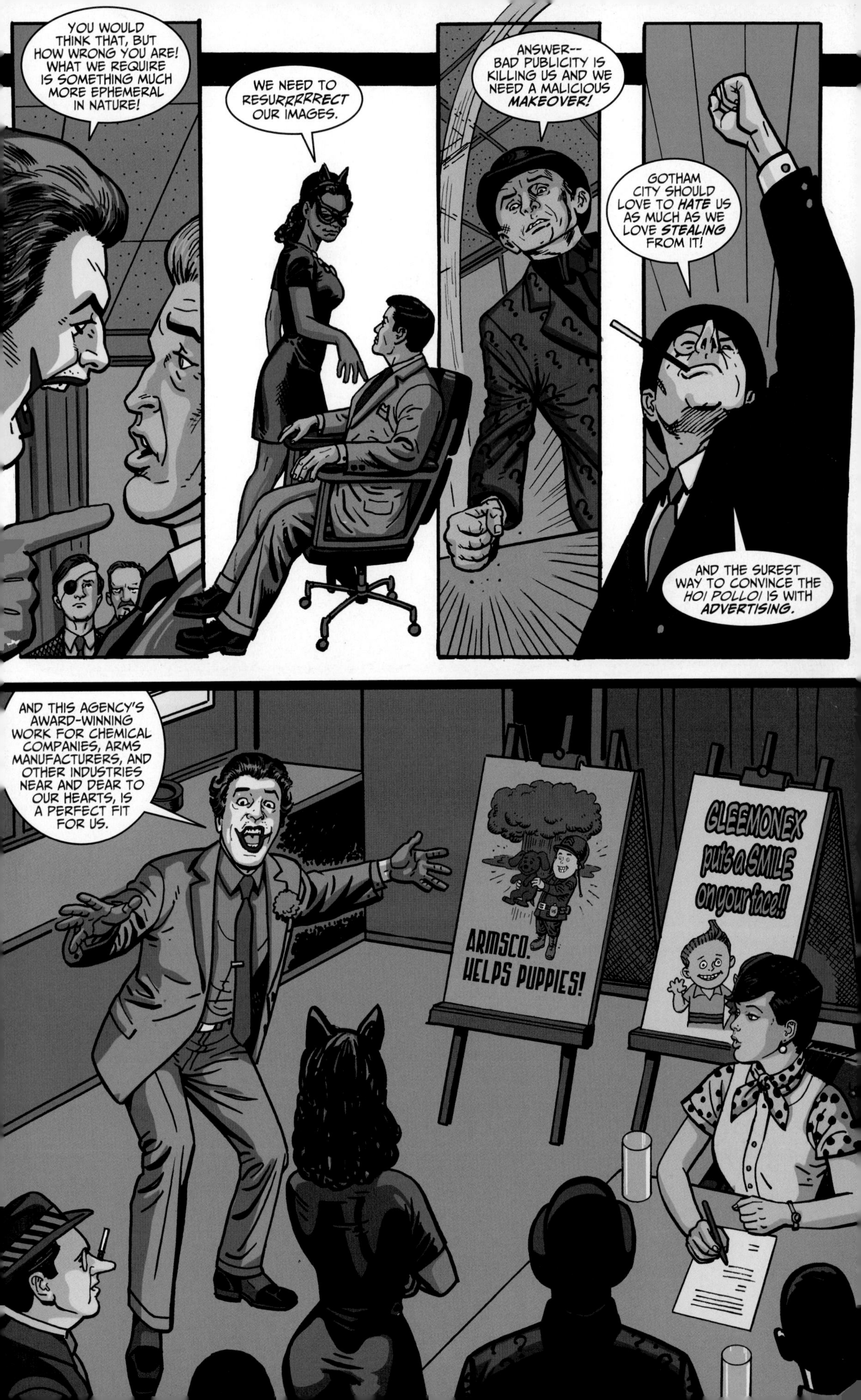

YOU WOULD THINK THAT, BUT HOW WRONG YOU ARE! WHAT WE REQUIRE IS SOMETHING MUCH MORE EPHEMERAL IN NATURE!
WE NEED TO RESURRRRRECT OUR IMAGES.
ANSWER-- BAD PUBLICITY IS KILLING US AND WE NEED A MALICIOUS MAKEOVER!
GOTHAM CITY SHOULD LOVE TO HATE US AS MUCH AS WE LOVE STEALING FROM IT!
AND THE SUREST WAY TO CONVINCE THE HOI POLLOI IS WITH ADVERTISING.
AND THIS AGENCY'S AWARD-WINNING WORK FOR CHEMICAL COMPANIES, ARMS MANUFACTURERS, AND OTHER INDUSTRIES NEAR AND DEAR TO OUR HEARTS, IS A PERFECT FIT FOR US.
ARMSCO. HELPS PUPPIES!
GLEEMONEX puts a SMILE on your face!!

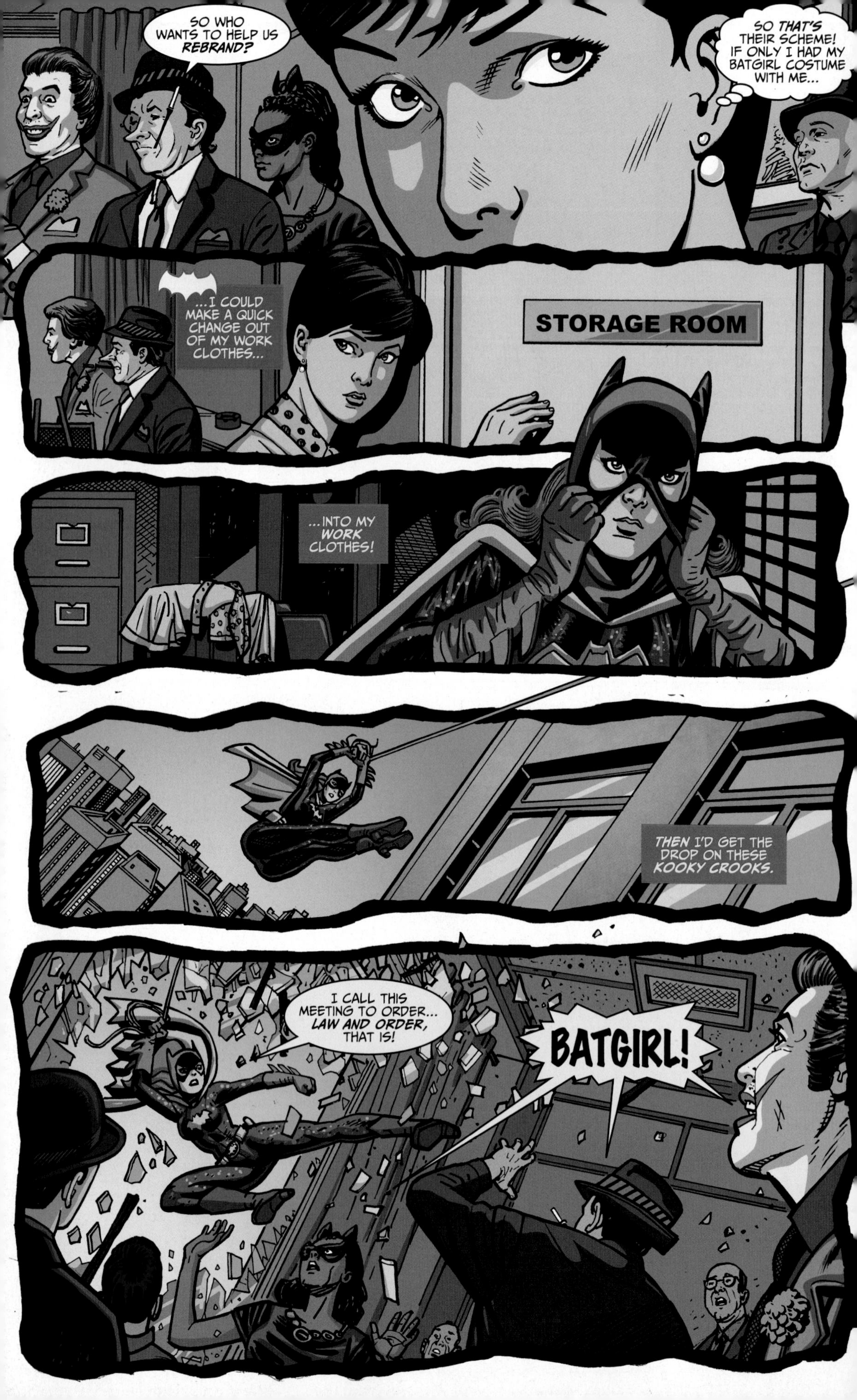
SO WHO WANTS TO HELP US *REBRAND?*
SO *THAT'S* THEIR SCHEME! IF ONLY I HAD MY BATGIRL COSTUME WITH ME...
...I COULD MAKE A QUICK CHANGE OUT OF MY WORK CLOTHES...
STORAGE ROOM
...INTO MY *WORK* CLOTHES!
*THEN* I'D GET THE DROP ON THESE *KOOKY CROOKS.*
I CALL THIS MEETING TO ORDER... *LAW AND ORDER,* THAT IS!
BATGIRL!

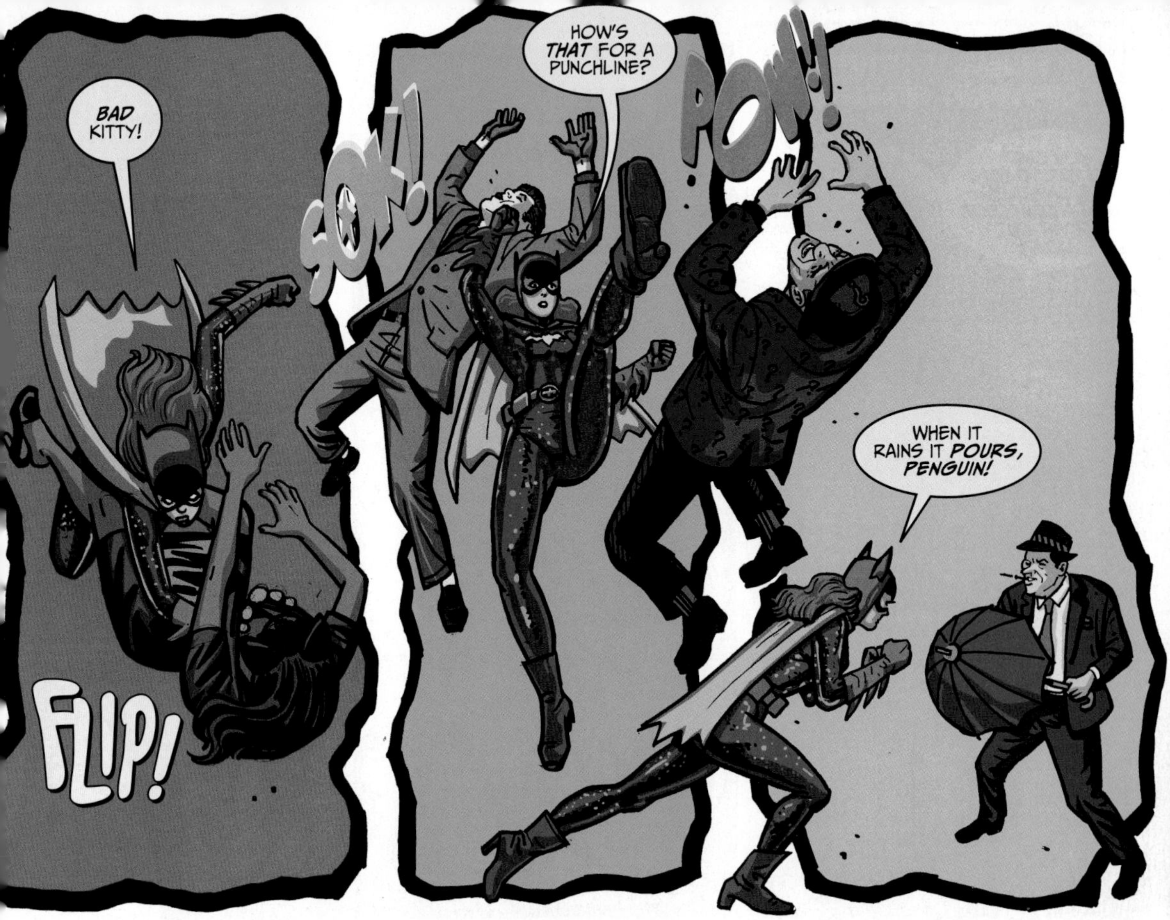
BAD KITTY!
FLIP!
SOK!
HOW'S THAT FOR A PUNCHLINE?
POW!!
WHEN IT RAINS IT POURS, PENGUIN!

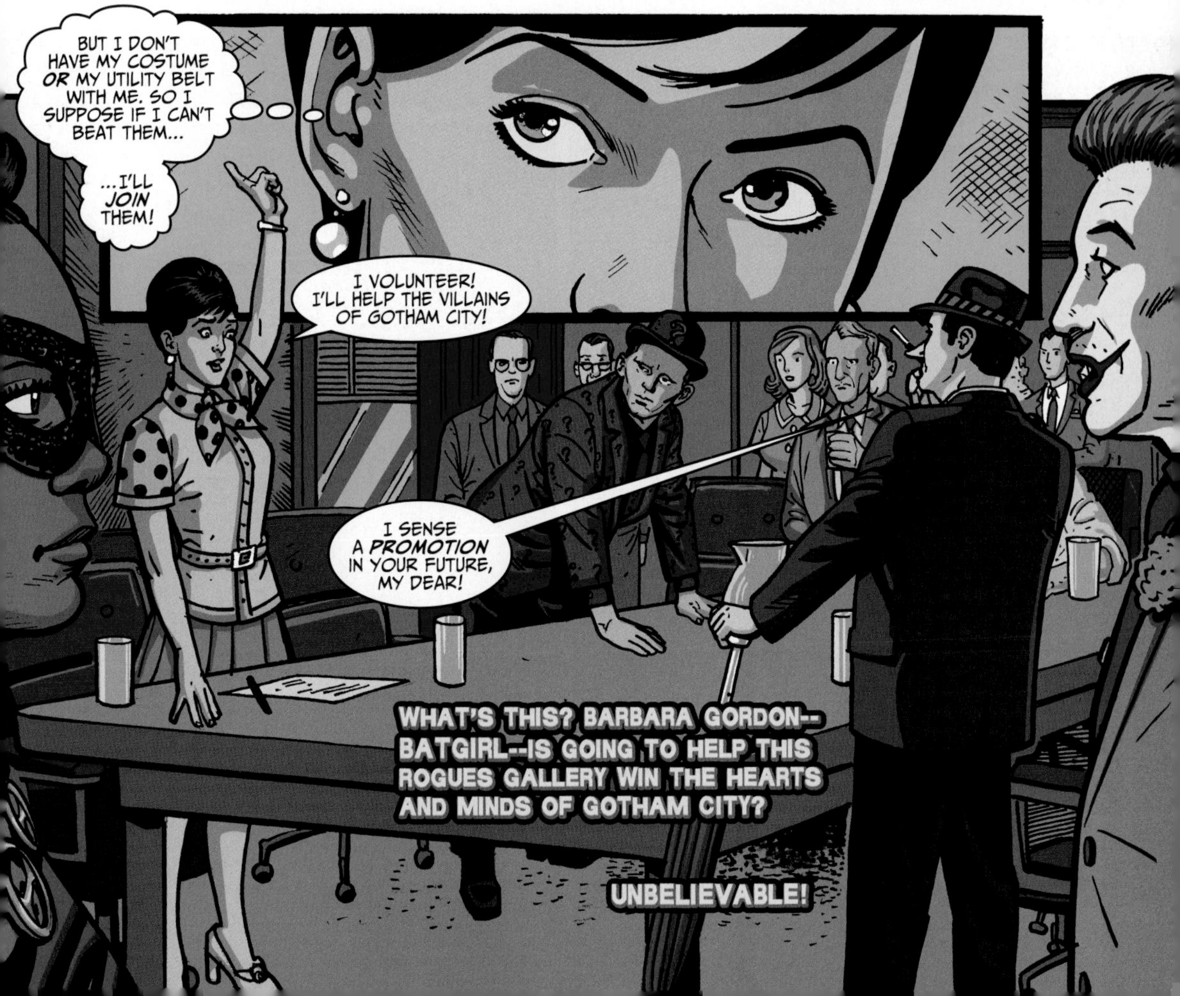
BUT I DON'T HAVE MY COSTUME OR MY UTILITY BELT WITH ME. SO I SUPPOSE IF I CAN'T BEAT THEM...
...I'LL JOIN THEM!
I VOLUNTEER! I'LL HELP THE VILLAINS OF GOTHAM CITY!
I SENSE A PROMOTION IN YOUR FUTURE, MY DEAR!
WHAT'S THIS? BARBARA GORDON--BATGIRL--IS GOING TO HELP THIS ROGUES GALLERY WIN THE HEARTS AND MINDS OF GOTHAM CITY?
UNBELIEVABLE!

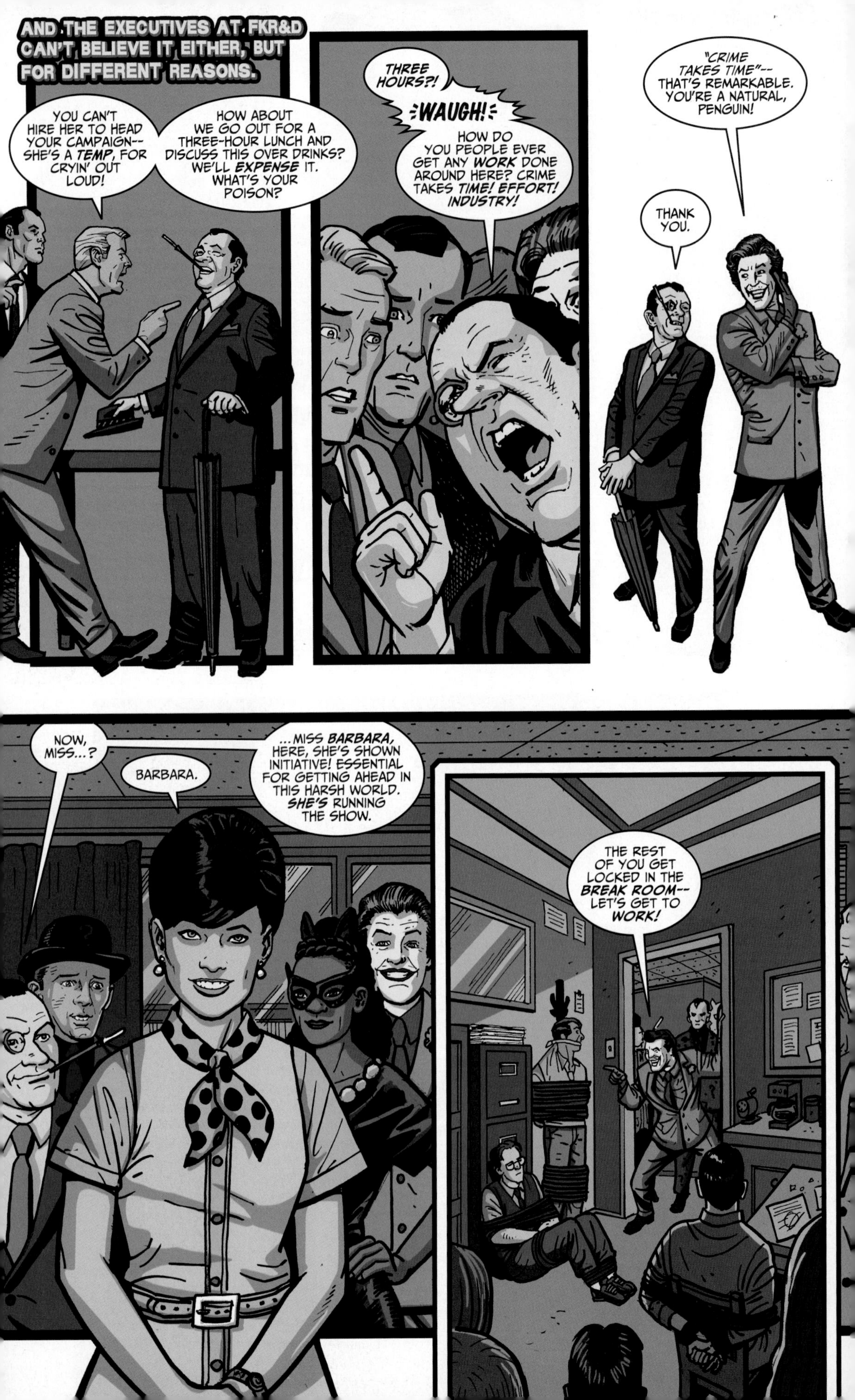
AND THE EXECUTIVES AT FKR&D CAN'T BELIEVE IT EITHER, BUT FOR DIFFERENT REASONS.
YOU CAN'T HIRE HER TO HEAD YOUR CAMPAIGN--SHE'S A TEMP, FOR CRYIN' OUT LOUD!
HOW ABOUT WE GO OUT FOR A THREE-HOUR LUNCH AND DISCUSS THIS OVER DRINKS? WE'LL EXPENSE IT. WHAT'S YOUR POISON?
THREE HOURS?!
WAUGH!
HOW DO YOU PEOPLE EVER GET ANY WORK DONE AROUND HERE? CRIME TAKES TIME! EFFORT! INDUSTRY!
"CRIME TAKES TIME"--THAT'S REMARKABLE. YOU'RE A NATURAL, PENGUIN!
THANK YOU.
NOW, MISS...?
BARBARA.
...MISS BARBARA, HERE, SHE'S SHOWN INITIATIVE! ESSENTIAL FOR GETTING AHEAD IN THIS HARSH WORLD. SHE'S RUNNING THE SHOW.
THE REST OF YOU GET LOCKED IN THE BREAK ROOM--LET'S GET TO WORK!

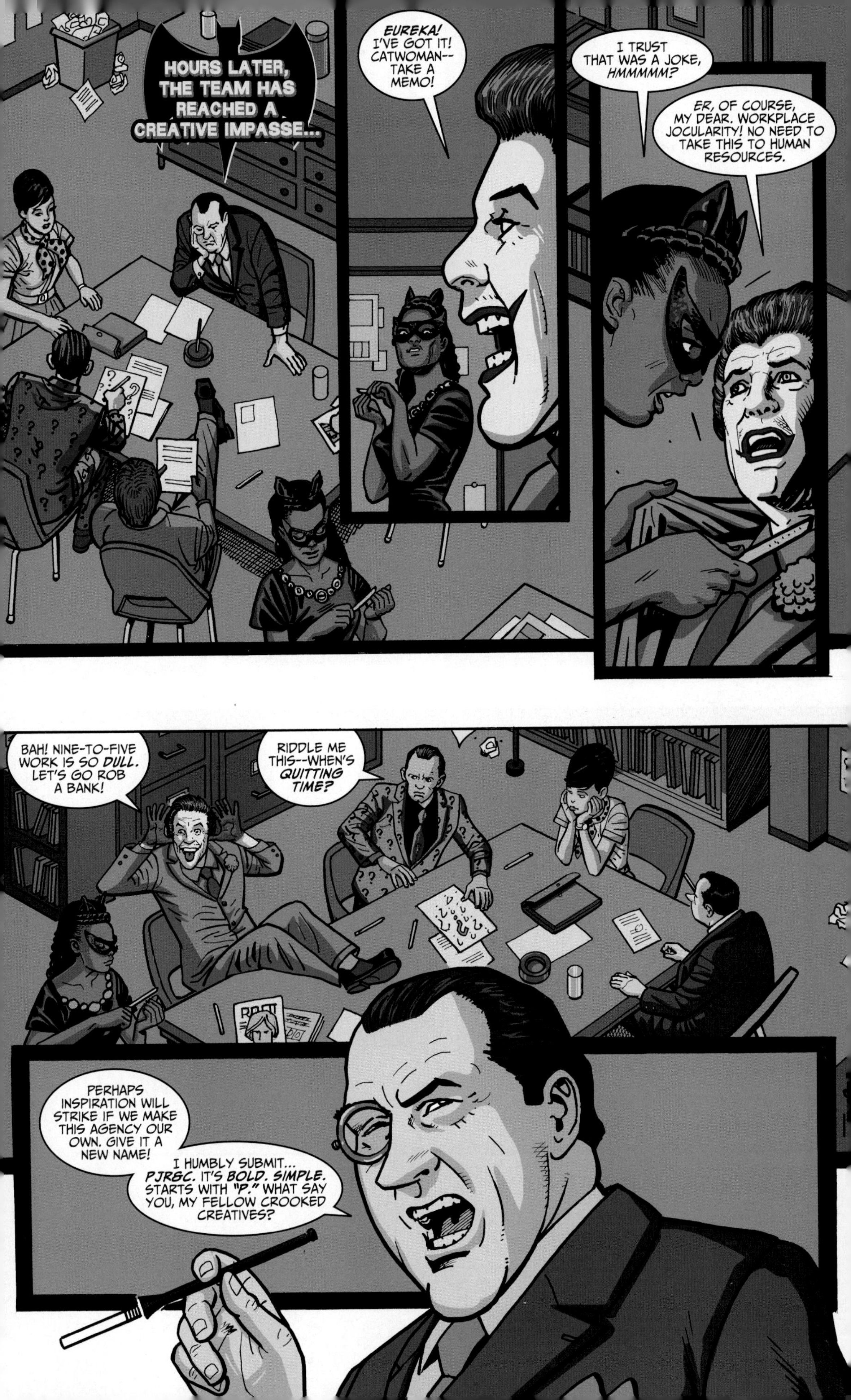
HOURS LATER, THE TEAM HAS REACHED A CREATIVE IMPASSE...
EUREKA! I'VE GOT IT! CATWOMAN-- TAKE A MEMO!
I TRUST THAT WAS A JOKE, HMMMMM?
ER, OF COURSE, MY DEAR. WORKPLACE JOCULARITY! NO NEED TO TAKE THIS TO HUMAN RESOURCES.
BAH! NINE-TO-FIVE WORK IS SO DULL. LET'S GO ROB A BANK!
RIDDLE ME THIS--WHEN'S QUITTING TIME?
PERHAPS INSPIRATION WILL STRIKE IF WE MAKE THIS AGENCY OUR OWN. GIVE IT A NEW NAME!
I HUMBLY SUBMIT... PJRGC. IT'S BOLD. SIMPLE. STARTS WITH "P." WHAT SAY YOU, MY FELLOW CROOKED CREATIVES?

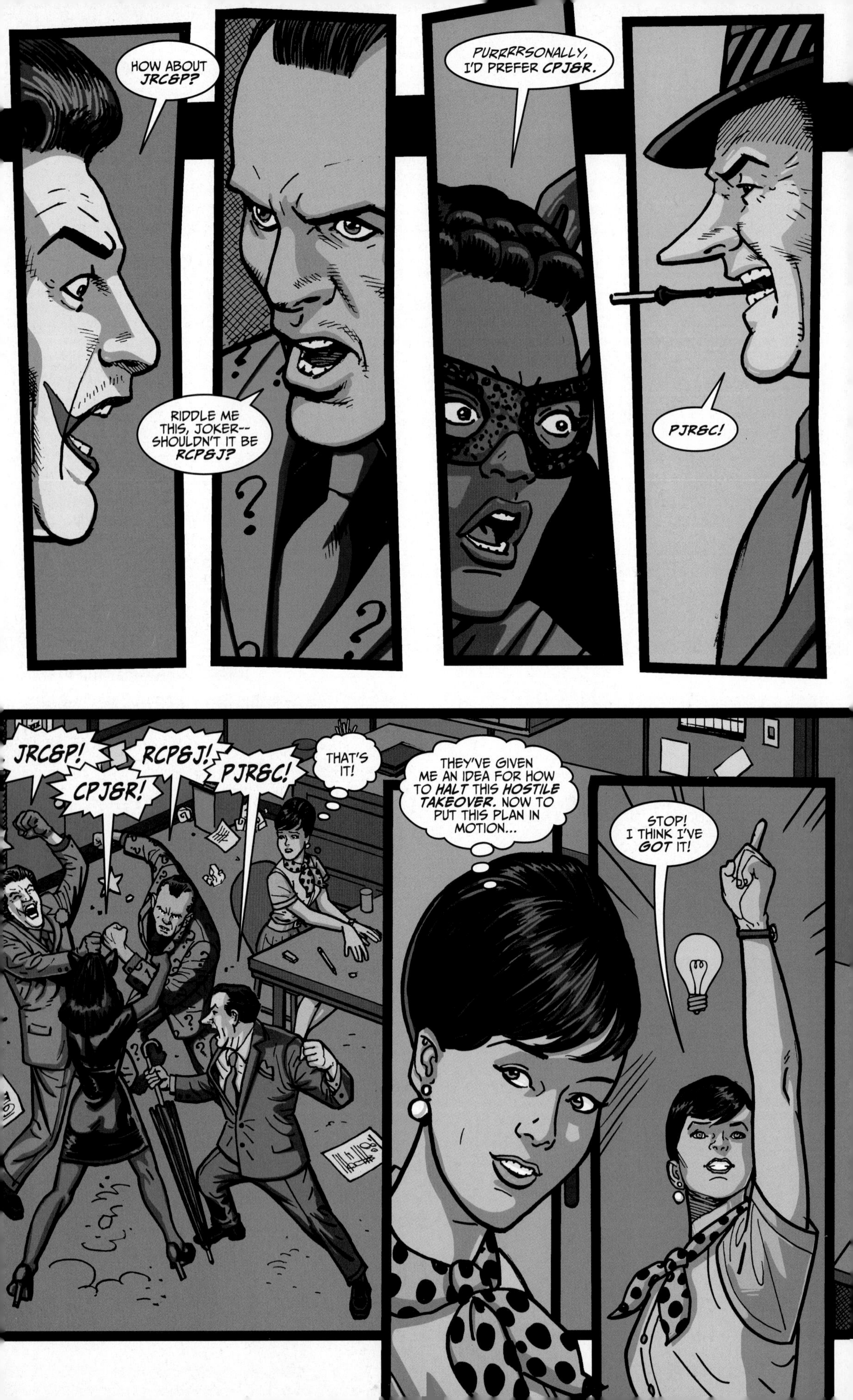
HOW ABOUT JRC&P?
RIDDLE ME THIS, JOKER-- SHOULDN'T IT BE RCP&J?
PURRRRSONALLY, I'D PREFER CPJ&R.
PJR&C!
JRC&P!
CPJ&R!
RCP&J!
PJR&C!
THAT'S IT!
THEY'VE GIVEN ME AN IDEA FOR HOW TO HALT THIS HOSTILE TAKEOVER. NOW TO PUT THIS PLAN IN MOTION...
STOP! I THINK I'VE GOT IT!

TO BEGIN WITH, LET'S FACE THE FACTS-- GOTHAM CITY IS *BORED* OF YOU.

*BORED?* OF THE *JOKER?* BUT I'M THE CLOWN PRINCE OF CRIME. I'M *VERY* ENTERTAINING!

QUIET! LET HER TALK.

YOU'VE ALL BECOME *OLD HAT.* ON MONDAY, CATWOMAN HEISTS A PET SHOW. TUESDAY, THE RIDDLER ROBS A MUSEUM, WEDNESDAY...WELL, YOU GET THE IDEA.

THEY'RE TAKING US FOR GRANTED.

EXACTLY! YOU NEED TO SHAKE THINGS UP. AND THEN THE ANSWER HIT ME. ACTUALLY, YOU WALKED IN WITH THE IDEA, PENGUIN.

I DID?

I GOT JESSICA HERE FROM THE ART DEPARTMENT TO HELP ME WHIP THIS CONCEPT TOGETHER.

IT'S NOT FINAL, BUT I THINK WE'VE GOT IT.

LADY AND GENTLEMEN, MAY WE PRESENT TO YOU...

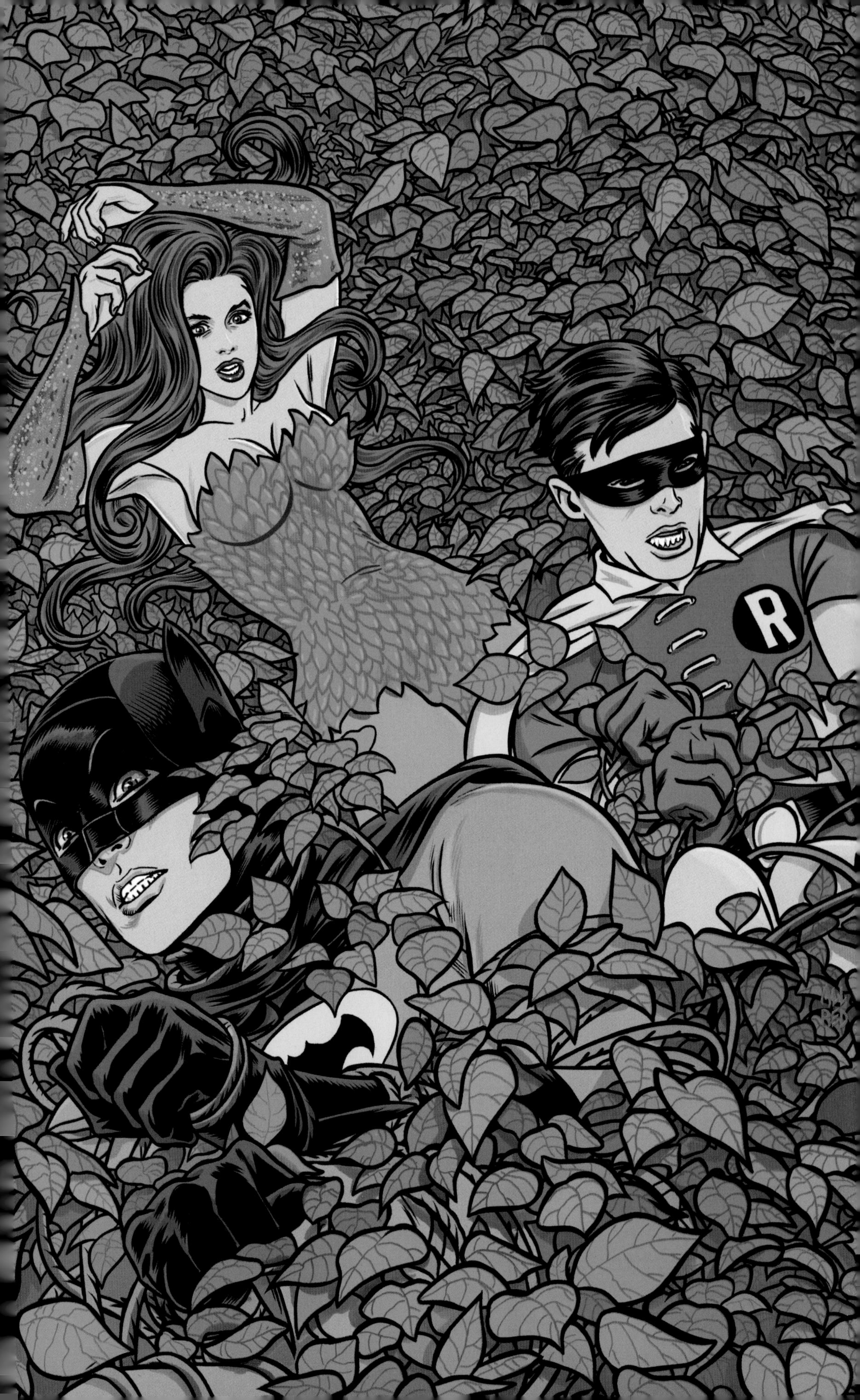

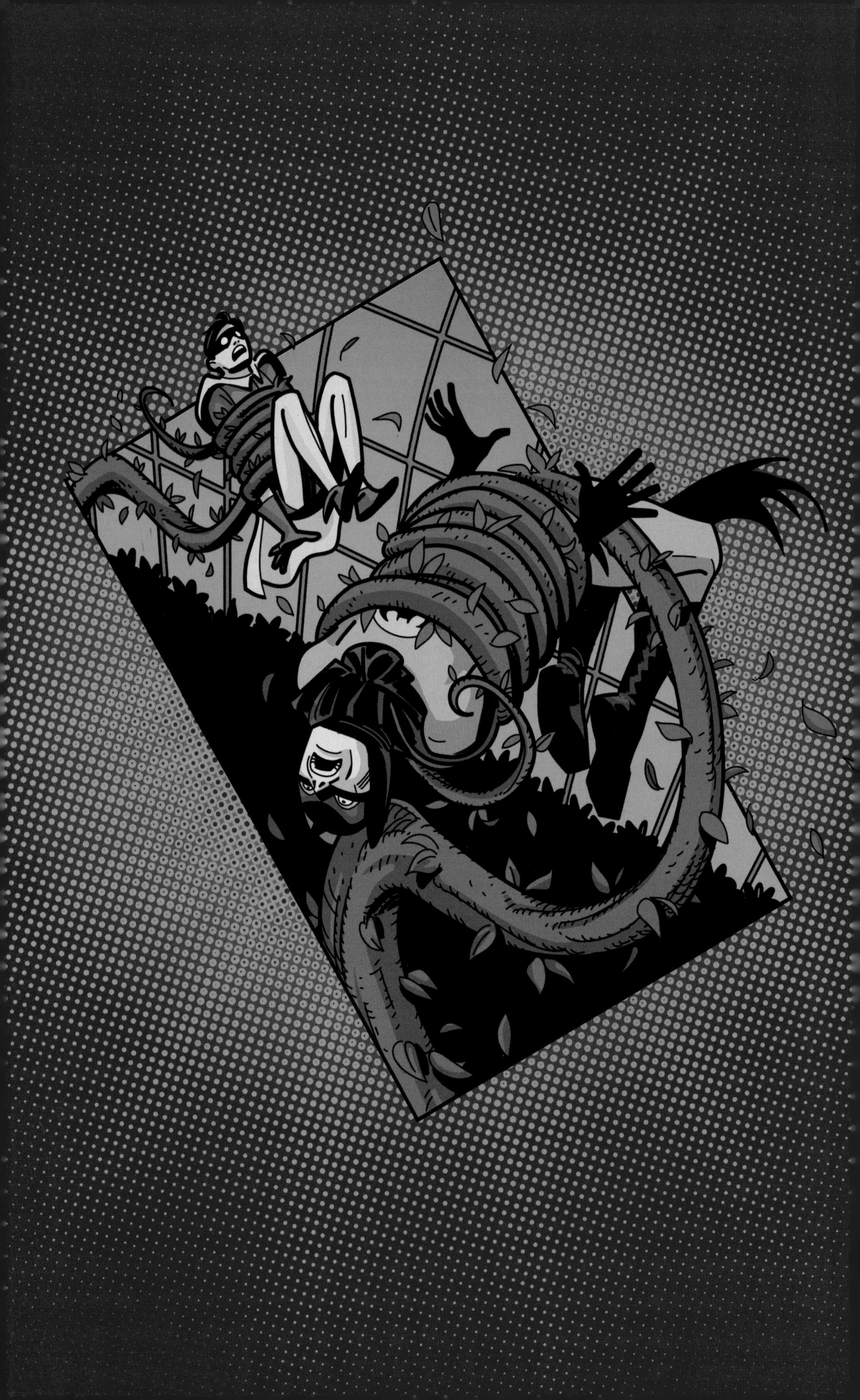

# "POISON IVY'S DEADLY KISS"

Written by JEFF PARKER   Art by JESSE HAMM
Colors by KELLY FITZPATRICK   Letters by WES ABBOTT
Cover by MICHAEL and LAURA ALLRED

HOW--HOW DO YOU KNOW IT'S *MURDER*, CAPED CRUSADER?

IT'S CERTAINLY NOT NATURAL CAUSES, COMMISSIONER. SOMEONE THE LILAC KNEW... WHO COULD GET IN CLOSE WITHOUT HIM GRABBING A WEAPON.

AND WHO LEFT A VERY *DEADLY* TRACE.

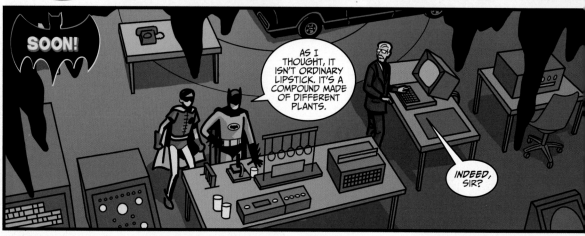

SOON!

AS I THOUGHT, IT ISN'T ORDINARY LIPSTICK. IT'S A COMPOUND MADE OF DIFFERENT PLANTS.

INDEED, SIR?

PARTICULARLY, A FLORAL CHEMICAL FROM *ROSA CARULEA*. AN EXTREMELY RARE AND DEADLY FLOWERING BUSH.

WHEN ABSORBED BY THE SKIN...

VWEEP
VWEEP
VWEEP

A KISS... FROM A *ROSE*...

YES, THANK YOU, COMMISSIONER. BATMAN *DOES* WANT TO BE AT THE QUESTIONING...

"ALL RIGHT, MACURDY, YE WANT TO PLAY HARDBALL, DO YE?"

THERE'S YER WATER... BUT NOT *COLD*, LIKE YE ASKED FOR. *LUKEWARM.*

I GOT *RIGHTS*, O'HARA!

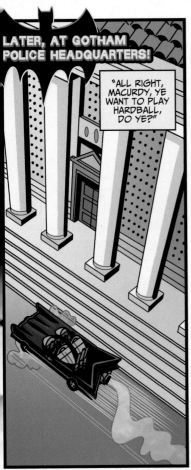

I'LL TAKE OVER QUESTIONING, CHIEF.

*GULP!*

LOOK, YOU GUYS CAN'T THINK I OFFED THE BOSS. I'M THE ONE WHO CALLED IT IN!

NO, WHAT I WANT TO KNOW IS WHERE LOUIE GOT HIS PLANTS.

SEEING YOUR HIDEOUT, THERE WASN'T ENOUGH OF A SETUP TO GROW SUCH SPECIALIZED HYBRIDS.

THE BOSS NEVER TOOK ANY OF US WITH HIM THE NIGHTS HE WENT. HE KEPT HIS SOURCE *TOP SECRET!*

YOU HAVE TO *THINK!* ANYTHING YOU REMEMBER ABOUT HIS TRIPS.

THERE'S A *KILLER* AT LARGE!

I GOT *NOTHING*, I MEAN, EXCEPT MAYBE...

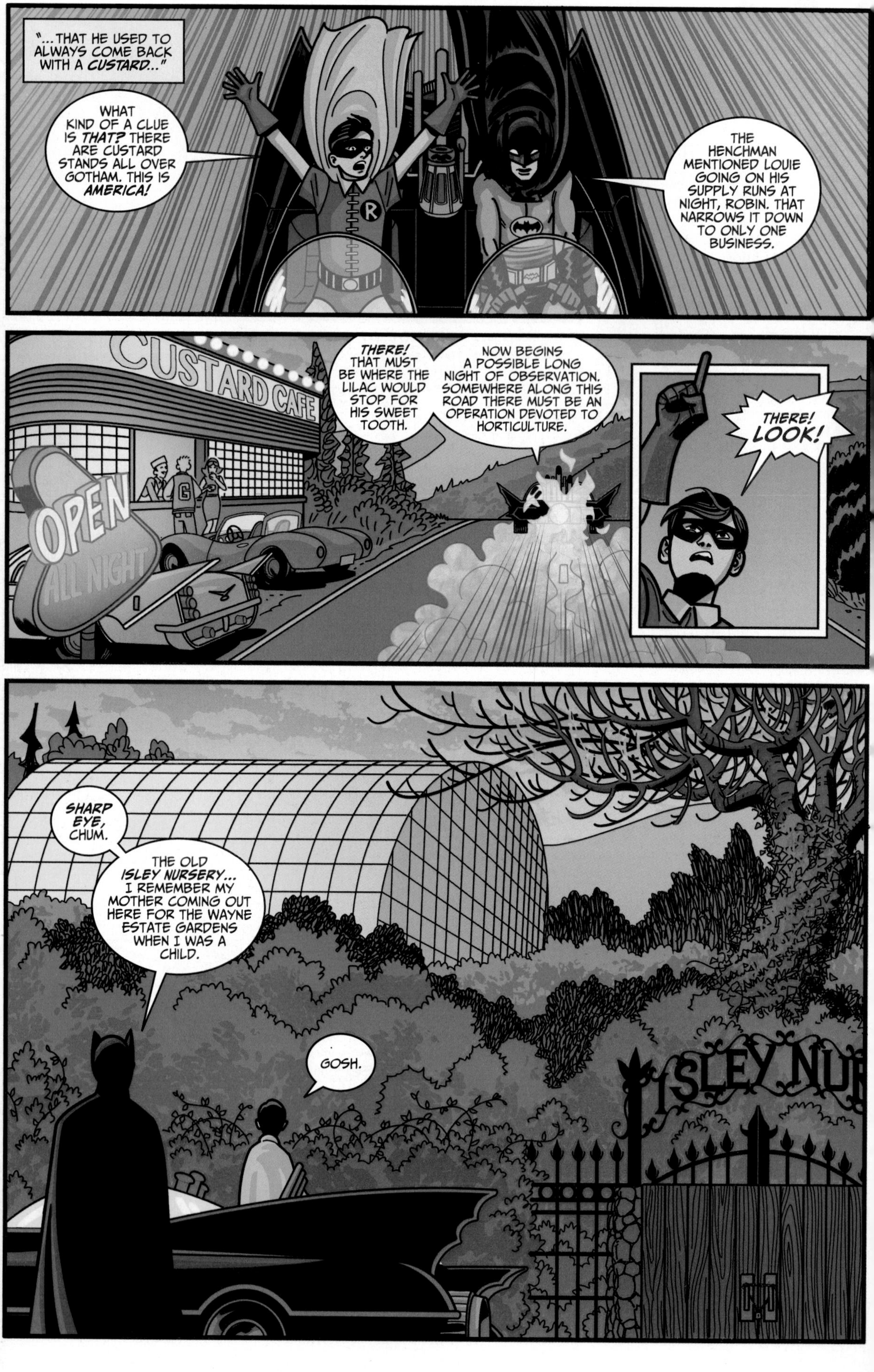
"...THAT HE USED TO ALWAYS COME BACK WITH A *CUSTARD*..."
WHAT KIND OF A CLUE IS *THAT?* THERE ARE CUSTARD STANDS ALL OVER GOTHAM. THIS IS *AMERICA!*
THE HENCHMAN MENTIONED LOUIE GOING ON HIS SUPPLY RUNS AT NIGHT, ROBIN. THAT NARROWS IT DOWN TO ONLY ONE BUSINESS.
CUSTARD CAFE
OPEN ALL NIGHT
*THERE!* THAT MUST BE WHERE THE LILAC WOULD STOP FOR HIS SWEET TOOTH.
NOW BEGINS A POSSIBLE LONG NIGHT OF OBSERVATION. SOMEWHERE ALONG THIS ROAD THERE MUST BE AN OPERATION DEVOTED TO HORTICULTURE.
*THERE! LOOK!*
*SHARP EYE,* CHUM.
THE OLD *ISLEY NURSERY*... I REMEMBER MY MOTHER COMING OUT HERE FOR THE WAYNE ESTATE GARDENS WHEN I WAS A CHILD.
GOSH.
ISLEY NU

BAT-SKELETON KEY SHOULD WORK FOR THIS...

SO... YOU HAVE BEEN HERE BEFORE?

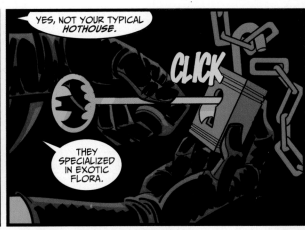

YES, NOT YOUR TYPICAL HOTHOUSE.

CLICK

THEY SPECIALIZED IN EXOTIC FLORA.

"THE ISLEYS WERE ESTEEMED BOTANISTS WHO HAD MOVED TO GOTHAM TO TEACH AT THE UNIVERSITY AND START THIS NURSERY."

GREAT, YOU'VE SUCCESSFULLY GRAFTED A STEM, PAMELA!

WE'D LOVE TO PLANT ORCHARDS AT WAYNE MANOR.

I'LL COME OUT AND DO A SOIL STUDY, AND WE CAN START RIGHT AWAY, MRS. WAYNE!

"THEY DID VERY WELL FOR MANY YEARS, A FIXTURE OF GOTHAM.

"THEN ONE DAY, DR. ISLEY TOOK ILL...HE HAD BEEN EXPOSED TO THE NETTLES OF A TROPICAL BUSH THAT HAD BEEN MISLABELED AS A HARMLESS PLANT.

"HIS HEALTH NEVER RECOVERED, AND NEITHER DID THE BUSINESS. HIS FAMILY MOVED BACK TO THE SOUTH AND THE NURSERY CLOSED."

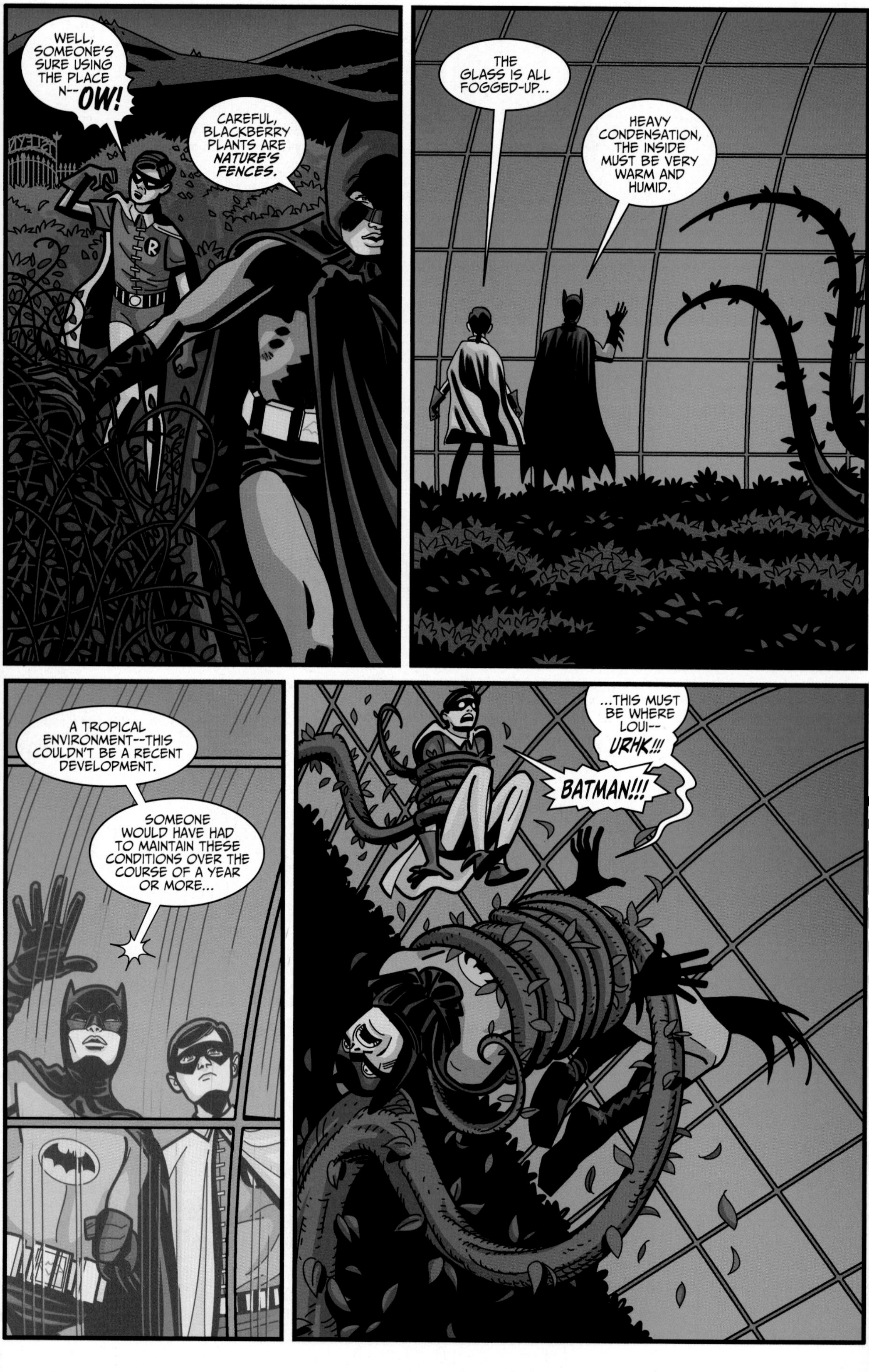
WELL, SOMEONE'S SURE USING THE PLACE N--OW!
CAREFUL, BLACKBERRY PLANTS ARE NATURE'S FENCES.
THE GLASS IS ALL FOGGED-UP...
HEAVY CONDENSATION, THE INSIDE MUST BE VERY WARM AND HUMID.
A TROPICAL ENVIRONMENT--THIS COULDN'T BE A RECENT DEVELOPMENT.
SOMEONE WOULD HAVE HAD TO MAINTAIN THESE CONDITIONS OVER THE COURSE OF A YEAR OR MORE...
...THIS MUST BE WHERE LOUI--URHK!!!
BATMAN!!!

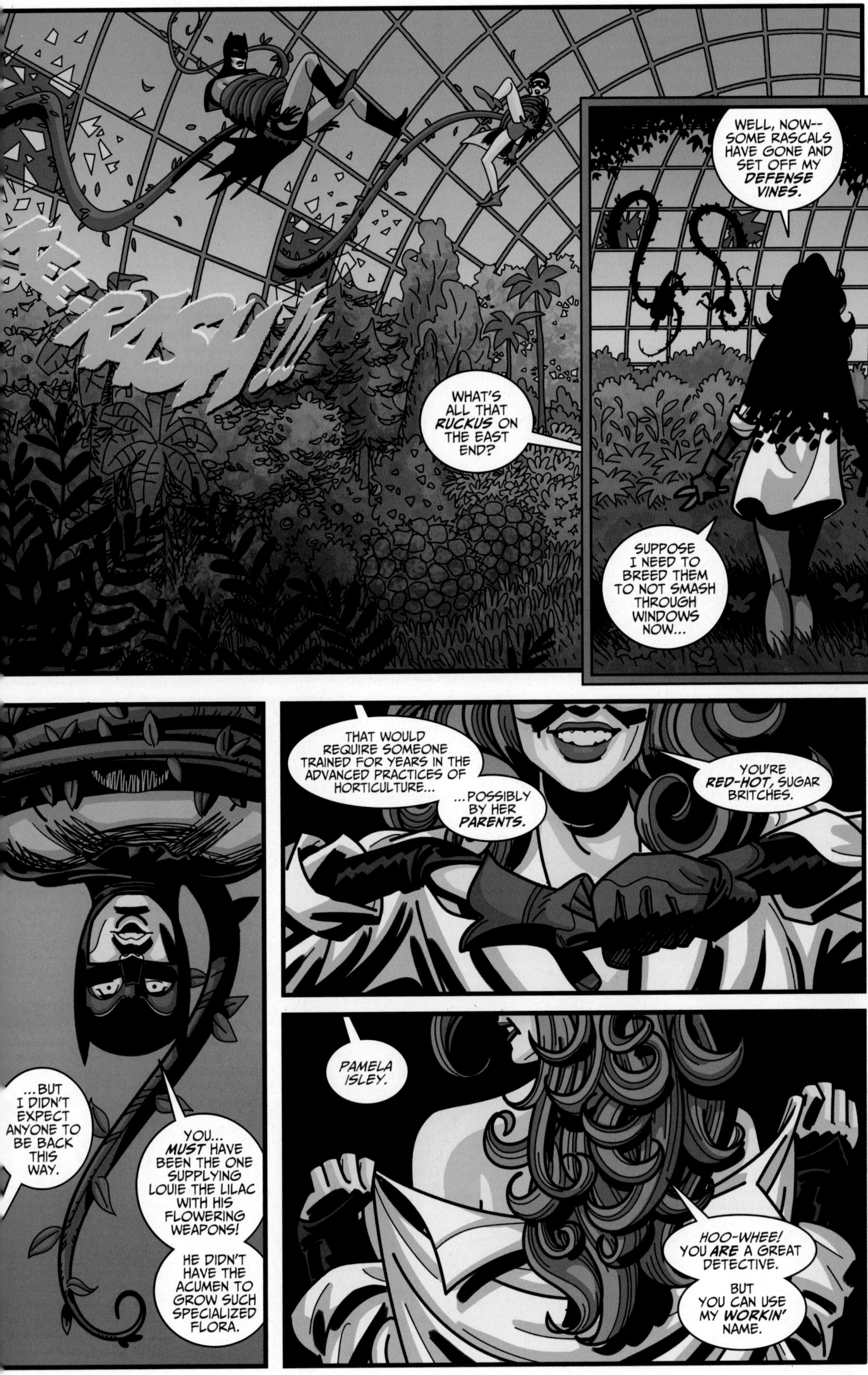
KER-RASH!!!
WHAT'S ALL THAT RUCKUS ON THE EAST END?
WELL, NOW-- SOME RASCALS HAVE GONE AND SET OFF MY DEFENSE VINES.
SUPPOSE I NEED TO BREED THEM TO NOT SMASH THROUGH WINDOWS NOW...
...BUT I DIDN'T EXPECT ANYONE TO BE BACK THIS WAY.
YOU... MUST HAVE BEEN THE ONE SUPPLYING LOUIE THE LILAC WITH HIS FLOWERING WEAPONS!
HE DIDN'T HAVE THE ACUMEN TO GROW SUCH SPECIALIZED FLORA.
THAT WOULD REQUIRE SOMEONE TRAINED FOR YEARS IN THE ADVANCED PRACTICES OF HORTICULTURE...
...POSSIBLY BY HER PARENTS.
YOU'RE RED-HOT, SUGAR BRITCHES.
PAMELA ISLEY.
HOO-WHEE! YOU ARE A GREAT DETECTIVE.
BUT YOU CAN USE MY WORKIN' NAME.

POISON IVY!

I'VE BEEN READYING MY DEBUT IN GOTHAM FOR *TWO YEARS* NOW, TESTING OUT MY CREATIONS THROUGH THE LILAC...

...WHO RECENTLY THOUGHT HE DIDN'T *NEED* TO PAY LITTLE OL' IVY FOR HER HARD WORK. SO I LEARNED HIM *OTHERWISE.*

POISON!

*HUSH UP,* BOY, I'M TALKIN' TO YOUR BOSS.

'SIDES, I ALREADY SAID IT IN MY NAME. BUT IT AIN'T POISON TO *ME.*

I SPENT MY LIFE SLOWLY INOCULATING M'SELF WITH THAT DEADLY PLANT THAT TOOK MY DADDY FROM ME.

I DETERMINED I'D *SHOW* THAT BUSH WHO WAS IN CHARGE.

DRIP   DRIP   DRIP

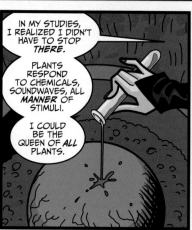

IN MY STUDIES, I REALIZED I DIDN'T HAVE TO STOP *THERE.*

PLANTS RESPOND TO CHEMICALS, SOUNDWAVES, ALL *MANNER* OF STIMULI.

I COULD BE THE QUEEN OF *ALL* PLANTS.

AND I DON'T NEED *MIDDLEMEN* MAKING ALL THE MONEY WHILE I DO ALL THE *REAL* WORK.

I DON'T NEED *MEN* AT ALL.

BBRRRRRTTRRR

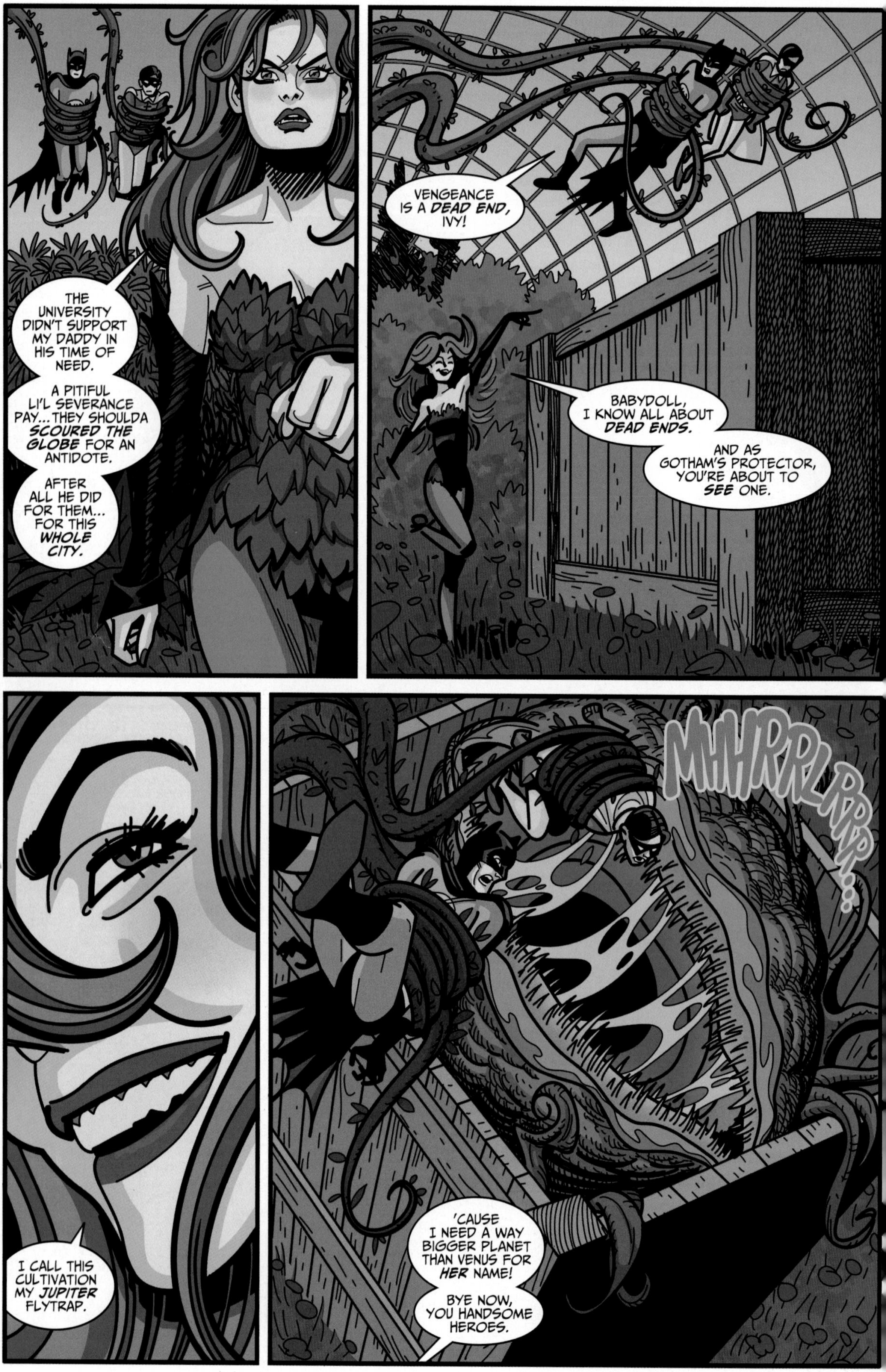
THE UNIVERSITY DIDN'T SUPPORT MY DADDY IN HIS TIME OF NEED.
A PITIFUL LI'L SEVERANCE PAY... THEY SHOULDA SCOURED THE GLOBE FOR AN ANTIDOTE.
AFTER ALL HE DID FOR THEM... FOR THIS WHOLE CITY.
VENGEANCE IS A DEAD END, IVY!
BABYDOLL, I KNOW ALL ABOUT DEAD ENDS.
AND AS GOTHAM'S PROTECTOR, YOU'RE ABOUT TO SEE ONE.
I CALL THIS CULTIVATION MY JUPITER FLYTRAP.
MHHRRLRRR...
'CAUSE I NEED A WAY BIGGER PLANET THAN VENUS FOR HER NAME!
BYE NOW, YOU HANDSOME HEROES.

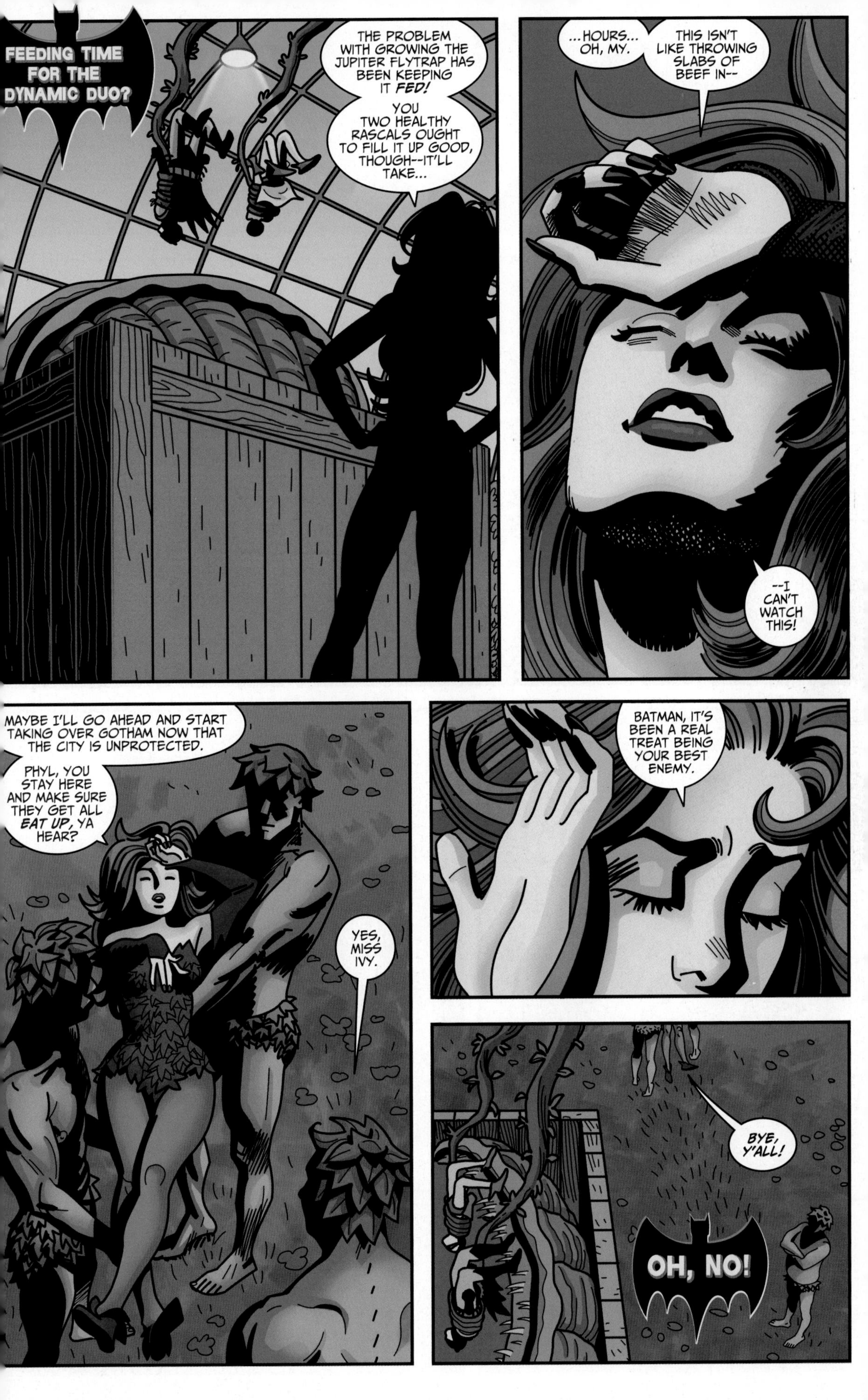
FEEDING TIME FOR THE DYNAMIC DUO?
THE PROBLEM WITH GROWING THE JUPITER FLYTRAP HAS BEEN KEEPING IT FED!
YOU TWO HEALTHY RASCALS OUGHT TO FILL IT UP GOOD, THOUGH--IT'LL TAKE...
...HOURS... OH, MY.
THIS ISN'T LIKE THROWING SLABS OF BEEF IN--
--I CAN'T WATCH THIS!
MAYBE I'LL GO AHEAD AND START TAKING OVER GOTHAM NOW THAT THE CITY IS UNPROTECTED.
PHYL, YOU STAY HERE AND MAKE SURE THEY GET ALL EAT UP, YA HEAR?
YES, MISS IVY.
BATMAN, IT'S BEEN A REAL TREAT BEING YOUR BEST ENEMY.
BYE, Y'ALL!
OH, NO!

THIS IS IT-- *NO ESCAPE!*

I'M NEVER GOING TO GROW UP AND INHERIT THE MANTLE OF *BATMAN!*

AH... *EASY,* CHUM, LET'S NOT PUT THE CART BEFORE THE HORSE.

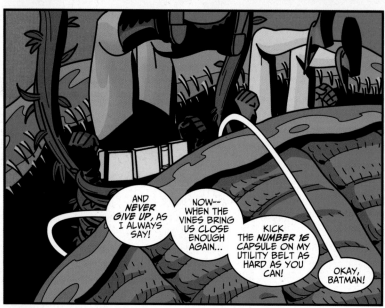

AND *NEVER GIVE UP,* AS I ALWAYS SAY!

NOW-- WHEN THE VINES BRING US CLOSE ENOUGH AGAIN...

KICK THE *NUMBER 16* CAPSULE ON MY UTILITY BELT AS HARD AS YOU CAN!

OKAY, BATMAN!

MOST IMPORTANTLY-- HOLD YOUR BREATH AS SOON AS IT BURSTS!

CLOSER... IF I CAN GET CLOSER...

PSSHHHH

NOW!

WHAT AM THAT?

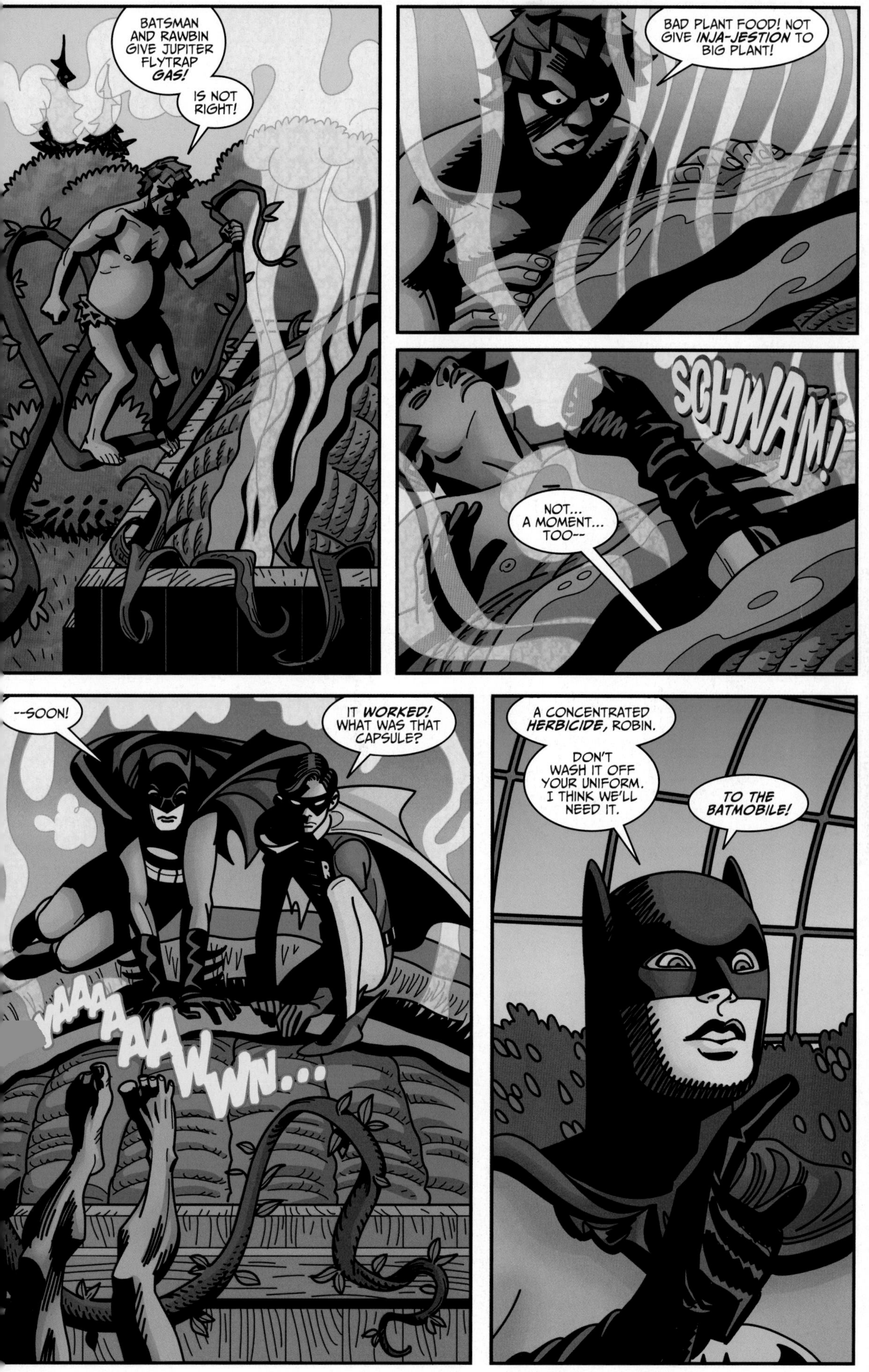

BATSMAN AND RAWBIN GIVE JUPITER FLYTRAP GAS!
IS NOT RIGHT!
BAD PLANT FOOD! NOT GIVE INJA-JESTION TO BIG PLANT!
SCHWAM!
NOT... A MOMENT... TOO--
--SOON!
IT WORKED! WHAT WAS THAT CAPSULE?
YAAAAAAWWN...
A CONCENTRATED HERBICIDE, ROBIN.
DON'T WASH IT OFF YOUR UNIFORM. I THINK WE'LL NEED IT.
TO THE BATMOBILE!

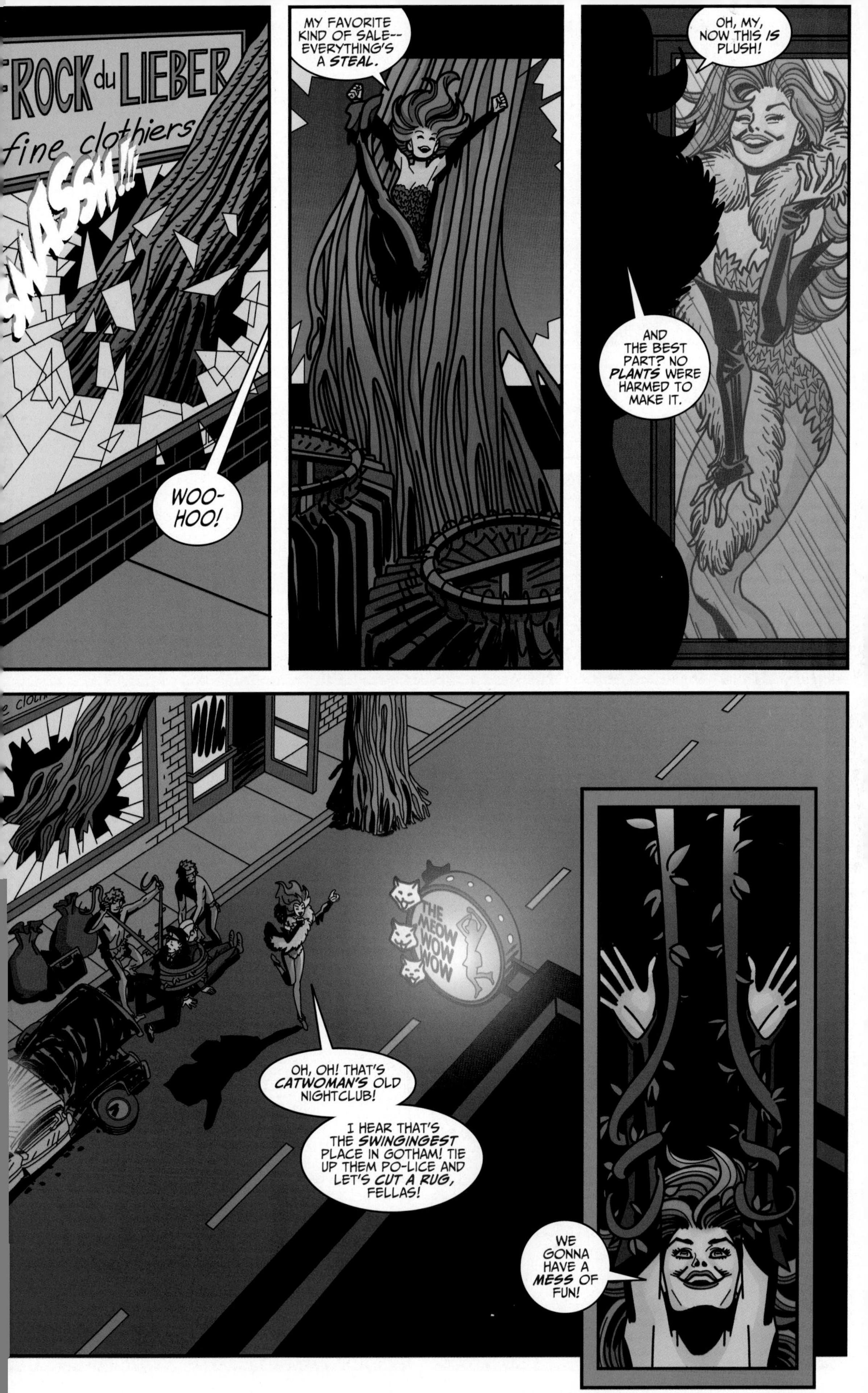
FROCK du LIEBER
fine clothiers
SMASSH!!!
WOO-HOO!
MY FAVORITE KIND OF SALE-- EVERYTHING'S A STEAL.
OH, MY, NOW THIS IS PLUSH!
AND THE BEST PART? NO PLANTS WERE HARMED TO MAKE IT.
THE MEOW WOW WOW
OH, OH! THAT'S CATWOMAN'S OLD NIGHTCLUB!
I HEAR THAT'S THE SWINGINGEST PLACE IN GOTHAM! TIE UP THEM PO-LICE AND LET'S CUT A RUG, FELLAS!
WE GONNA HAVE A MESS OF FUN!

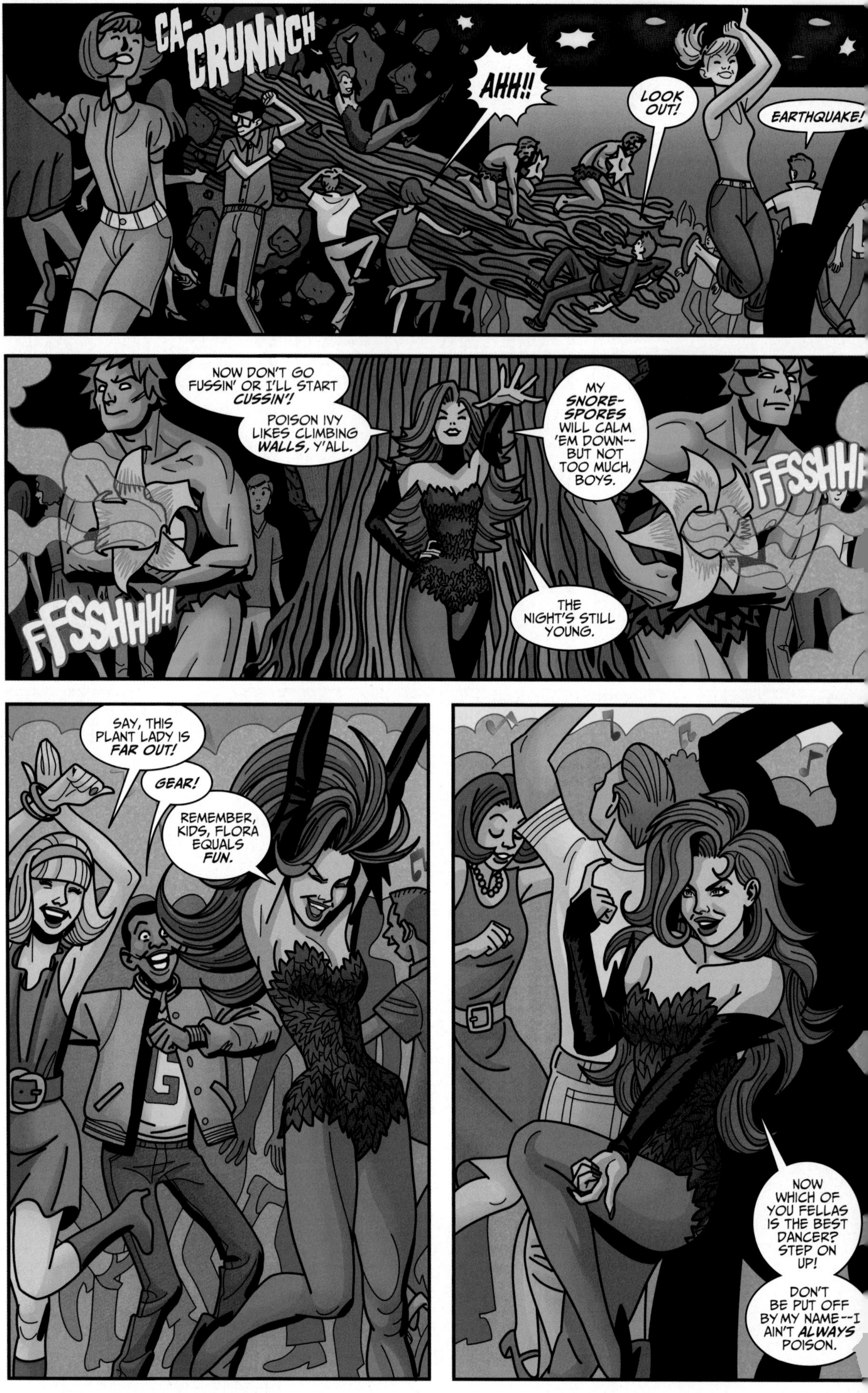
CA-CRUNNCH
AHH!!
LOOK OUT!
EARTHQUAKE!
NOW DON'T GO FUSSIN' OR I'LL START CUSSIN'!
POISON IVY LIKES CLIMBING WALLS, Y'ALL.
MY SNORE-SPORES WILL CALM 'EM DOWN-- BUT NOT TOO MUCH, BOYS.
FFSSHHH
FFSSHHHH
THE NIGHT'S STILL YOUNG.
SAY, THIS PLANT LADY IS FAR OUT!
GEAR!
REMEMBER, KIDS, FLORA EQUALS FUN.
NOW WHICH OF YOU FELLAS IS THE BEST DANCER? STEP ON UP!
DON'T BE PUT OFF BY MY NAME--I AIN'T ALWAYS POISON.

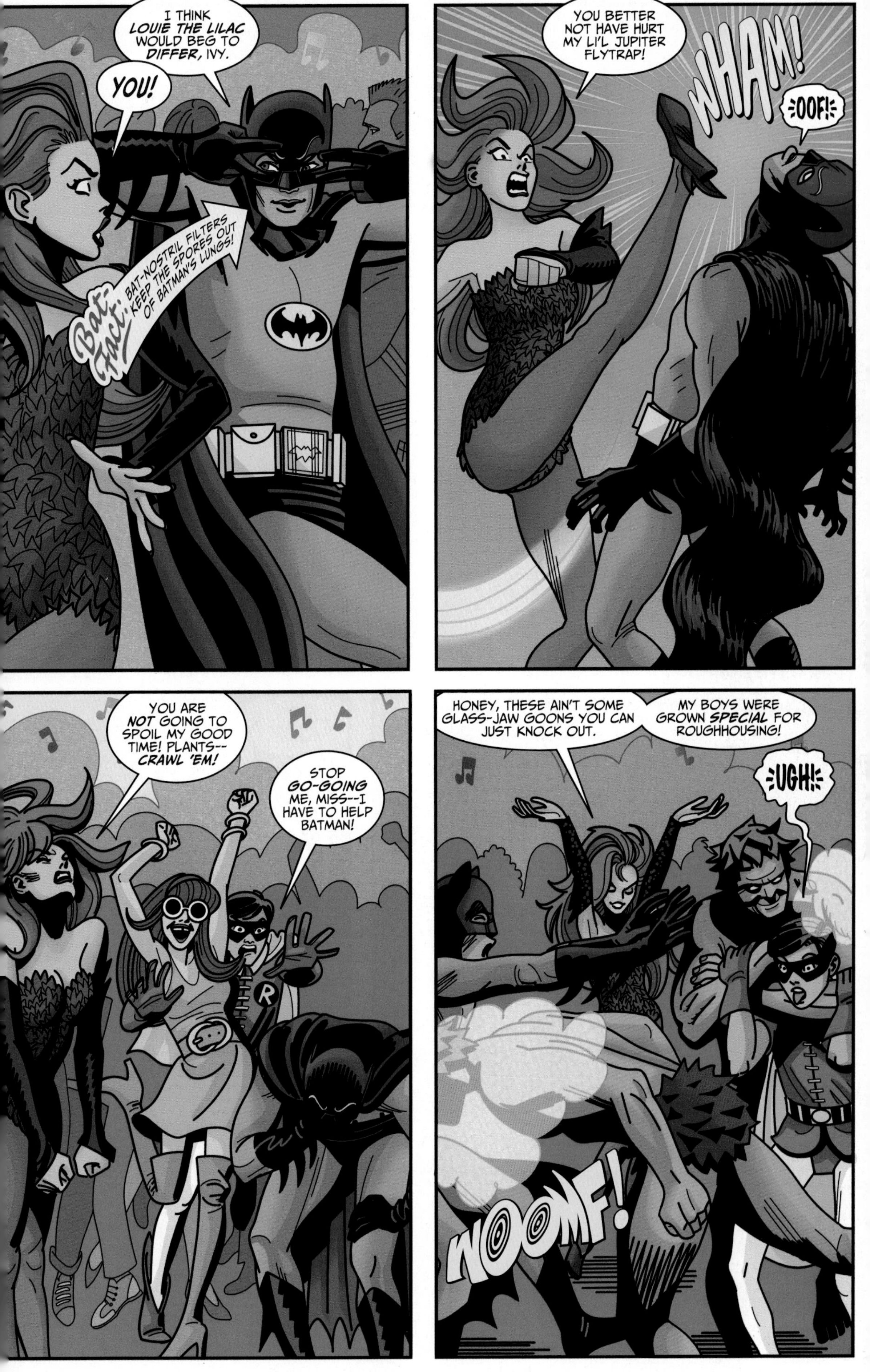
I THINK LOUIE THE LILAC WOULD BEG TO DIFFER, IVY.
YOU!
Bat-Fact: BAT-NOSTRIL FILTERS KEEP THE SPORES OUT OF BATMAN'S LUNGS!
YOU BETTER NOT HAVE HURT MY LI'L JUPITER FLYTRAP!
WHAM!
OOF!
YOU ARE NOT GOING TO SPOIL MY GOOD TIME! PLANTS-- CRAWL 'EM!
STOP GO-GOING ME, MISS--I HAVE TO HELP BATMAN!
HONEY, THESE AIN'T SOME GLASS-JAW GOONS YOU CAN JUST KNOCK OUT.
MY BOYS WERE GROWN SPECIAL FOR ROUGHHOUSING!
UGH!
WOOMF!

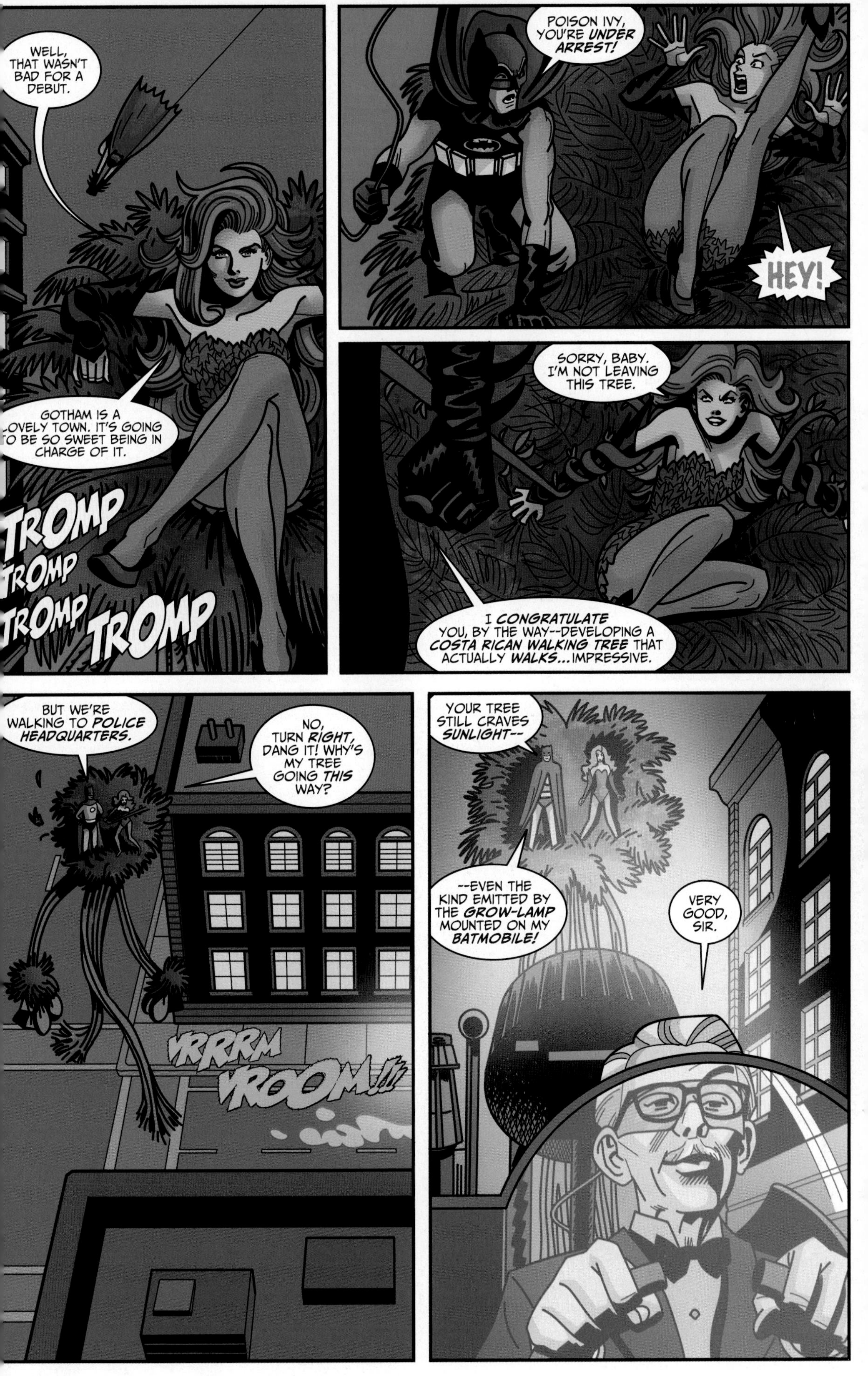
WELL, THAT WASN'T BAD FOR A DEBUT.
GOTHAM IS A LOVELY TOWN. IT'S GOING TO BE SO SWEET BEING IN CHARGE OF IT.
TROMP TROMP TROMP TROMP
POISON IVY, YOU'RE UNDER ARREST!
HEY!
SORRY, BABY. I'M NOT LEAVING THIS TREE.
I CONGRATULATE YOU, BY THE WAY--DEVELOPING A COSTA RICAN WALKING TREE THAT ACTUALLY WALKS...IMPRESSIVE.
BUT WE'RE WALKING TO POLICE HEADQUARTERS.
NO, TURN RIGHT, DANG IT! WHY'S MY TREE GOING THIS WAY?
VRRRM VROOM!!
YOUR TREE STILL CRAVES SUNLIGHT--
--EVEN THE KIND EMITTED BY THE GROW-LAMP MOUNTED ON MY BATMOBILE!
VERY GOOD, SIR.

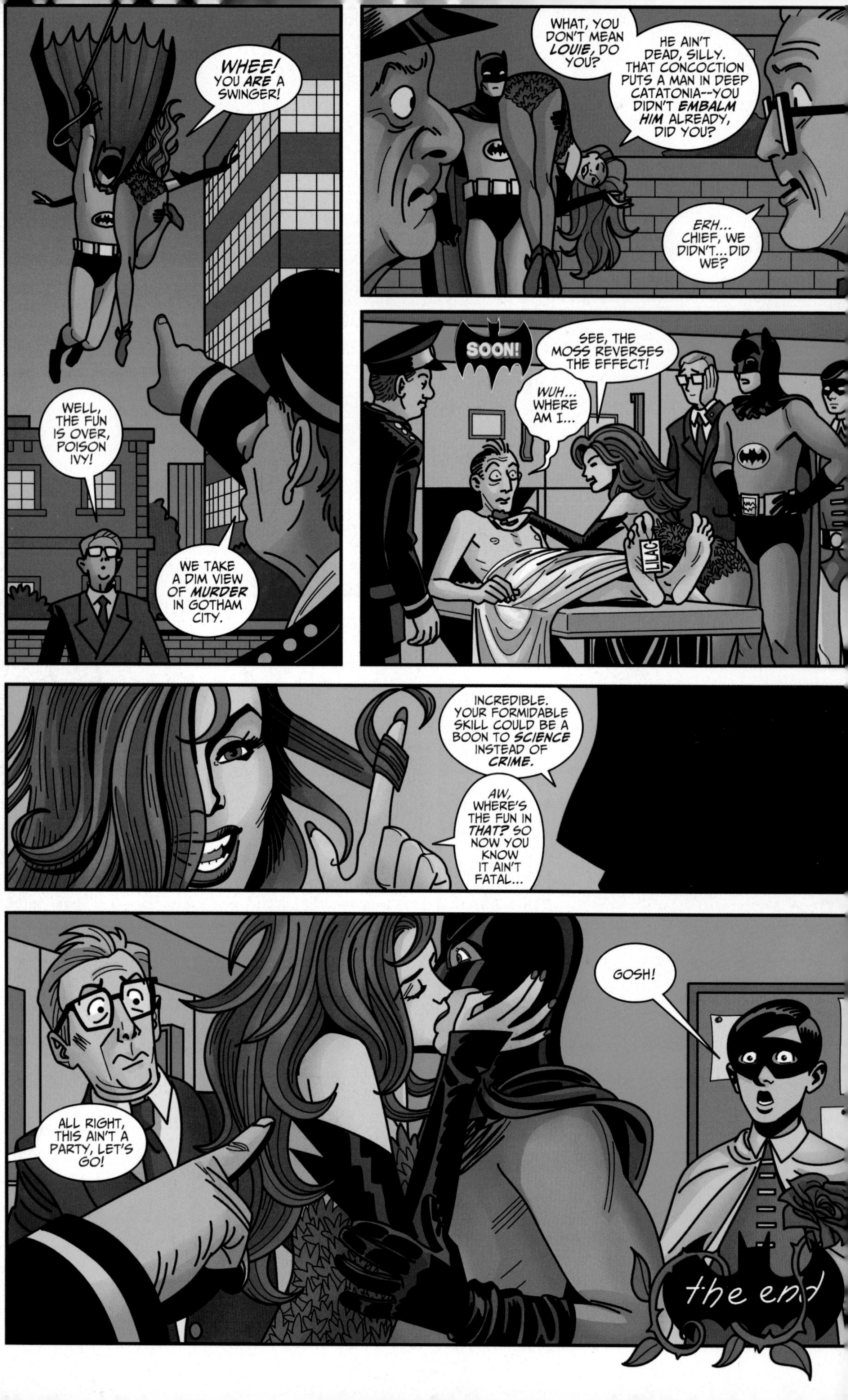
WHEE! YOU ARE A SWINGER!
WELL, THE FUN IS OVER, POISON IVY!
WE TAKE A DIM VIEW OF MURDER IN GOTHAM CITY.
WHAT, YOU DON'T MEAN LOUIE, DO YOU?
HE AIN'T DEAD, SILLY. THAT CONCOCTION PUTS A MAN IN DEEP CATATONIA--YOU DIDN'T EMBALM HIM ALREADY, DID YOU?
ERH... CHIEF, WE DIDN'T...DID WE?
SOON!
SEE, THE MOSS REVERSES THE EFFECT!
WUH... WHERE AM I...
LILAC
INCREDIBLE. YOUR FORMIDABLE SKILL COULD BE A BOON TO SCIENCE INSTEAD OF CRIME.
AW, WHERE'S THE FUN IN THAT? SO NOW YOU KNOW IT AIN'T FATAL...
GOSH!
ALL RIGHT, THIS AIN'T A PARTY, LET'S GO!
the end

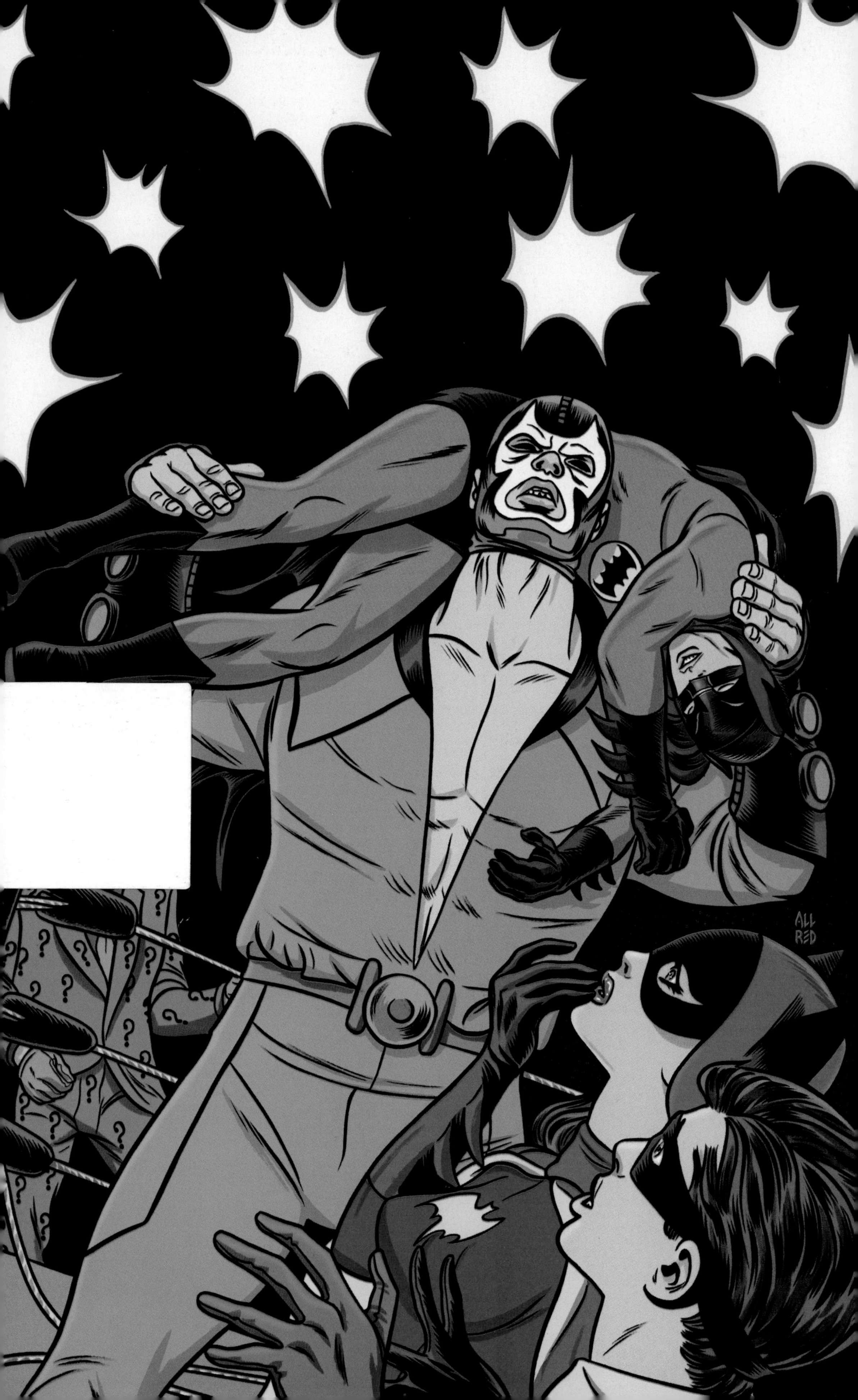
ALL
RED

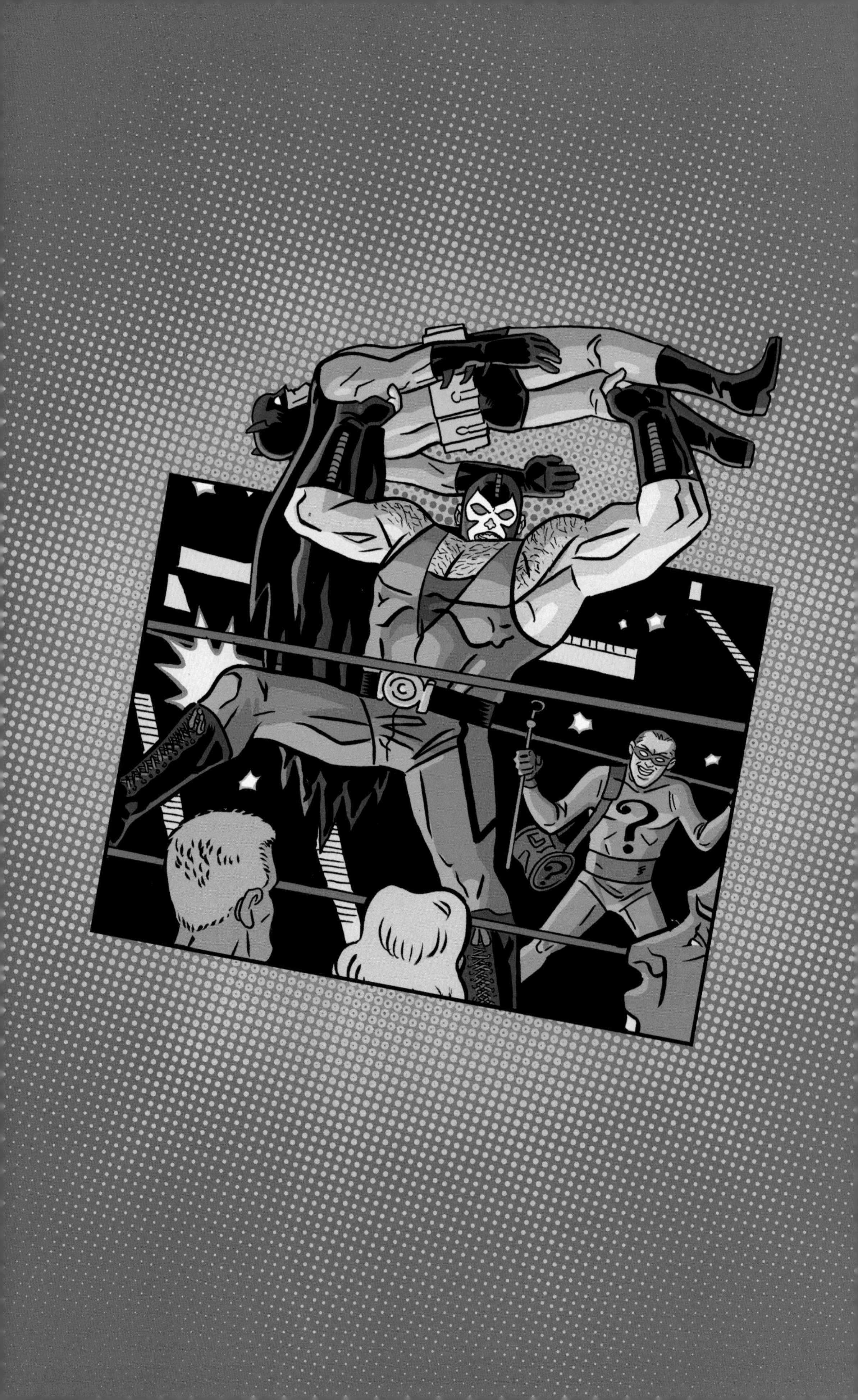

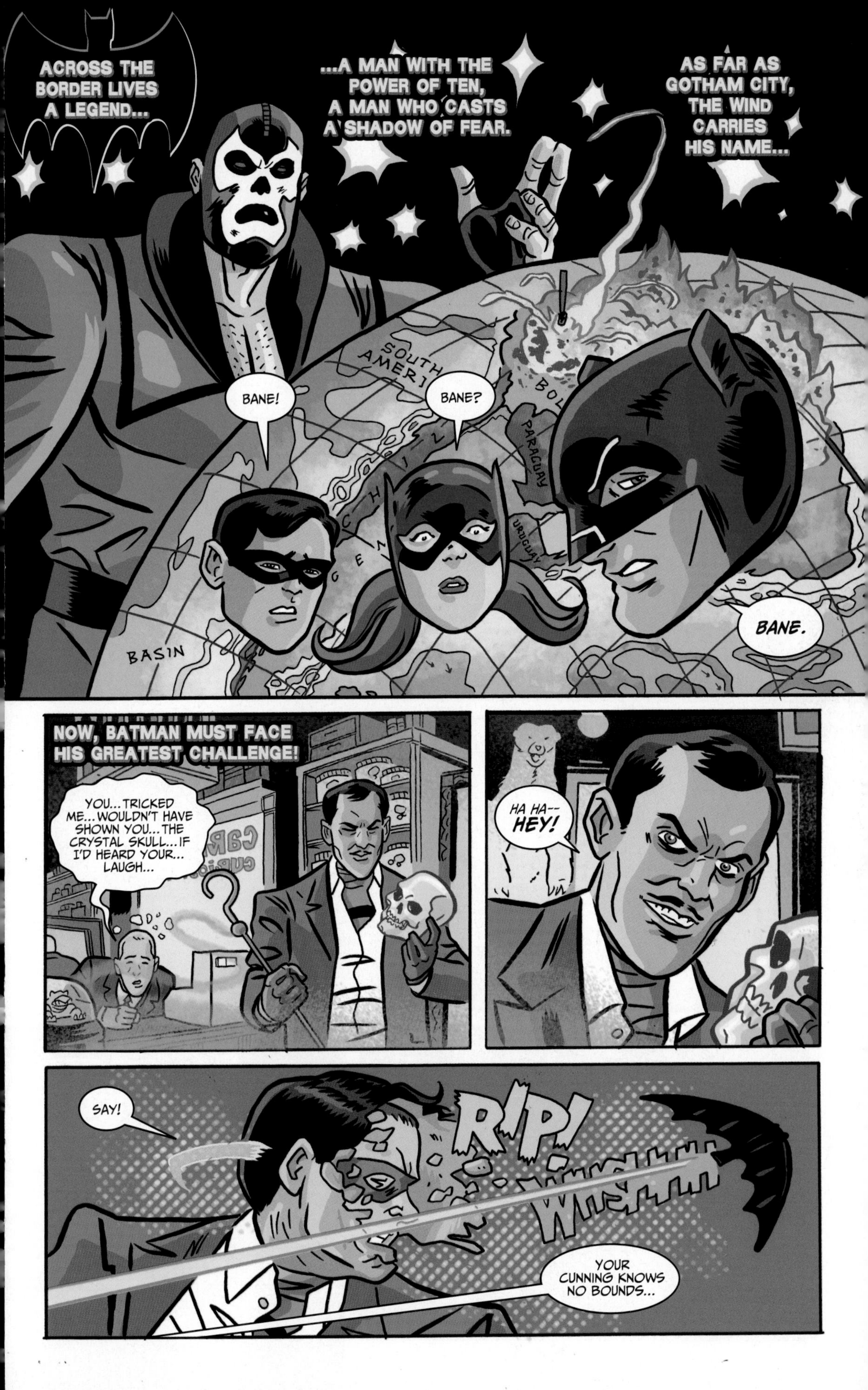

ACROSS THE BORDER LIVES A LEGEND...
...A MAN WITH THE POWER OF TEN, A MAN WHO CASTS A SHADOW OF FEAR.
AS FAR AS GOTHAM CITY, THE WIND CARRIES HIS NAME...
SOUTH AMERI
PARAGUAY
URUGUAY
BASIN
BANE!
BANE?
BANE.
NOW, BATMAN MUST FACE HIS GREATEST CHALLENGE!
YOU...TRICKED ME...WOULDN'T HAVE SHOWN YOU...THE CRYSTAL SKULL...IF I'D HEARD YOUR... LAUGH...
HA HA-- HEY!
SAY!
RIP!
YOUR CUNNING KNOWS NO BOUNDS...

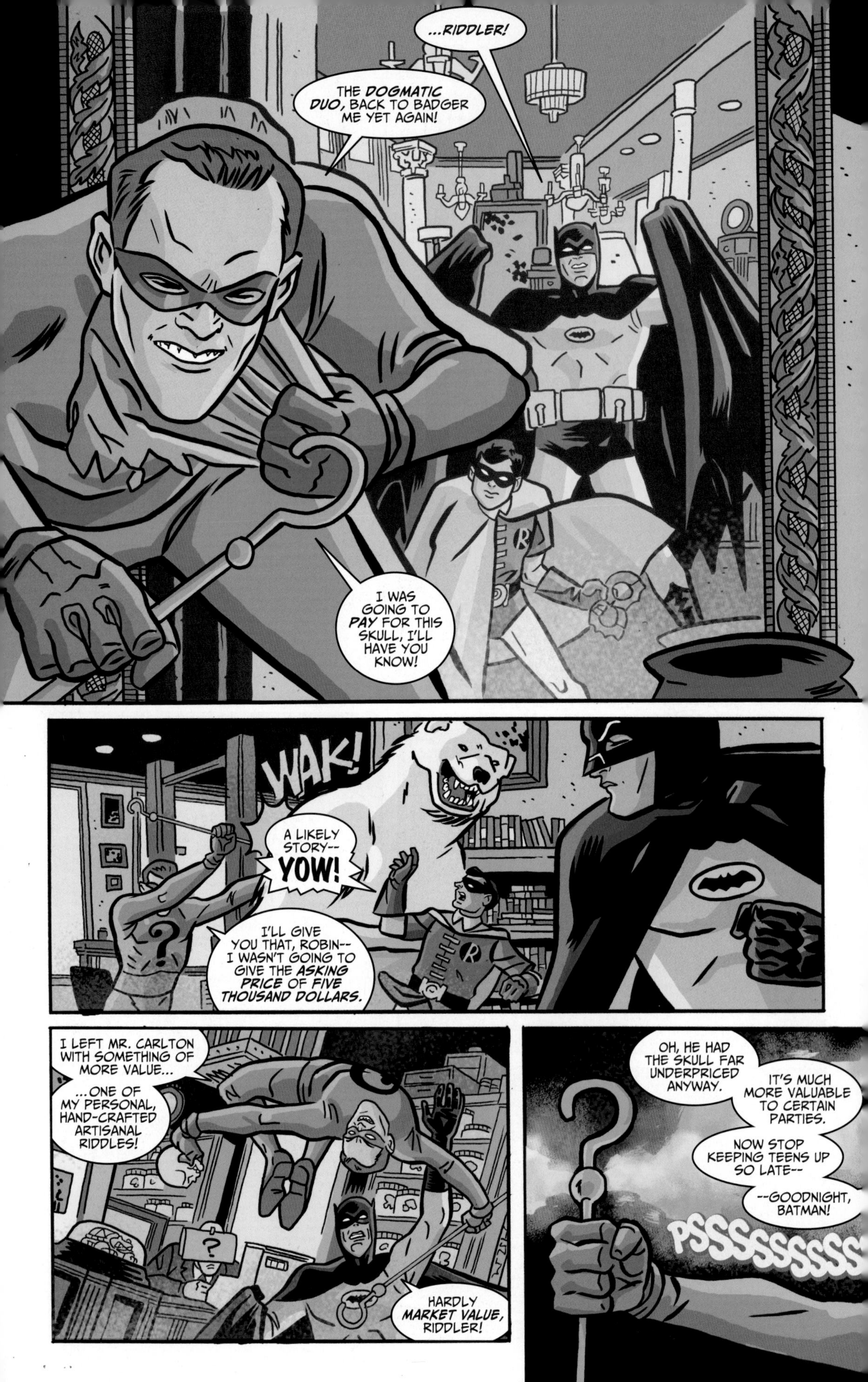
THE DOGMATIC DUO, BACK TO BADGER ME YET AGAIN!
...RIDDLER!
I WAS GOING TO PAY FOR THIS SKULL, I'LL HAVE YOU KNOW!
WAK!
A LIKELY STORY-- YOW!
I'LL GIVE YOU THAT, ROBIN-- I WASN'T GOING TO GIVE THE ASKING PRICE OF FIVE THOUSAND DOLLARS.
I LEFT MR. CARLTON WITH SOMETHING OF MORE VALUE...
...ONE OF MY PERSONAL, HAND-CRAFTED ARTISANAL RIDDLES!
HARDLY MARKET VALUE, RIDDLER!
OH, HE HAD THE SKULL FAR UNDERPRICED ANYWAY.
IT'S MUCH MORE VALUABLE TO CERTAIN PARTIES.
NOW STOP KEEPING TEENS UP SO LATE--
--GOODNIGHT, BATMAN!
PSSSSSSSSS

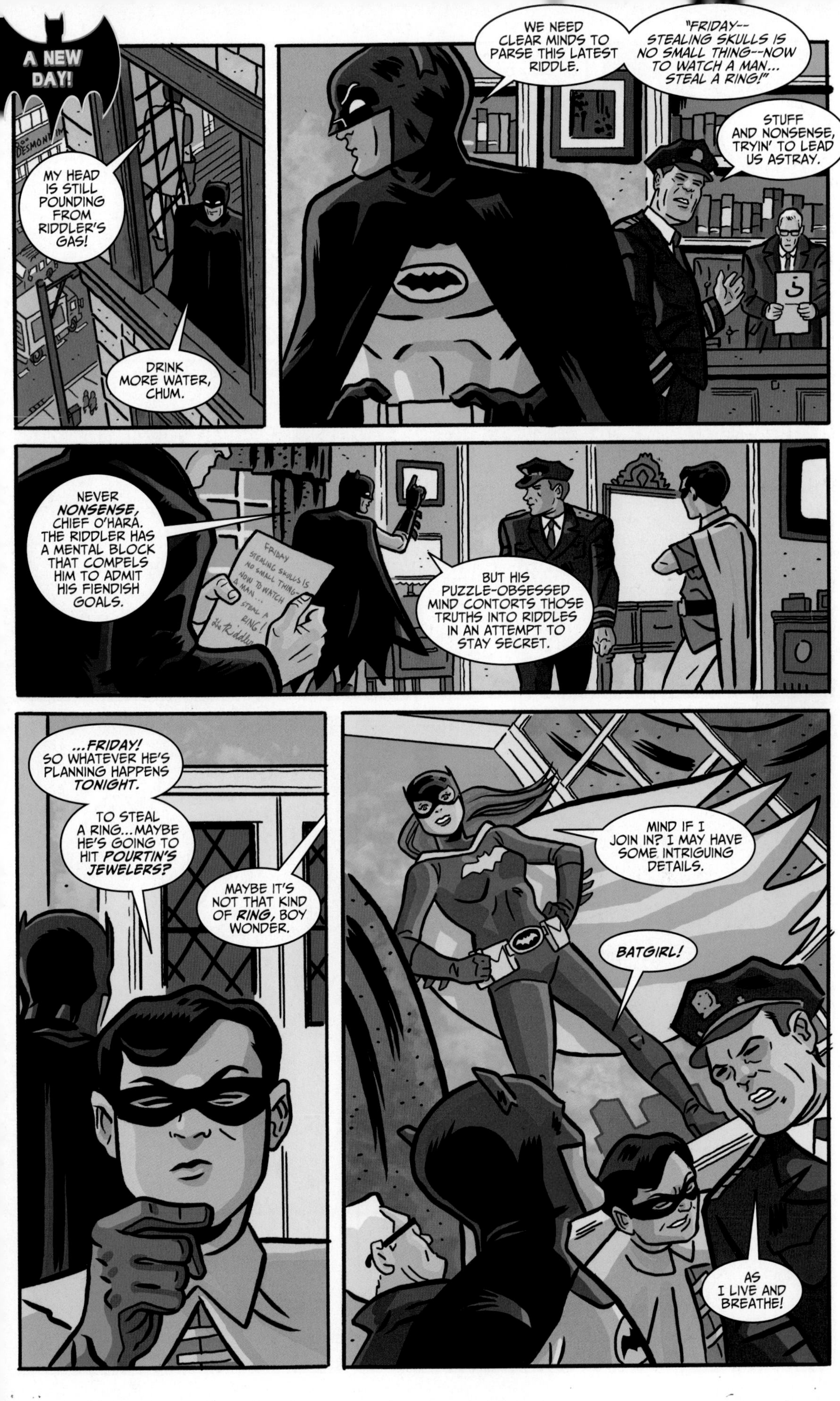

A NEW DAY!
MY HEAD IS STILL POUNDING FROM RIDDLER'S GAS!
DRINK MORE WATER, CHUM.
WE NEED CLEAR MINDS TO PARSE THIS LATEST RIDDLE.
"FRIDAY-- STEALING SKULLS IS NO SMALL THING--NOW TO WATCH A MAN... STEAL A RING!"
STUFF AND NONSENSE, TRYIN' TO LEAD US ASTRAY.
NEVER NONSENSE, CHIEF O'HARA. THE RIDDLER HAS A MENTAL BLOCK THAT COMPELS HIM TO ADMIT HIS FIENDISH GOALS.
BUT HIS PUZZLE-OBSESSED MIND CONTORTS THOSE TRUTHS INTO RIDDLES IN AN ATTEMPT TO STAY SECRET.
...FRIDAY! SO WHATEVER HE'S PLANNING HAPPENS TONIGHT.
TO STEAL A RING... MAYBE HE'S GOING TO HIT POURTIN'S JEWELERS?
MAYBE IT'S NOT THAT KIND OF RING, BOY WONDER.
MIND IF I JOIN IN? I MAY HAVE SOME INTRIGUING DETAILS.
BATGIRL!
AS I LIVE AND BREATHE!

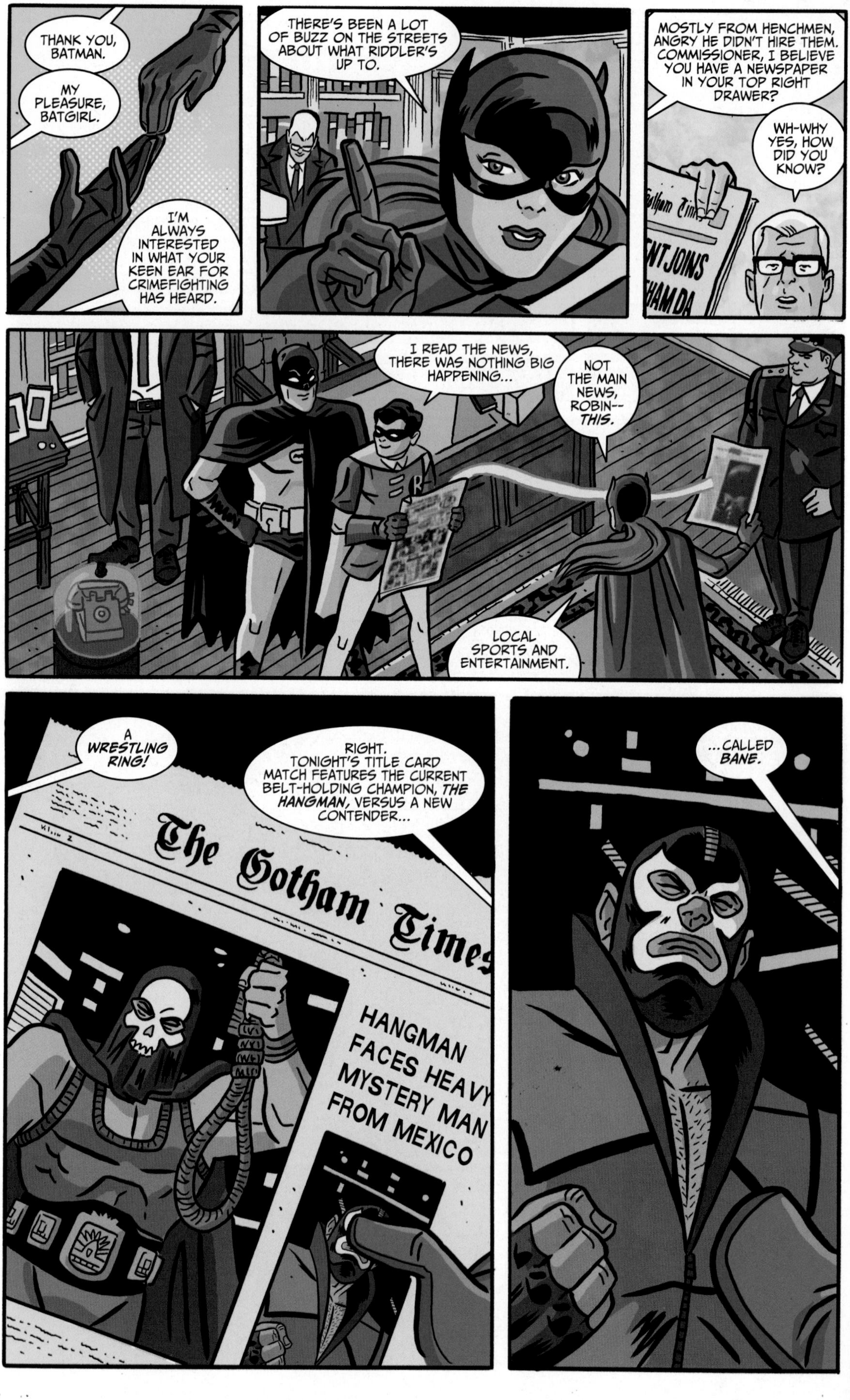
THANK YOU, BATMAN.
MY PLEASURE, BATGIRL.
I'M ALWAYS INTERESTED IN WHAT YOUR KEEN EAR FOR CRIMEFIGHTING HAS HEARD.
THERE'S BEEN A LOT OF BUZZ ON THE STREETS ABOUT WHAT RIDDLER'S UP TO.
MOSTLY FROM HENCHMEN, ANGRY HE DIDN'T HIRE THEM. COMMISSIONER, I BELIEVE YOU HAVE A NEWSPAPER IN YOUR TOP RIGHT DRAWER?
WH-WHY YES, HOW DID YOU KNOW?
I READ THE NEWS, THERE WAS NOTHING BIG HAPPENING...
NOT THE MAIN NEWS, ROBIN-- THIS.
LOCAL SPORTS AND ENTERTAINMENT.
A WRESTLING RING!
RIGHT. TONIGHT'S TITLE CARD MATCH FEATURES THE CURRENT BELT-HOLDING CHAMPION, THE HANGMAN, VERSUS A NEW CONTENDER...
The Gotham Times
HANGMAN FACES HEAVY MYSTERY MAN FROM MEXICO
...CALLED BANE.

"BANE ENTERS THE RING"

Written by JEFF PARKER
Art and Color by SCOTT KOWALCHUK
Letters by WES ABBOTT
Cover by MICHAEL and LAURA ALLRED

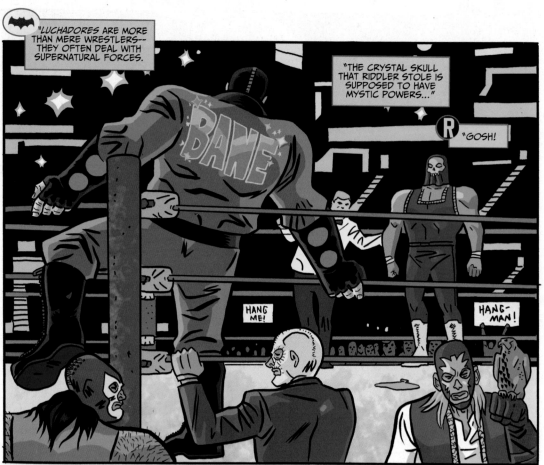

"LUCHADORES ARE MORE THAN MERE WRESTLERS-- THEY OFTEN DEAL WITH SUPERNATURAL FORCES.

"THE CRYSTAL SKULL THAT RIDDLER STOLE IS SUPPOSED TO HAVE MYSTIC POWERS..."

"GOSH!

HANG ME!

HANG- MAN!

AND LOOK WHO'S BANE'S CORNER MAN!

HEEHEHEHEHEEE! THE HANGMAN IS A 12-1 FAVORITE, I'M GOING TO CLEAN UP ON THIS FIGHT!

JUST MAKE SURE EL CRANEO ES SAFE, RIDDLER.

DING DING DING DING!

GENTLEMEN... BEGIN!

WHOOM!

SHOULDN'T WE GO ARREST RIDDLER?

HE'S STAYING PUT, NO NEED TO RILE THE CROWD--LET'S WAIT UNTIL THE MATCH IS FINISHED.

DING! DING!

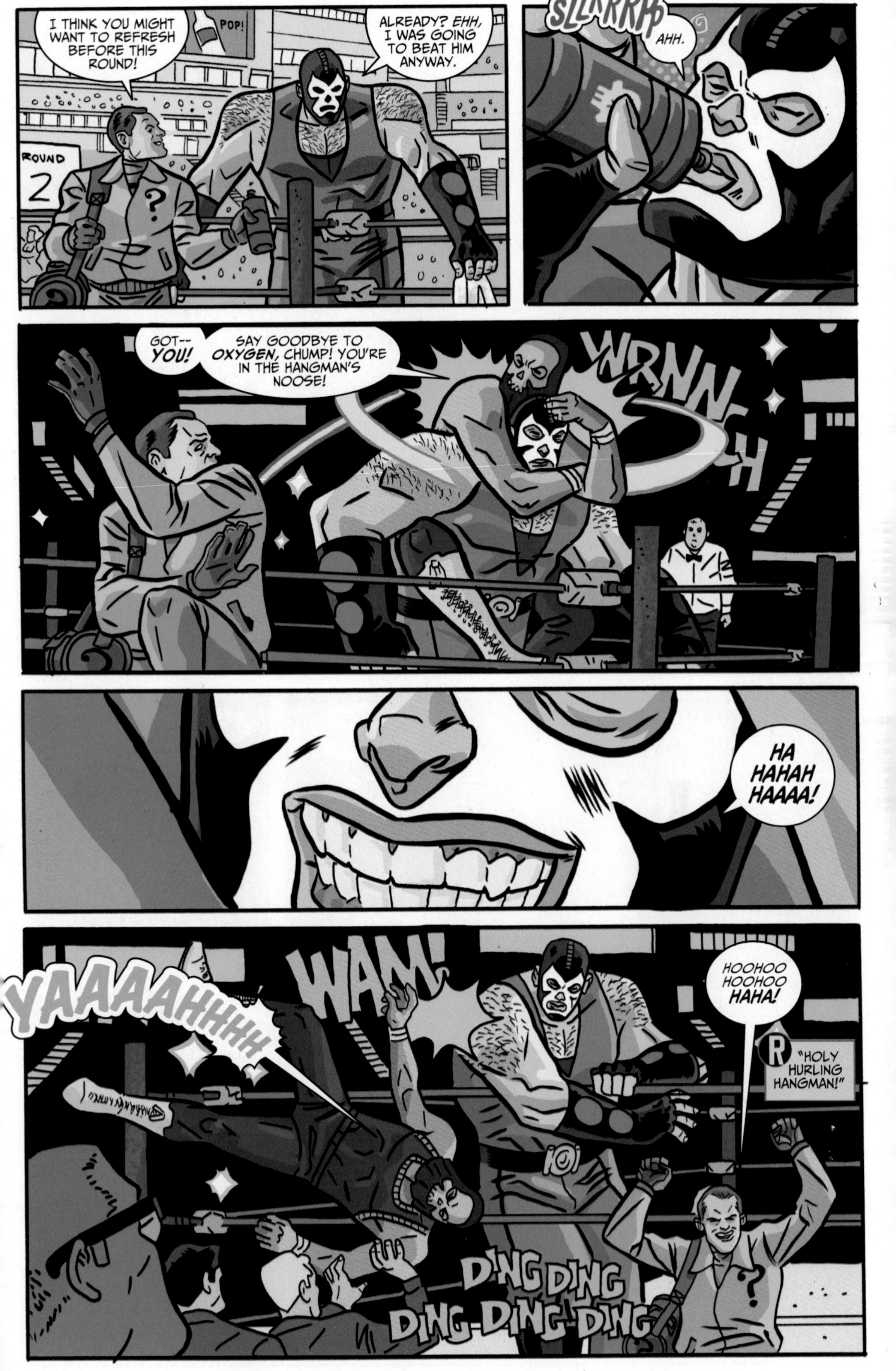
I THINK YOU MIGHT WANT TO REFRESH BEFORE THIS ROUND!
POP!
ALREADY? EHH, I WAS GOING TO BEAT HIM ANYWAY.
ROUND 2
SLLRRRRP
AHH.
GOT-- YOU!
SAY GOODBYE TO OXYGEN, CHUMP! YOU'RE IN THE HANGMAN'S NOOSE!
WRNNCH
HA HAHAH HAAAA!
YAAAAAHHHH
WAM!
HOOHOO HOOHOO HAHA!
"HOLY HURLING HANGMAN!"
DING DING DING DING DING

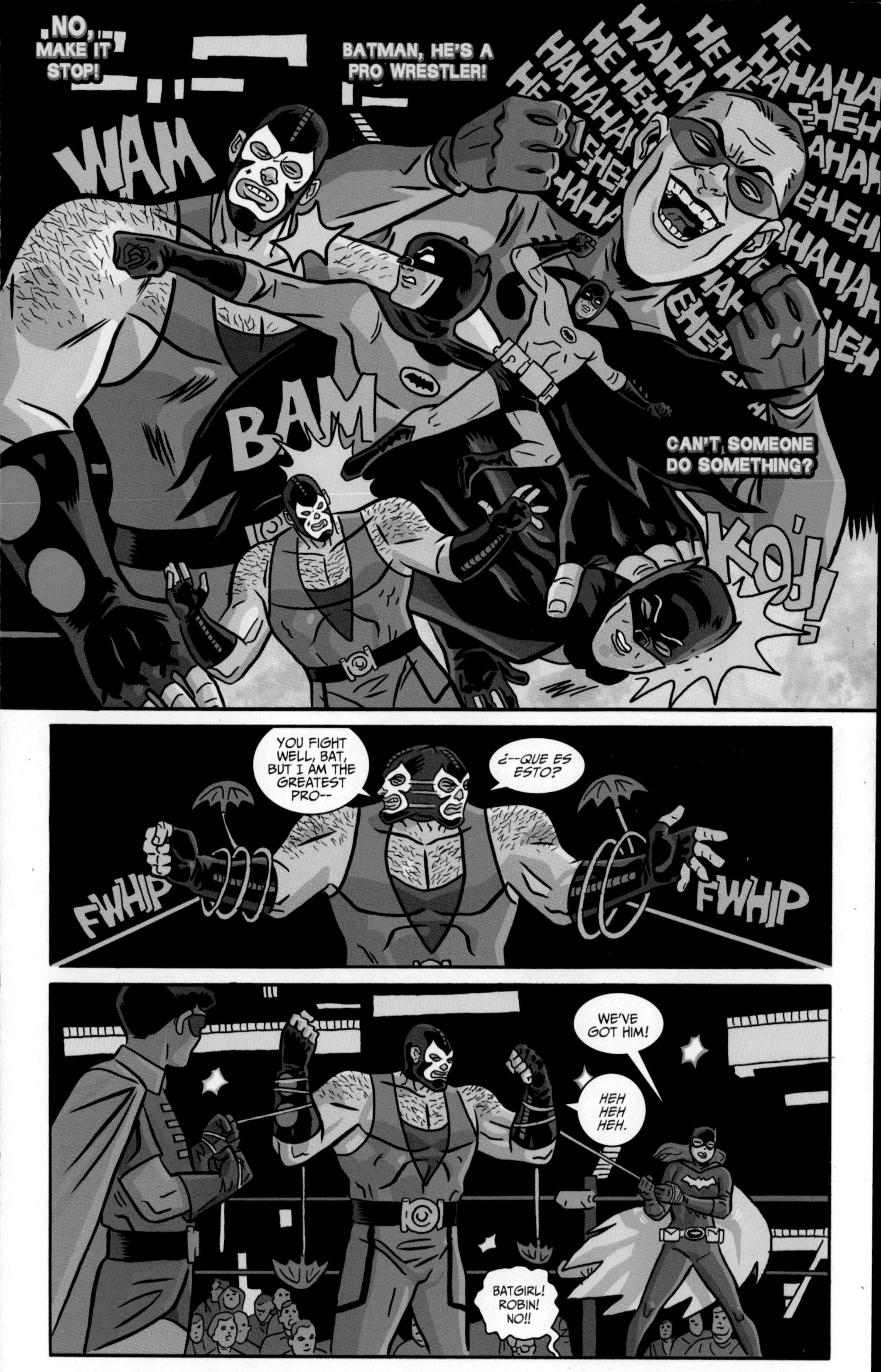
NO, MAKE IT STOP!
BATMAN, HE'S A PRO WRESTLER!
WAM
BAM
CAN'T SOMEONE DO SOMETHING?
KO'J!
YOU FIGHT WELL, BAT, BUT I AM THE GREATEST PRO--
¿--QUE ES ESTO?
FWHIP
FWHIP
WE'VE GOT HIM!
HEH HEH HEH.
BATGIRL! ROBIN! NO!!

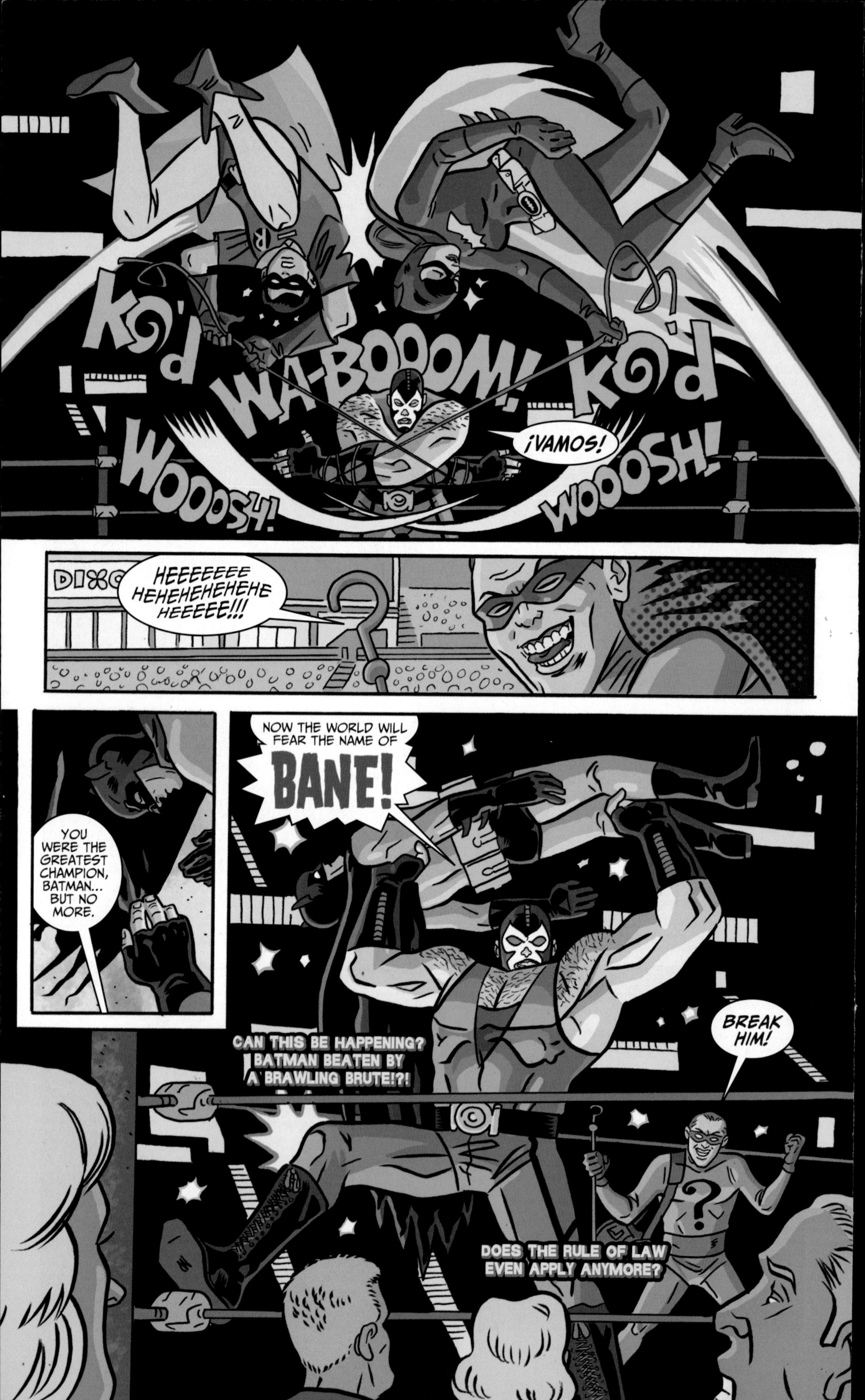
KO'd
WA-BOOOM!
KO'd
WOOOSH!
¡VAMOS!
WOOOSH!
HEEEEEEE HEHEHEHEHEHE HEEEEE!!!
YOU WERE THE GREATEST CHAMPION, BATMAN... BUT NO MORE.
NOW THE WORLD WILL FEAR THE NAME OF
BANE!
CAN THIS BE HAPPENING? BATMAN BEATEN BY A BRAWLING BRUTE!?!
BREAK HIM!
DOES THE RULE OF LAW EVEN APPLY ANYMORE?

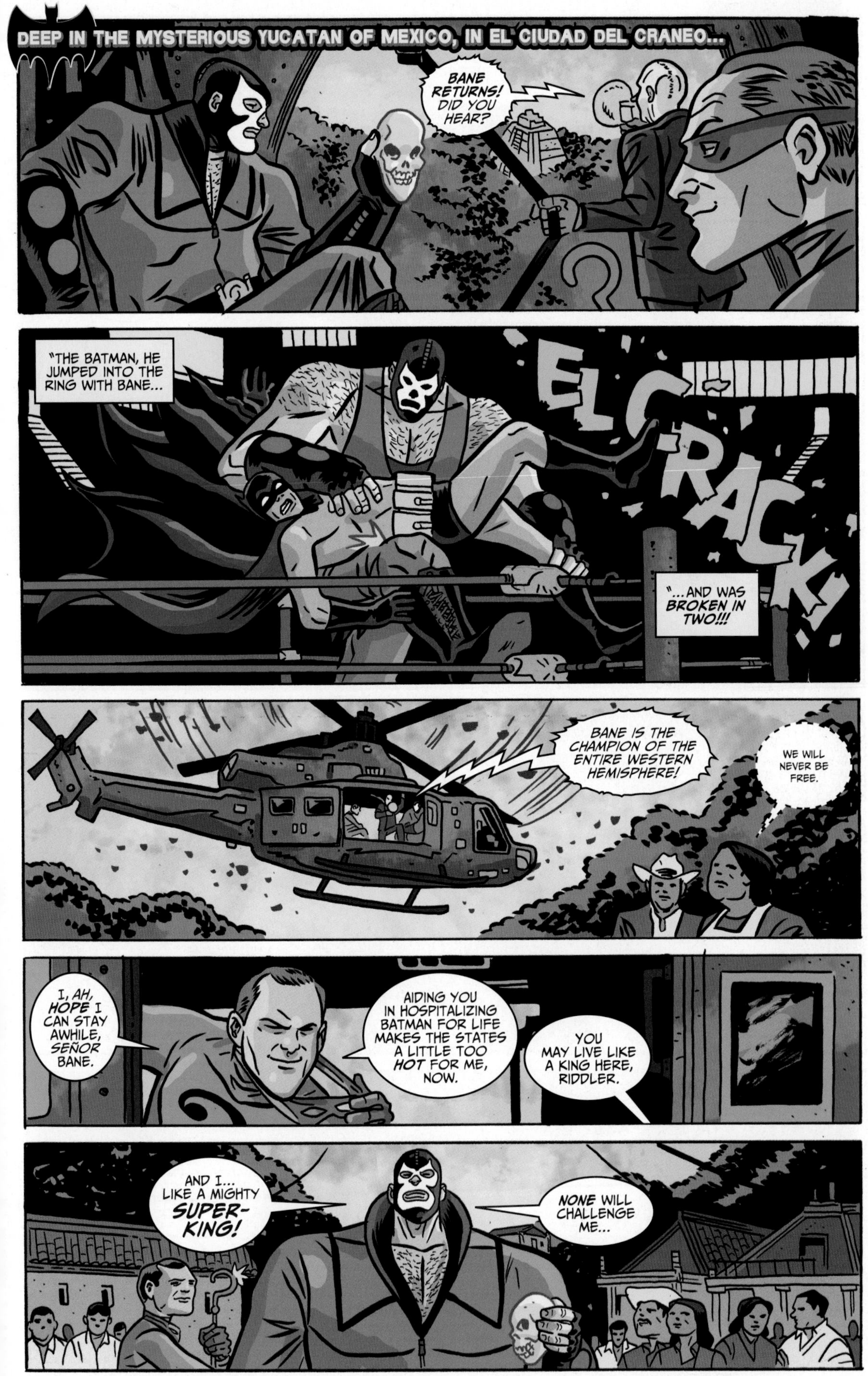
DEEP IN THE MYSTERIOUS YUCATAN OF MEXICO, IN EL CIUDAD DEL CRANEO...
BANE RETURNS! DID YOU HEAR?
"THE BATMAN, HE JUMPED INTO THE RING WITH BANE...
EL CRACK!
"...AND WAS BROKEN IN TWO!!!
BANE IS THE CHAMPION OF THE ENTIRE WESTERN HEMISPHERE!
WE WILL NEVER BE FREE.
I, AH, HOPE I CAN STAY AWHILE, SEÑOR BANE.
AIDING YOU IN HOSPITALIZING BATMAN FOR LIFE MAKES THE STATES A LITTLE TOO HOT FOR ME, NOW.
YOU MAY LIVE LIKE A KING HERE, RIDDLER.
AND I... LIKE A MIGHTY SUPER-KING!
NONE WILL CHALLENGE ME...

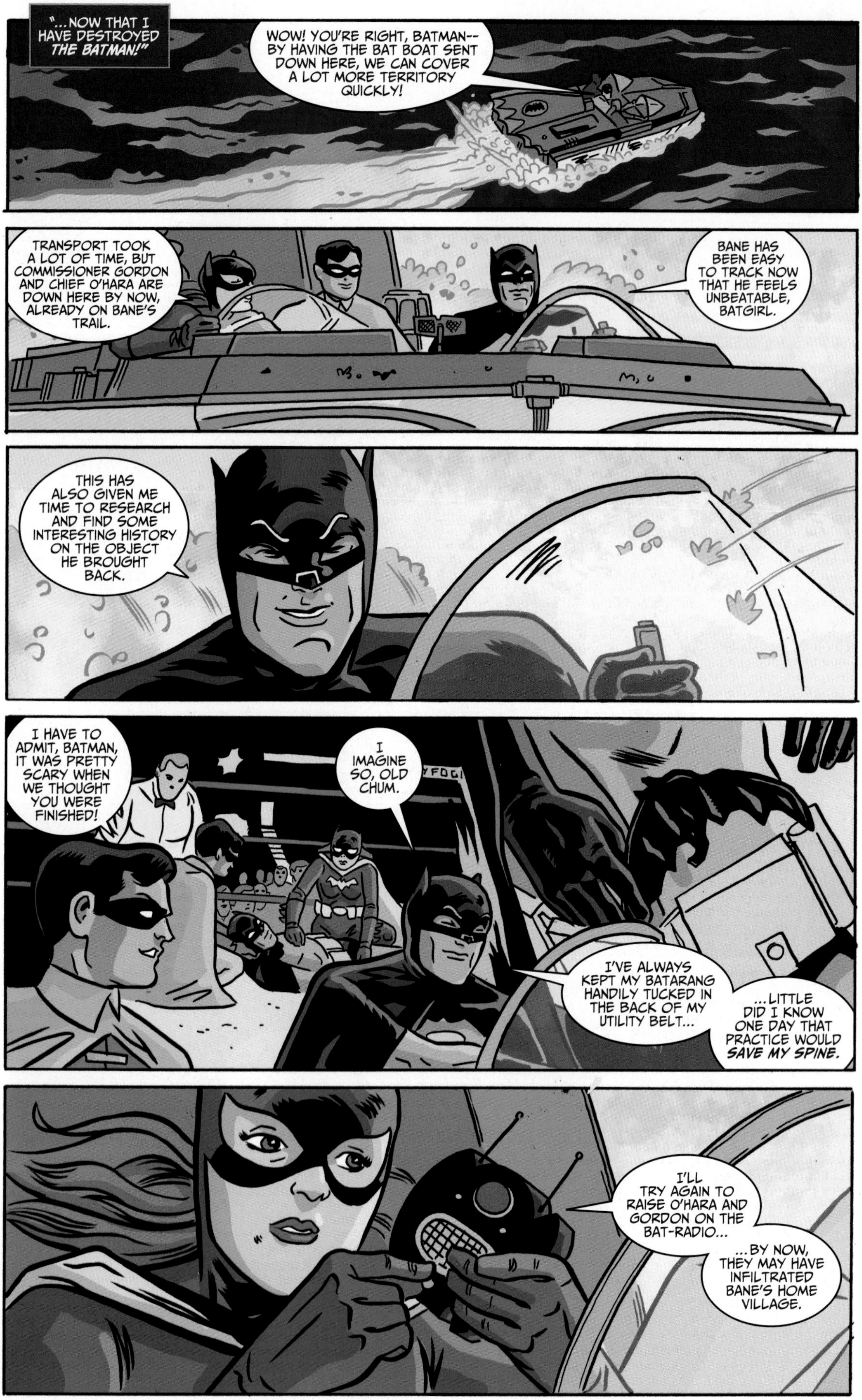
"...NOW THAT I HAVE DESTROYED *THE BATMAN!*"
WOW! YOU'RE RIGHT, BATMAN-- BY HAVING THE BAT BOAT SENT DOWN HERE, WE CAN COVER A LOT MORE TERRITORY QUICKLY!
TRANSPORT TOOK A LOT OF TIME, BUT COMMISSIONER GORDON AND CHIEF O'HARA ARE DOWN HERE BY NOW, ALREADY ON BANE'S TRAIL.
BANE HAS BEEN EASY TO TRACK NOW THAT HE FEELS UNBEATABLE, BATGIRL.
THIS HAS ALSO GIVEN ME TIME TO RESEARCH AND FIND SOME INTERESTING HISTORY ON THE OBJECT HE BROUGHT BACK.
I HAVE TO ADMIT, BATMAN, IT WAS PRETTY SCARY WHEN WE THOUGHT YOU WERE FINISHED!
I IMAGINE SO, OLD CHUM.
I'VE ALWAYS KEPT MY BATARANG HANDILY TUCKED IN THE BACK OF MY UTILITY BELT...
...LITTLE DID I KNOW ONE DAY THAT PRACTICE WOULD ***SAVE MY SPINE.***
I'LL TRY AGAIN TO RAISE O'HARA AND GORDON ON THE BAT-RADIO...
...BY NOW, THEY MAY HAVE INFILTRATED BANE'S HOME VILLAGE.

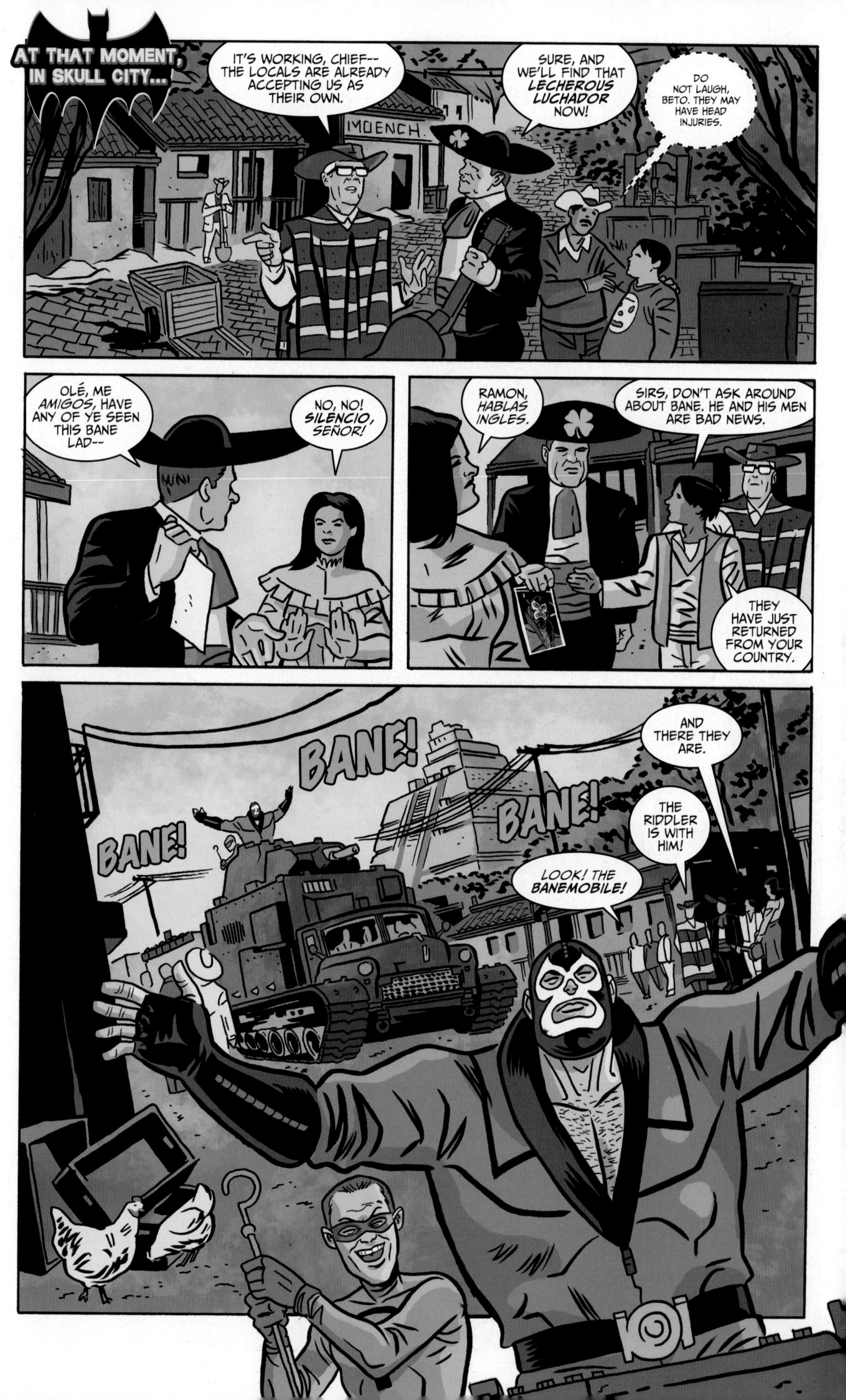
AT THAT MOMENT, IN SKULL CITY...
IT'S WORKING, CHIEF-- THE LOCALS ARE ALREADY ACCEPTING US AS THEIR OWN.
SURE, AND WE'LL FIND THAT LECHEROUS LUCHADOR NOW!
DO NOT LAUGH, BETO. THEY MAY HAVE HEAD INJURIES.
IMOENCH
OLÉ, ME AMIGOS, HAVE ANY OF YE SEEN THIS BANE LAD--
NO, NO! SILENCIO, SEÑOR!
RAMON, HABLAS INGLES.
SIRS, DON'T ASK AROUND ABOUT BANE. HE AND HIS MEN ARE BAD NEWS.
THEY HAVE JUST RETURNED FROM YOUR COUNTRY.
BANE!
BANE!
BANE!
AND THERE THEY ARE.
THE RIDDLER IS WITH HIM!
LOOK! THE BANEMOBILE!

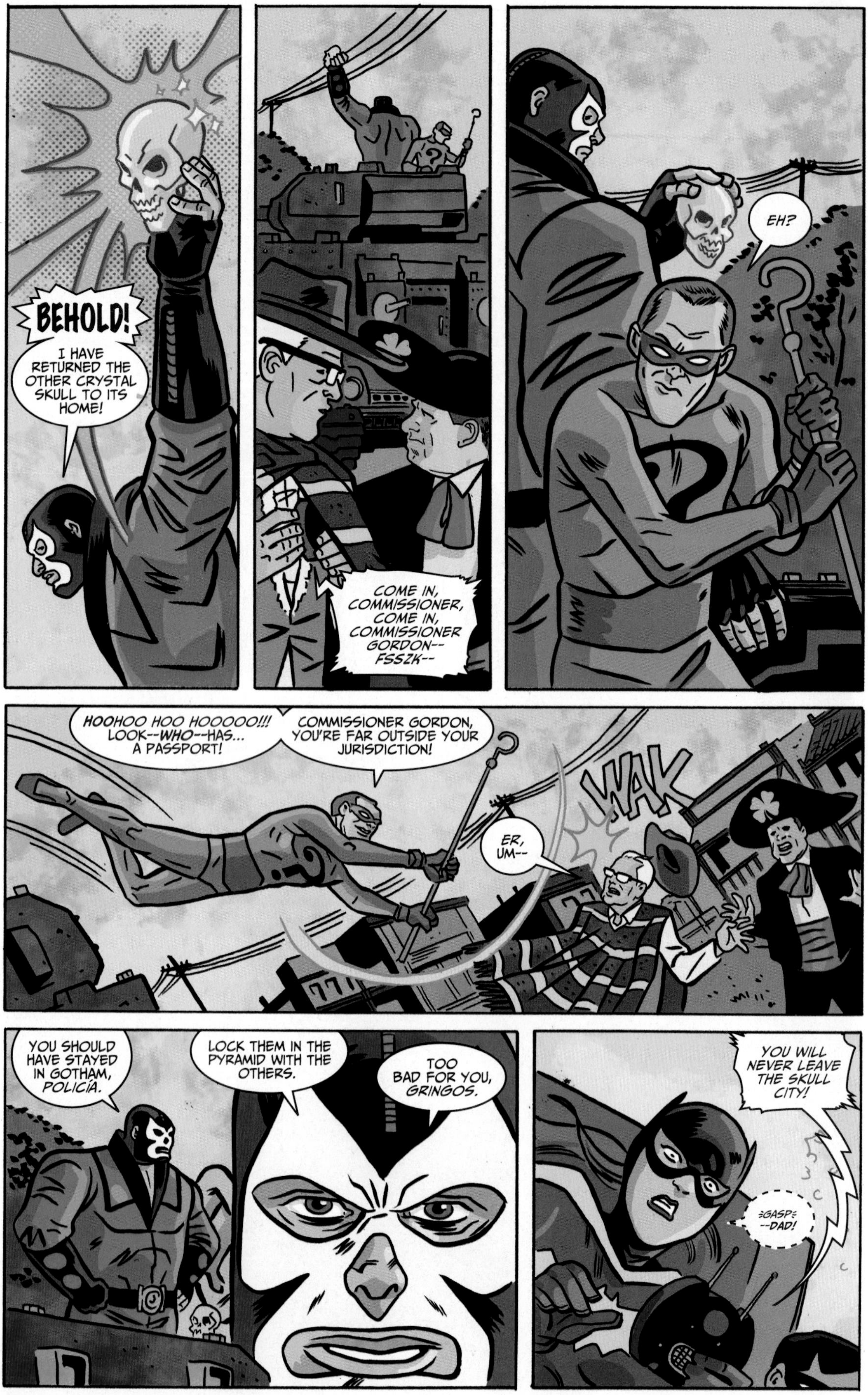
BEHOLD!
I HAVE RETURNED THE OTHER CRYSTAL SKULL TO ITS HOME!
COME IN, COMMISSIONER, COME IN, COMMISSIONER GORDON-- FSSZK--
EH?
HOOHOO HOO HOOOOO!!! LOOK--WHO--HAS... A PASSPORT!
COMMISSIONER GORDON, YOU'RE FAR OUTSIDE YOUR JURISDICTION!
WAK
ER, UM--
YOU SHOULD HAVE STAYED IN GOTHAM, POLICÍA.
LOCK THEM IN THE PYRAMID WITH THE OTHERS.
TOO BAD FOR YOU, GRINGOS.
YOU WILL NEVER LEAVE THE SKULL CITY!
GASP --DAD!

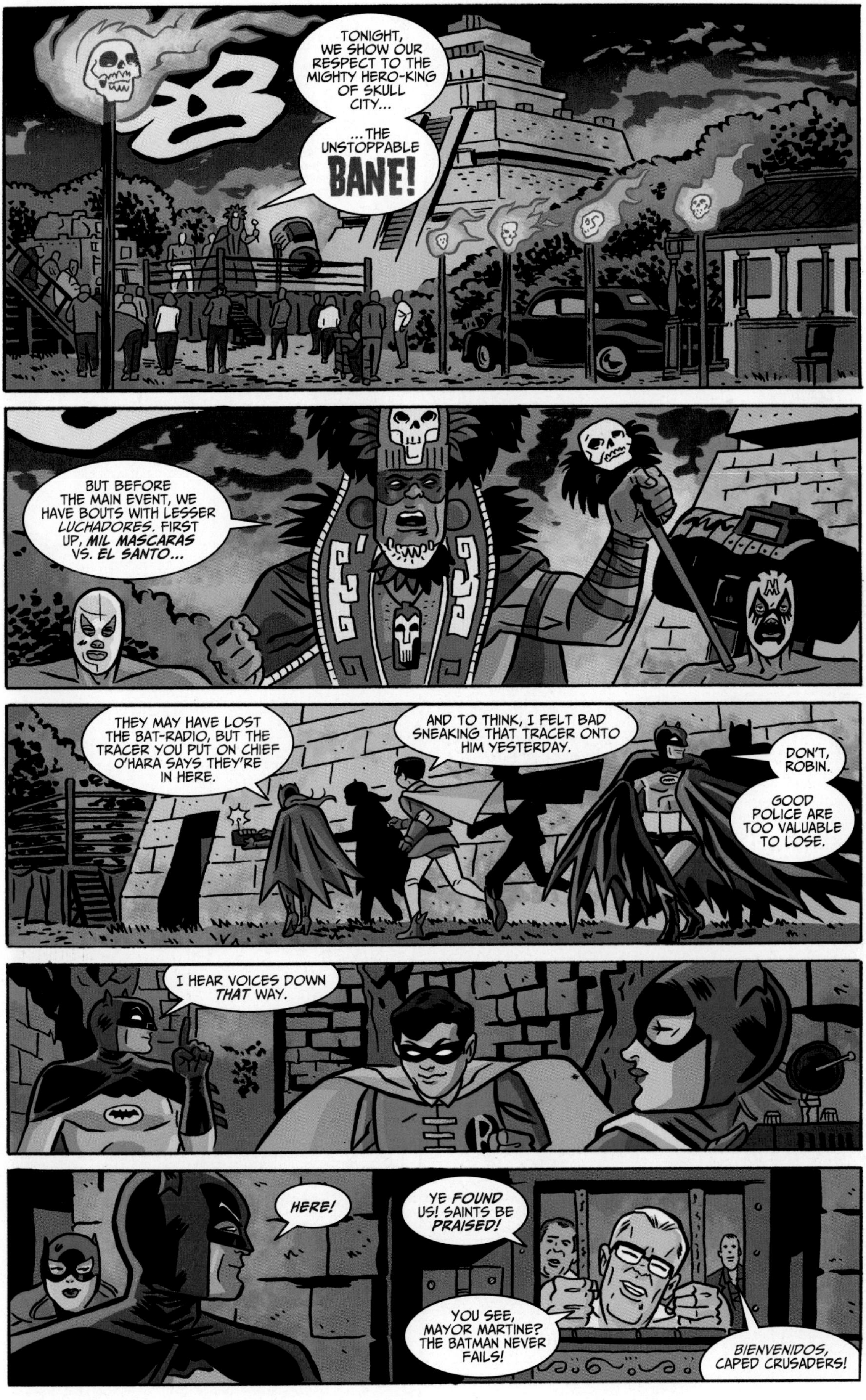
TONIGHT, WE SHOW OUR RESPECT TO THE MIGHTY HERO-KING OF SKULL CITY...
...THE UNSTOPPABLE BANE!
BUT BEFORE THE MAIN EVENT, WE HAVE BOUTS WITH LESSER *LUCHADORES*. FIRST UP, ***MIL MASCARAS*** VS. ***EL SANTO...***
THEY MAY HAVE LOST THE BAT-RADIO, BUT THE TRACER YOU PUT ON CHIEF O'HARA SAYS THEY'RE IN HERE.
AND TO THINK, I FELT BAD SNEAKING THAT TRACER ONTO HIM YESTERDAY.
DON'T, ROBIN.
GOOD POLICE ARE TOO VALUABLE TO LOSE.
I HEAR VOICES DOWN *THAT* WAY.
*HERE!*
YE *FOUND* US! SAINTS BE *PRAISED!*
YOU SEE, MAYOR MARTINE? THE BATMAN NEVER FAILS!
*BIENVENIDOS,* CAPED CRUSADERS!

THIS IS THE MAYOR OF SKULL CITY. BANE'S MEN LOCKED HIM AWAY FOR SMASHING THEIR ORIGINAL CRYSTAL SKULL.

ANOTHER SKULL-- WHY?

THE CRYSTAL SKULL IS THE SECRET TO MAKING THE ELIXIR WHICH GIVES BANE HIS GREAT *POWER!*

IT LASTS ONLY A FEW MINUTES AFTER DRINKING, BUT DURING THAT TIME, BANE IS *UNBEATABLE.* IT IS HOW HE HAS DOMINATED THE WRESTLING CIRCUIT HERE...

"...AND MY *CITY.*"

THAT SOUNDS LIKE THE EXACT ANCIENT PRACTICE I READ OF, WHERE AZTEC PRIESTS SENT MIGHTY WARRIORS INTO BATTLE.

I PREPARED FOR THAT THIS TIME--

BANE! BANE! BANE!

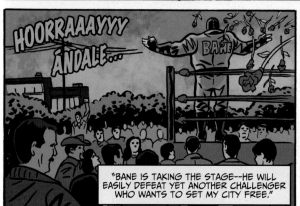

HOORRAAAYYY

ÁNDALE...

"BANE IS TAKING THE STAGE--HE WILL EASILY DEFEAT YET ANOTHER CHALLENGER WHO WANTS TO SET MY CITY FREE."

BATGIRL AND ROBIN, FREE THE CAPTIVES!

I HAVE TO REACH BANE IN TIME!

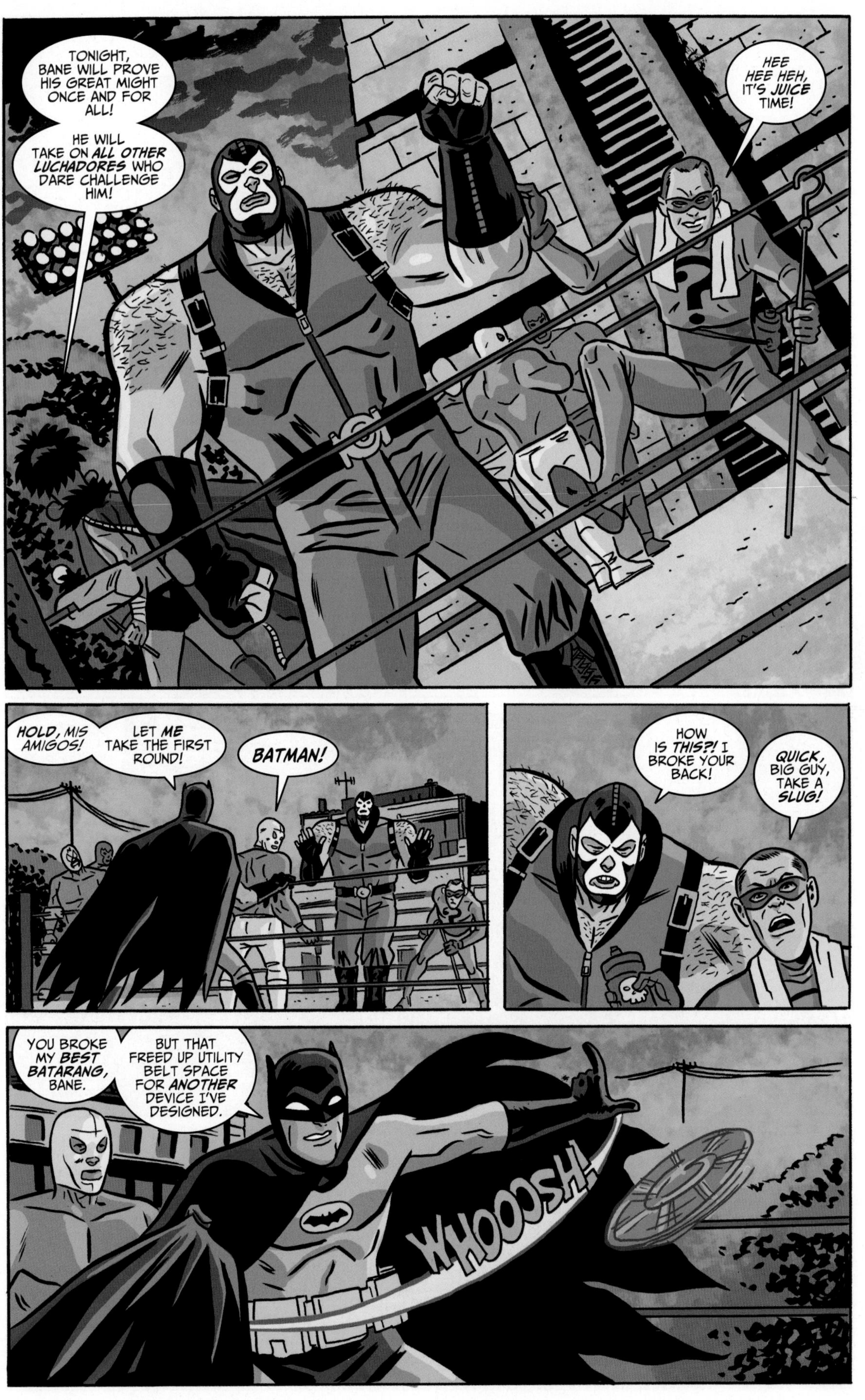
TONIGHT, BANE WILL PROVE HIS GREAT MIGHT ONCE AND FOR ALL!
HE WILL TAKE ON ALL OTHER LUCHADORES WHO DARE CHALLENGE HIM!
HEE HEE HEH, IT'S JUICE TIME!
HOLD, MIS AMIGOS!
LET ME TAKE THE FIRST ROUND!
BATMAN!
HOW IS THIS?! I BROKE YOUR BACK!
QUICK, BIG GUY, TAKE A SLUG!
YOU BROKE MY BEST BATARANG, BANE.
BUT THAT FREED UP UTILITY BELT SPACE FOR ANOTHER DEVICE I'VE DESIGNED.
WHOOOSH

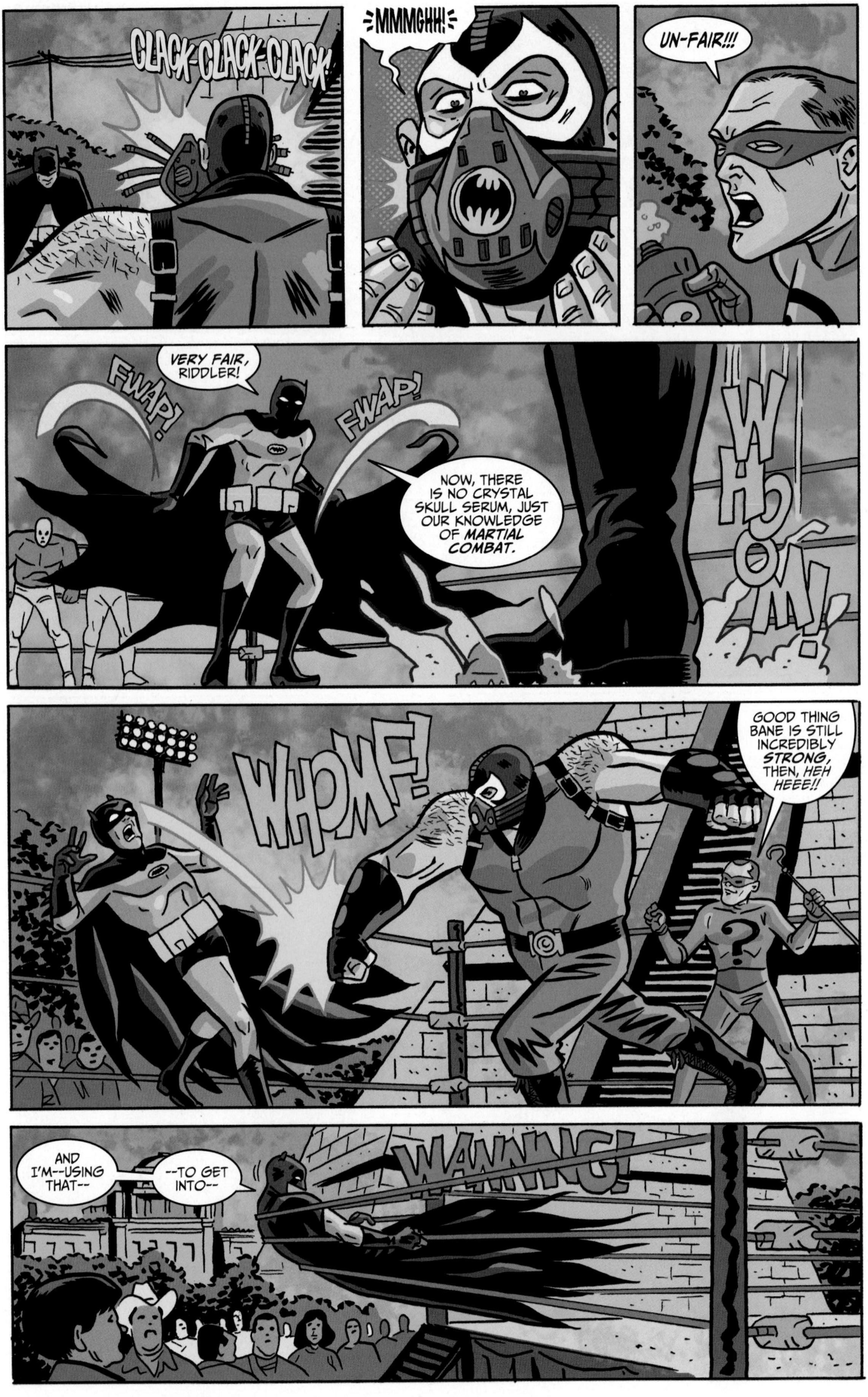
CLACK-CLACK-CLACK!
MMMGHH!
UN-FAIR!!!
VERY FAIR, RIDDLER!
FWAP!
FWAP!
NOW, THERE IS NO CRYSTAL SKULL SERUM, JUST OUR KNOWLEDGE OF MARTIAL COMBAT.
WHOOOM!
WHOMF!
GOOD THING BANE IS STILL INCREDIBLY STRONG, THEN, HEH HEEE!!
AND I'M--USING THAT--
--TO GET INTO--
WANNNG!

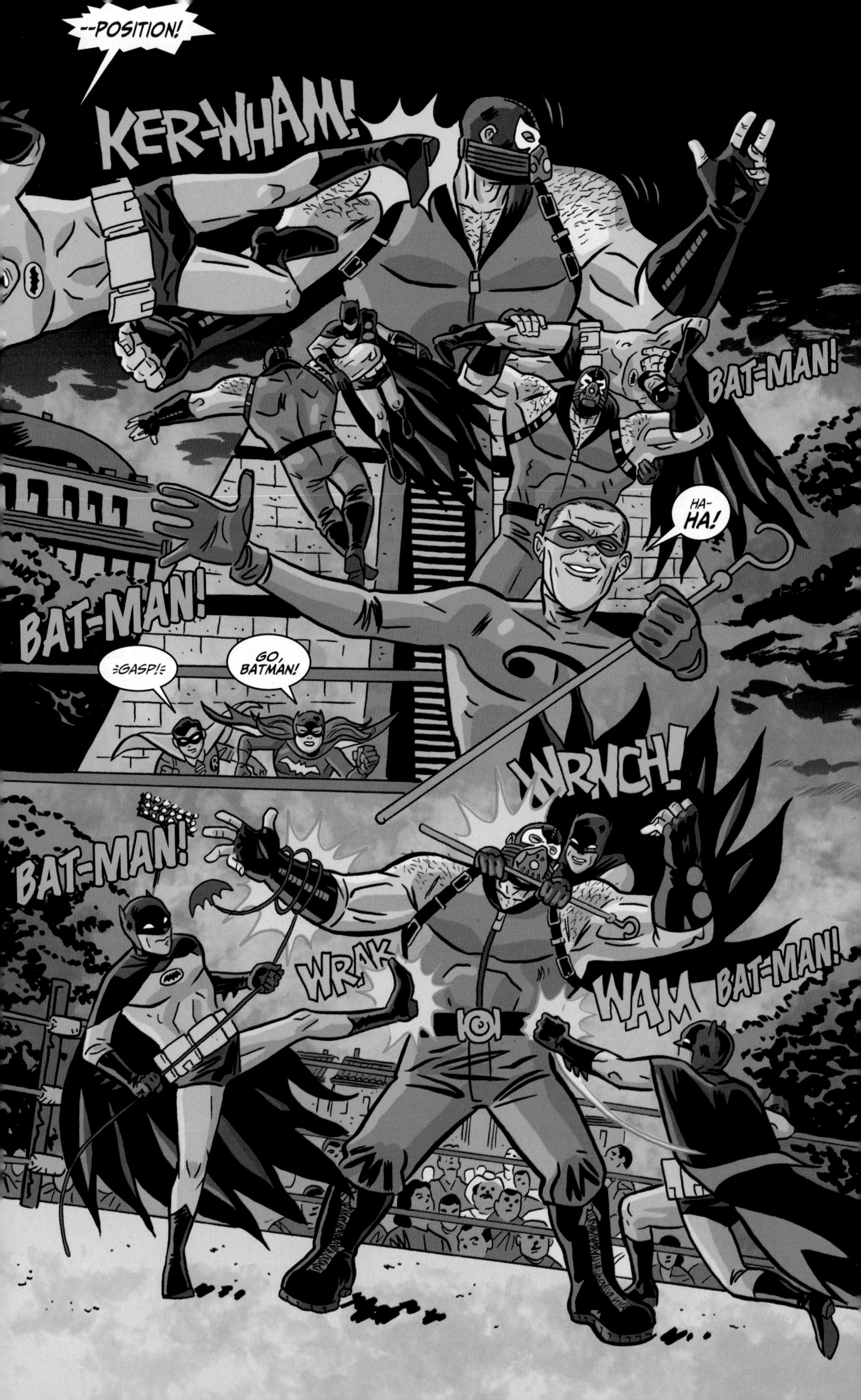
--POSITION!
KER-WHAM!
BAT-MAN!
HA-HA!
BAT-MAN!
≥GASP!≤
GO, BATMAN!
WRNCH!
BAT-MAN!
WRAK
WAM
BAT-MAN!

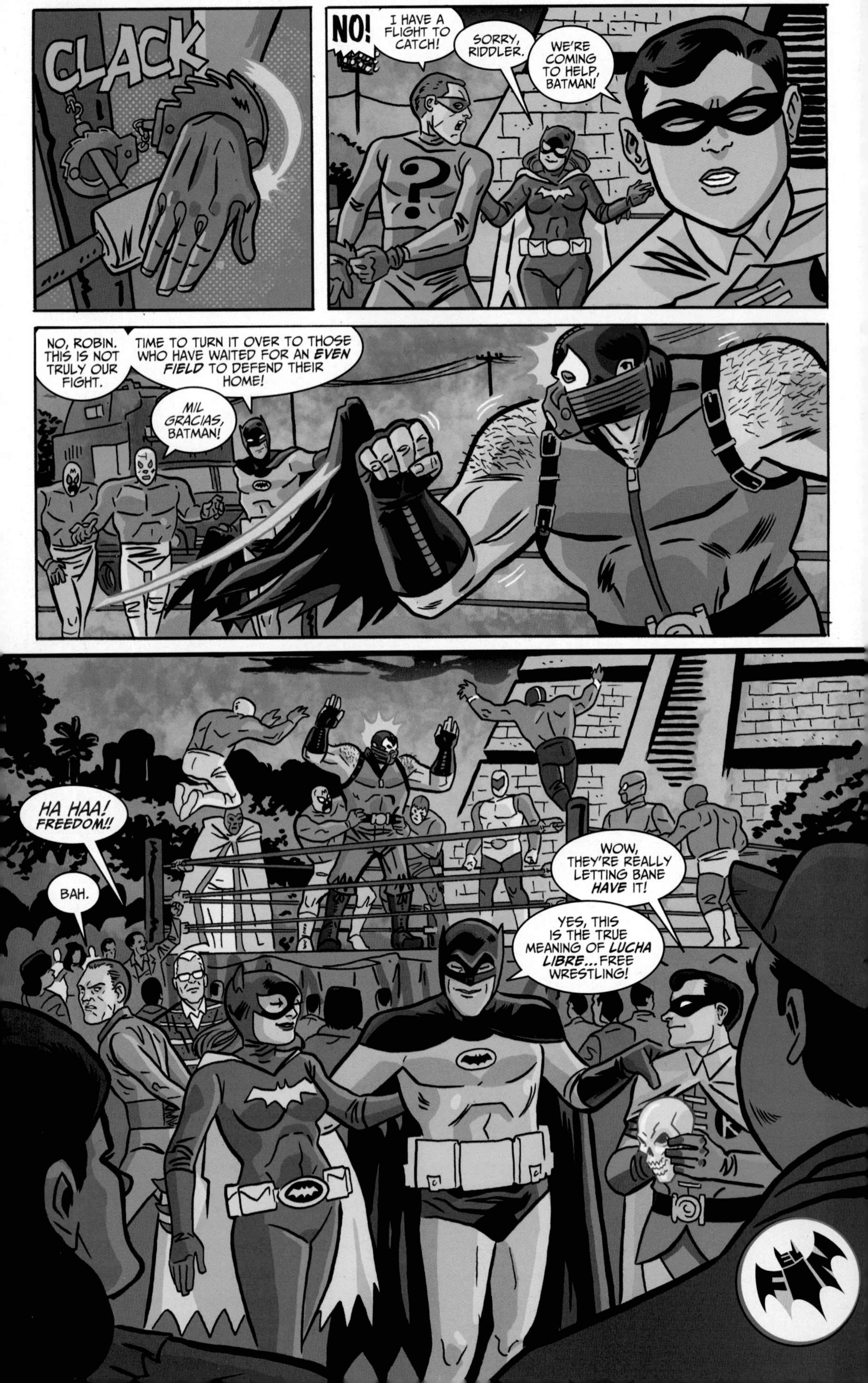
CLACK
NO!
I HAVE A FLIGHT TO CATCH!
SORRY, RIDDLER.
WE'RE COMING TO HELP, BATMAN!
NO, ROBIN. THIS IS NOT TRULY OUR FIGHT.
TIME TO TURN IT OVER TO THOSE WHO HAVE WAITED FOR AN EVEN FIELD TO DEFEND THEIR HOME!
MIL GRACIAS, BATMAN!
HA HAA! FREEDOM!!
BAH.
WOW, THEY'RE REALLY LETTING BANE HAVE IT!
YES, THIS IS THE TRUE MEANING OF LUCHA LIBRE... FREE WRESTLING!
EL FIN

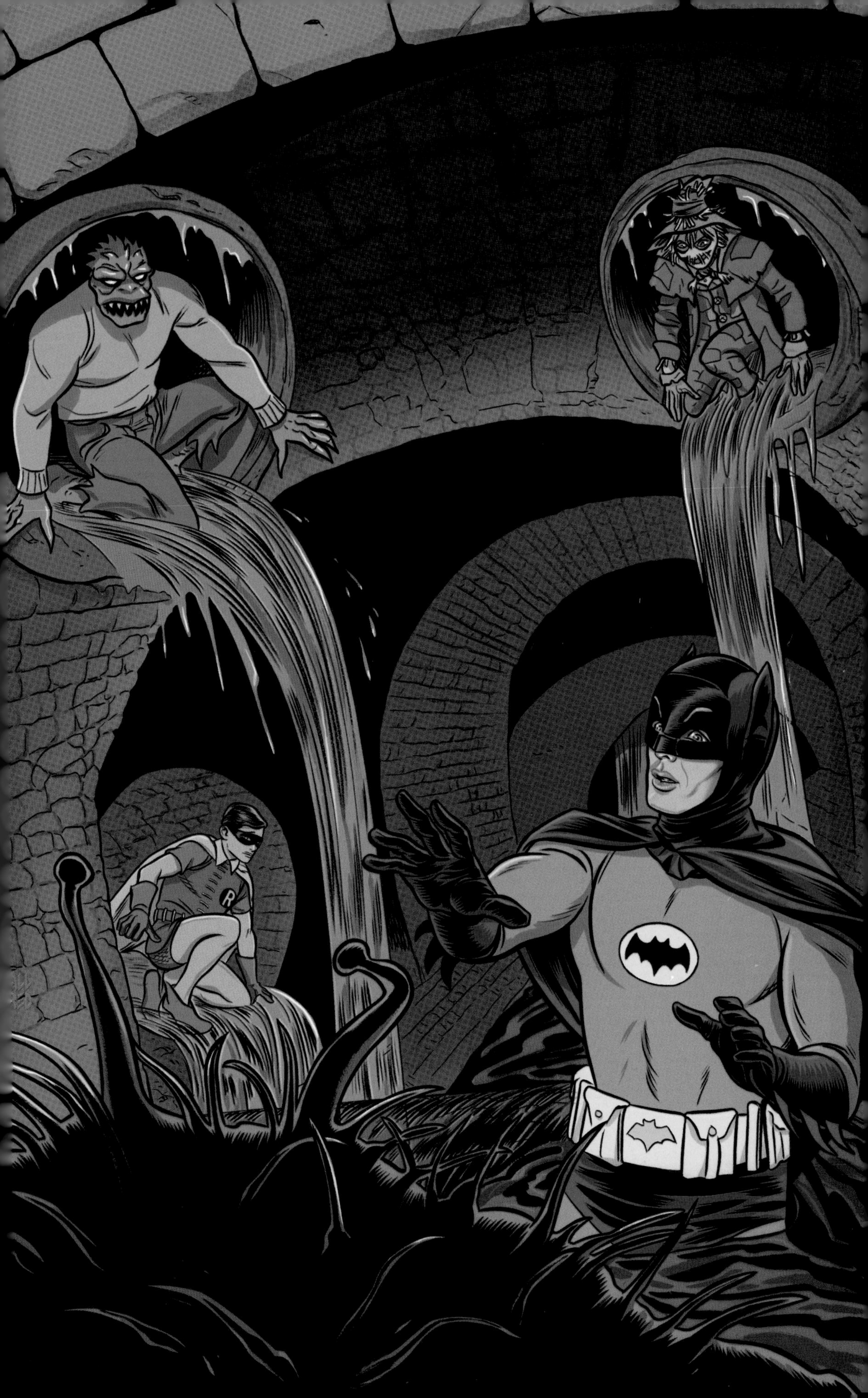

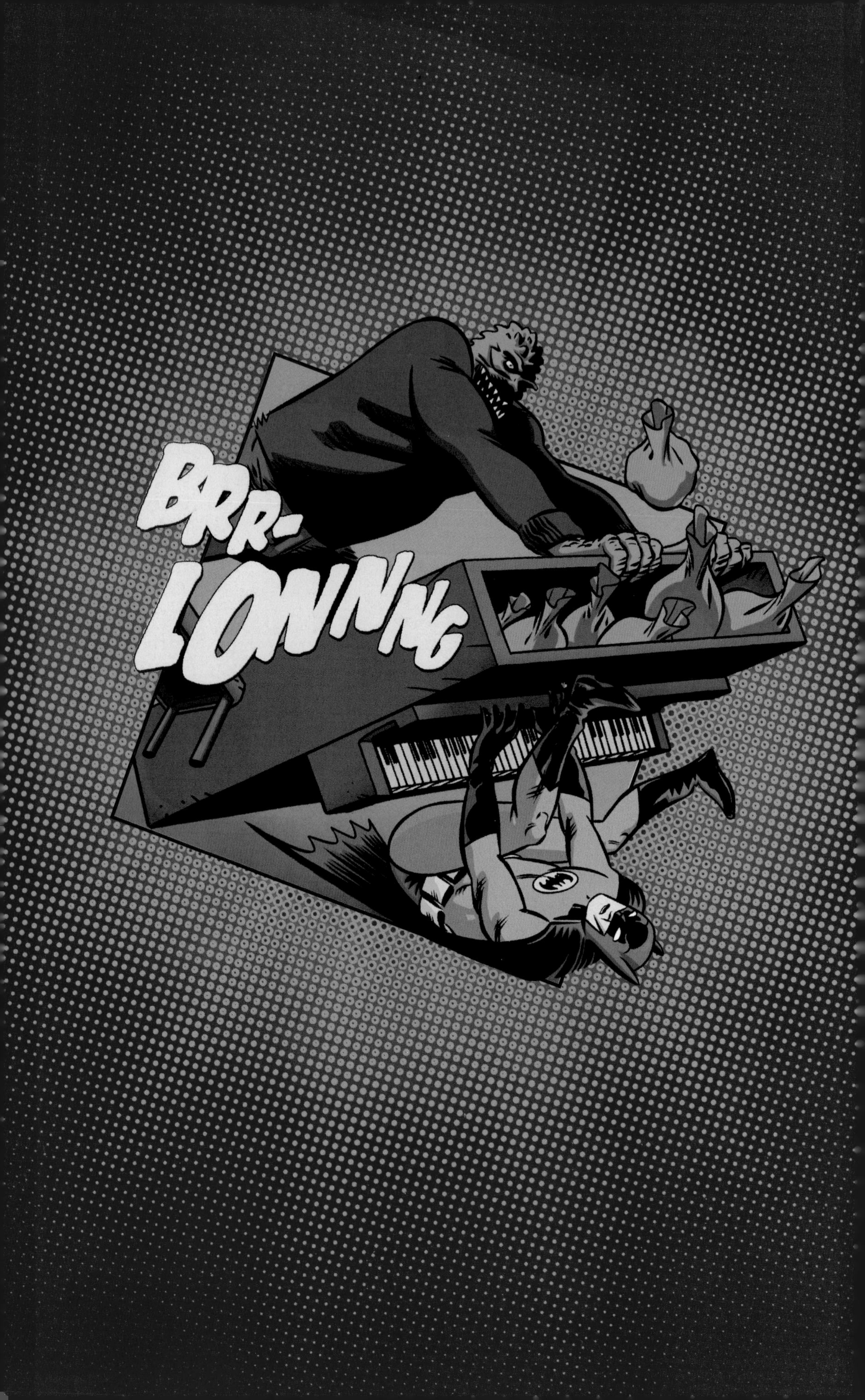
BRR-
LONNNG

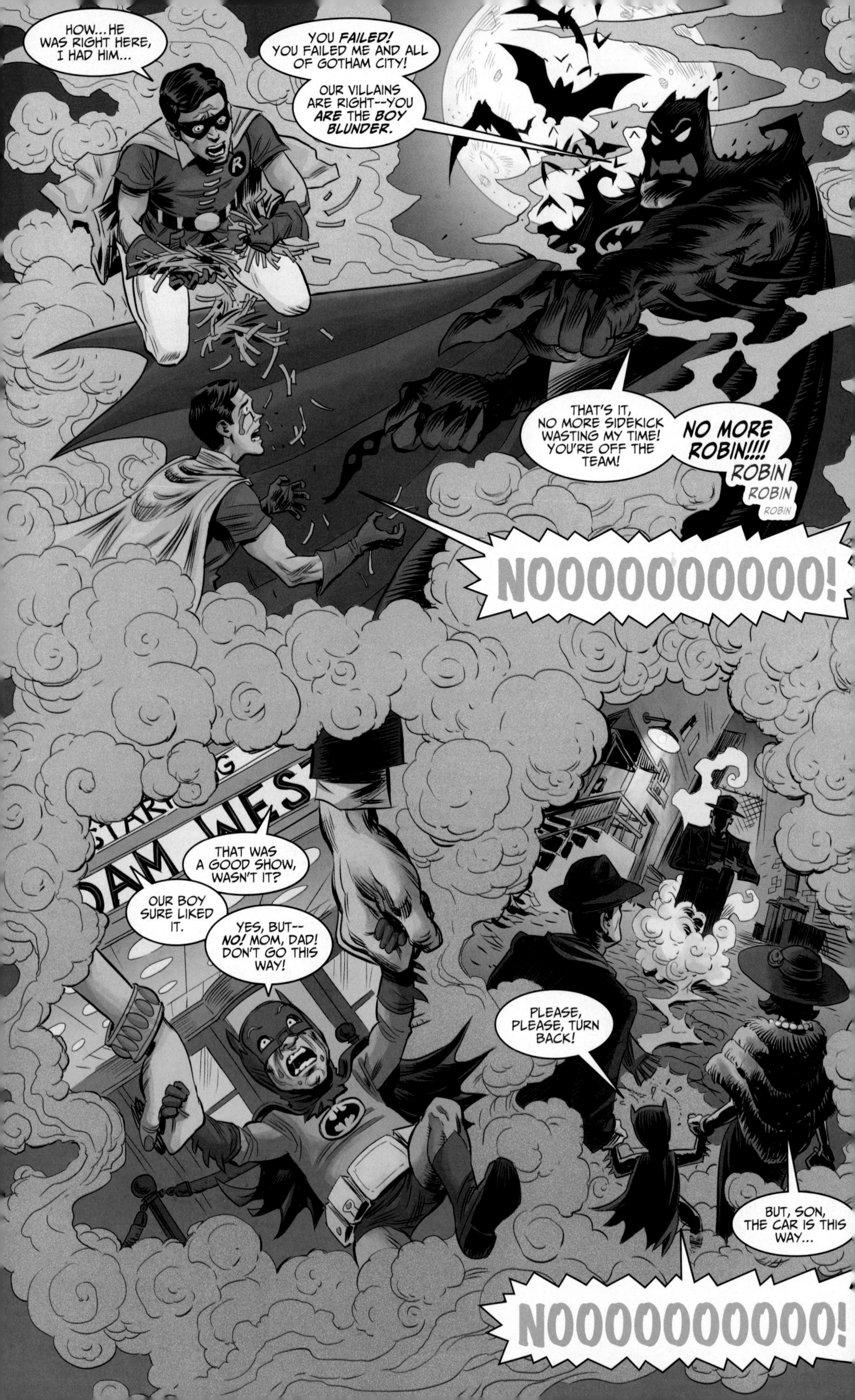
HOW...HE WAS RIGHT HERE, I HAD HIM...
YOU FAILED! YOU FAILED ME AND ALL OF GOTHAM CITY!
OUR VILLAINS ARE RIGHT--YOU ARE THE BOY BLUNDER.
THAT'S IT, NO MORE SIDEKICK WASTING MY TIME! YOU'RE OFF THE TEAM!
NO MORE ROBIN!!!! ROBIN ROBIN ROBIN
NOOOOOOOOOO!
STARRING ADAM WEST
THAT WAS A GOOD SHOW, WASN'T IT?
OUR BOY SURE LIKED IT.
YES, BUT-- NO! MOM, DAD! DON'T GO THIS WAY!
PLEASE, PLEASE, TURN BACK!
BUT, SON, THE CAR IS THIS WAY...
NOOOOOOOOOO!

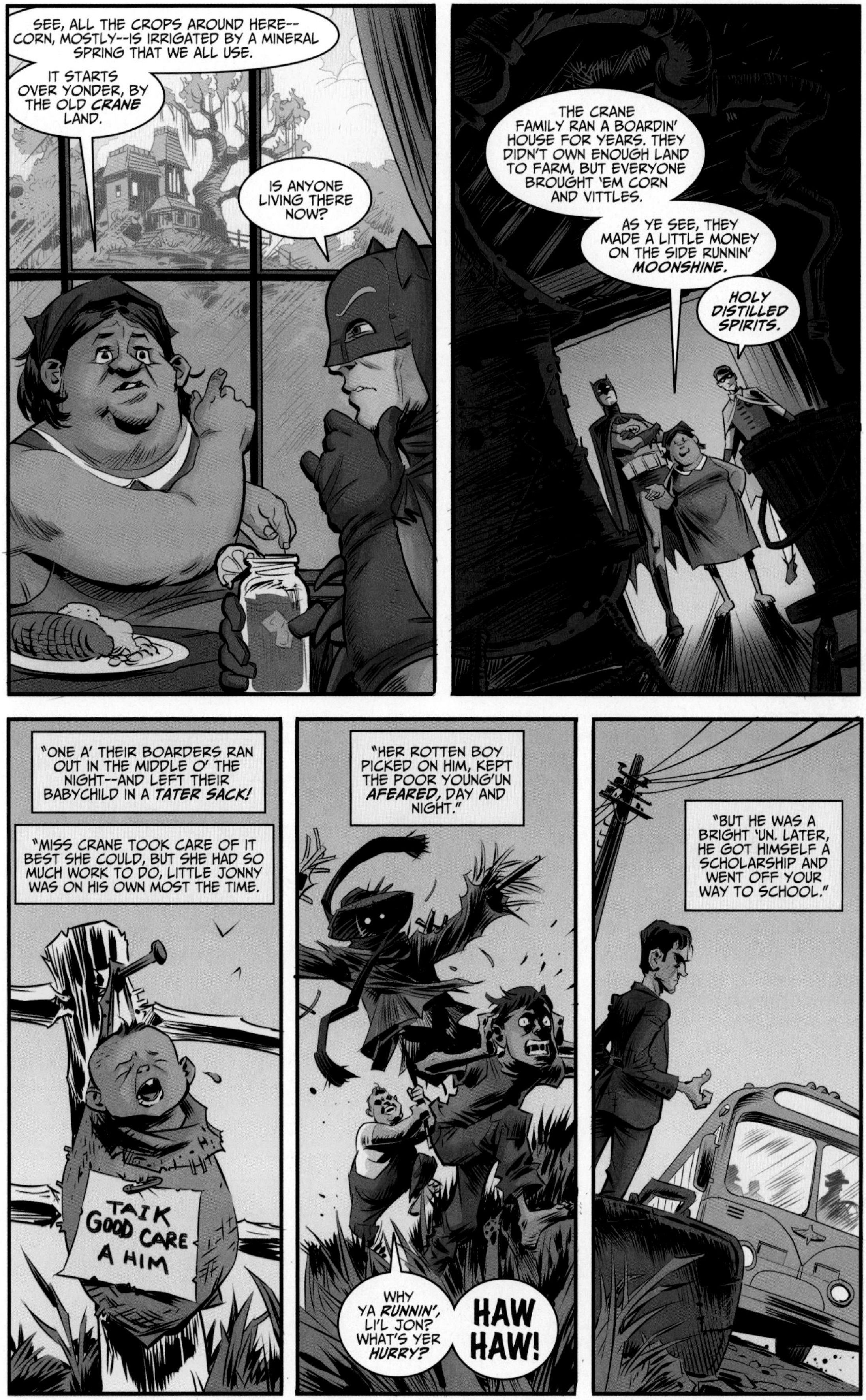
SEE, ALL THE CROPS AROUND HERE--CORN, MOSTLY--IS IRRIGATED BY A MINERAL SPRING THAT WE ALL USE.
IT STARTS OVER YONDER, BY THE OLD CRANE LAND.
IS ANYONE LIVING THERE NOW?
THE CRANE FAMILY RAN A BOARDIN' HOUSE FOR YEARS. THEY DIDN'T OWN ENOUGH LAND TO FARM, BUT EVERYONE BROUGHT 'EM CORN AND VITTLES.
AS YE SEE, THEY MADE A LITTLE MONEY ON THE SIDE RUNNIN' MOONSHINE.
HOLY DISTILLED SPIRITS.
"ONE A' THEIR BOARDERS RAN OUT IN THE MIDDLE O' THE NIGHT--AND LEFT THEIR BABYCHILD IN A TATER SACK!
"MISS CRANE TOOK CARE OF IT BEST SHE COULD, BUT SHE HAD SO MUCH WORK TO DO, LITTLE JONNY WAS ON HIS OWN MOST THE TIME.
TAIK GOOD CARE A HIM
"HER ROTTEN BOY PICKED ON HIM, KEPT THE POOR YOUNG'UN AFEARED, DAY AND NIGHT."
WHY YA RUNNIN', LI'L JON? WHAT'S YER HURRY?
HAW HAW!
"BUT HE WAS A BRIGHT 'UN. LATER, HE GOT HIMSELF A SCHOLARSHIP AND WENT OFF YOUR WAY TO SCHOOL."

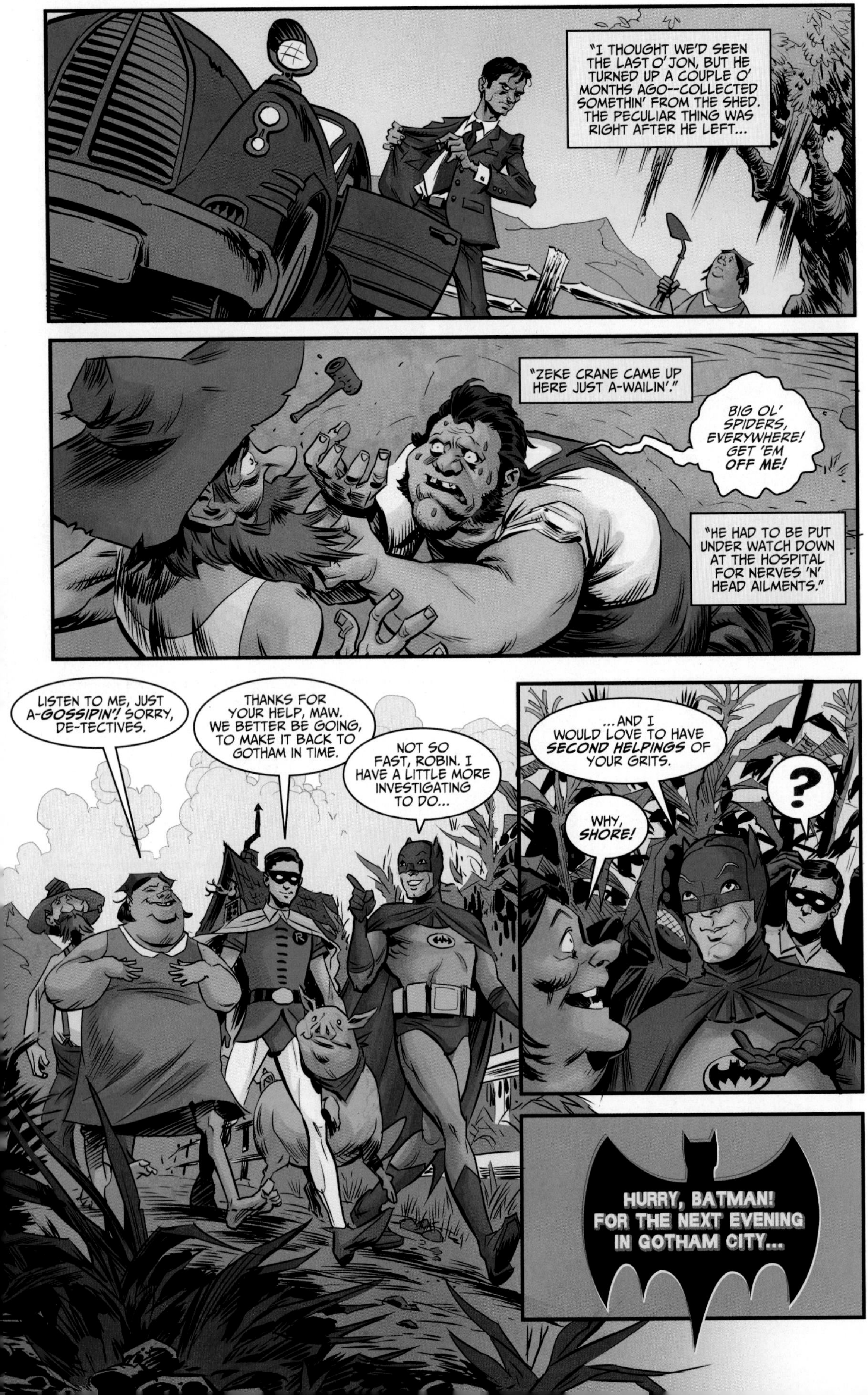
"I THOUGHT WE'D SEEN THE LAST O' JON, BUT HE TURNED UP A COUPLE O' MONTHS AGO--COLLECTED SOMETHIN' FROM THE SHED. THE PECULIAR THING WAS RIGHT AFTER HE LEFT...
"ZEKE CRANE CAME UP HERE JUST A-WAILIN'."
BIG OL' SPIDERS, EVERYWHERE! GET 'EM OFF ME!
"HE HAD TO BE PUT UNDER WATCH DOWN AT THE HOSPITAL FOR NERVES 'N' HEAD AILMENTS."
LISTEN TO ME, JUST A-GOSSIPIN'! SORRY, DE-TECTIVES.
THANKS FOR YOUR HELP, MAW. WE BETTER BE GOING, TO MAKE IT BACK TO GOTHAM IN TIME.
NOT SO FAST, ROBIN. I HAVE A LITTLE MORE INVESTIGATING TO DO...
...AND I WOULD LOVE TO HAVE SECOND HELPINGS OF YOUR GRITS.
WHY, SHORE!
?
HURRY, BATMAN! FOR THE NEXT EVENING IN GOTHAM CITY...

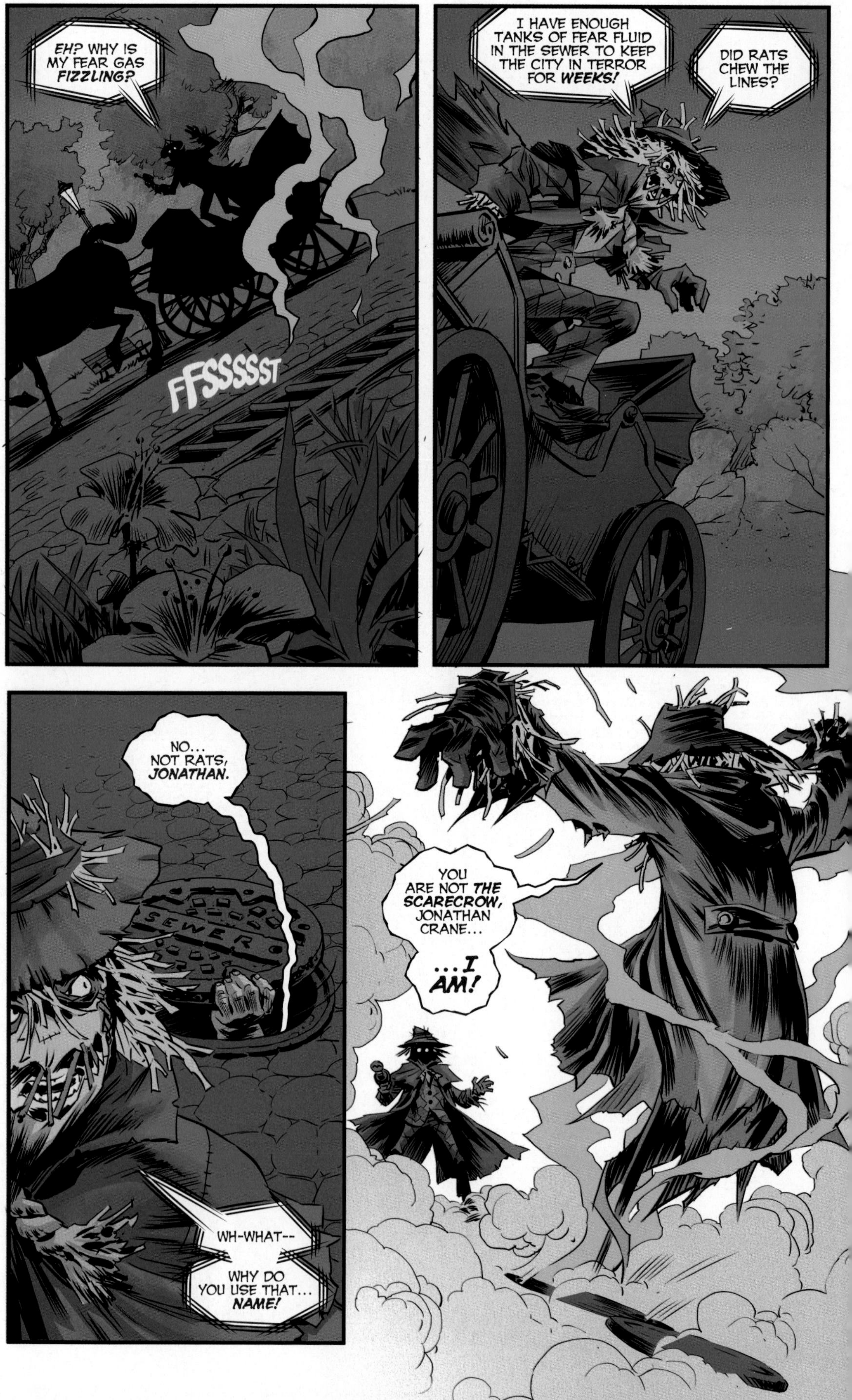
EH? WHY IS MY FEAR GAS FIZZLING?
FFSSSSST
I HAVE ENOUGH TANKS OF FEAR FLUID IN THE SEWER TO KEEP THE CITY IN TERROR FOR WEEKS!
DID RATS CHEW THE LINES?
NO... NOT RATS, JONATHAN.
SEWER
WH-WHAT--
WHY DO YOU USE THAT... NAME!
YOU ARE NOT THE SCARECROW, JONATHAN CRANE...
...I AM!

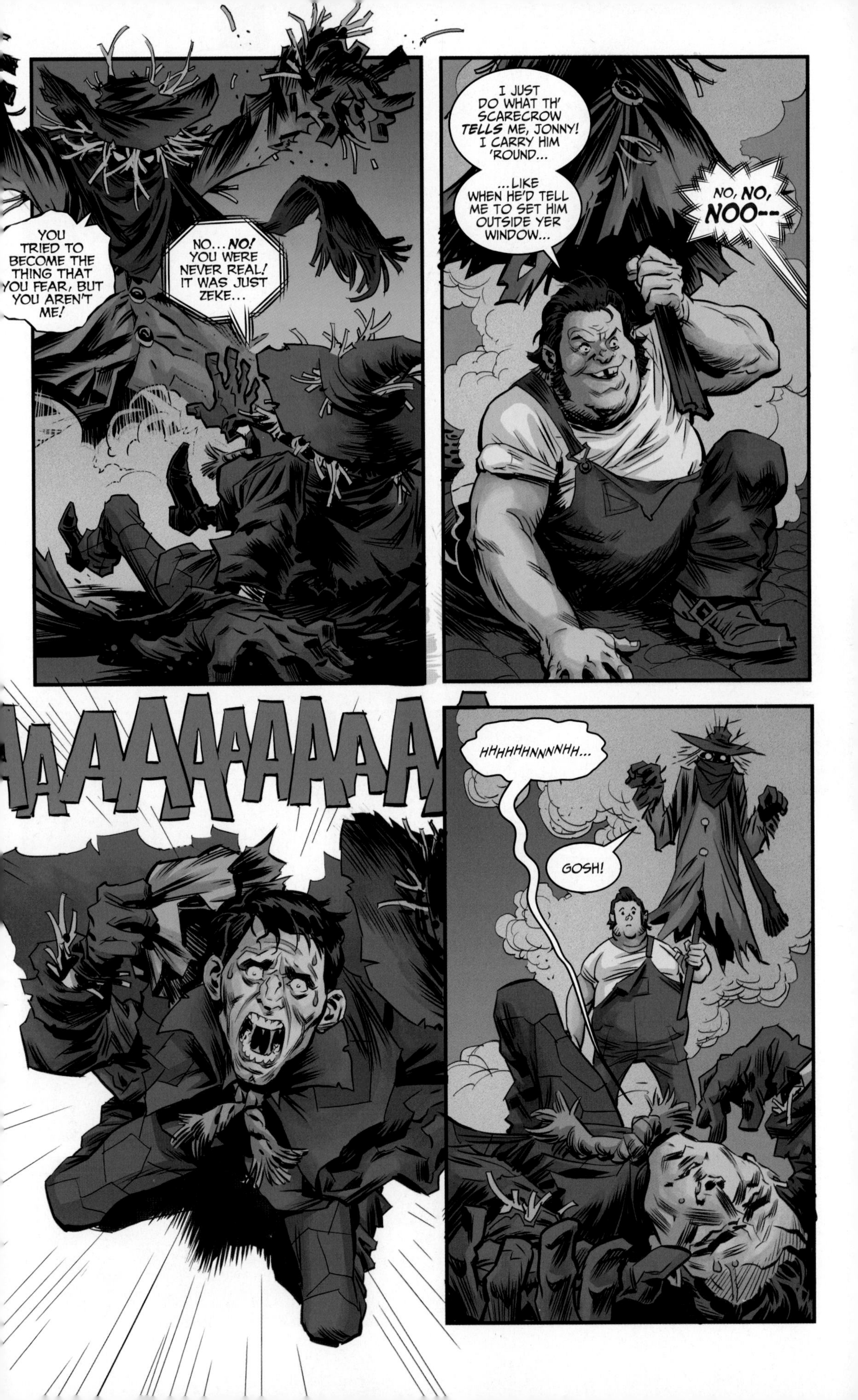
YOU TRIED TO BECOME THE THING THAT YOU FEAR, BUT YOU AREN'T ME!
NO... NO! YOU WERE NEVER REAL! IT WAS JUST ZEKE...
I JUST DO WHAT TH' SCARECROW TELLS ME, JONNY! I CARRY HIM 'ROUND...
...LIKE WHEN HE'D TELL ME TO SET HIM OUTSIDE YER WINDOW...
NO, NO, NOO--
AAAAAAAAAA
HHHHHHNNNNHH...
GOSH!

BRINGING BACK HIS MEMORIES *SHUT HIM DOWN,* LIKE YOU SAID, BATMAN!

I DID NOT RELISH DOING THAT, BUT HE WAS TAKING OUT HIS ISSUES ON OUR FAIR CITY.

HE USED THE DISTILLED CORN FROM JITTERS HOLLOW, REFINED TO MAXIMUM POTENCY.

EATING THE GRITS HELPED *INURE* US TO THE FEAR GAS, ENOUGH TO EMPLOY MENTAL EXERCISES AND RESIST IT.

THE KIND OF DEFENSES IT TOOK CRANE A LIFETIME TO ADOPT.

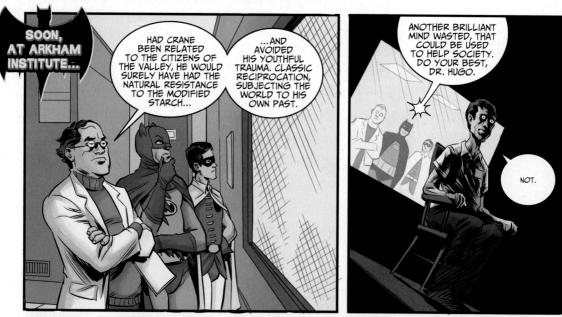

SOON, AT ARKHAM INSTITUTE...

HAD CRANE BEEN RELATED TO THE CITIZENS OF THE VALLEY, HE WOULD SURELY HAVE HAD THE NATURAL RESISTANCE TO THE MODIFIED STARCH...

...AND AVOIDED HIS YOUTHFUL TRAUMA. CLASSIC RECIPROCATION, SUBJECTING THE WORLD TO HIS OWN PAST.

ANOTHER BRILLIANT MIND WASTED, THAT COULD BE USED TO HELP SOCIETY. DO YOUR BEST, DR. HUGO.

NOT.

NOT...

...AFRAID.

THE END

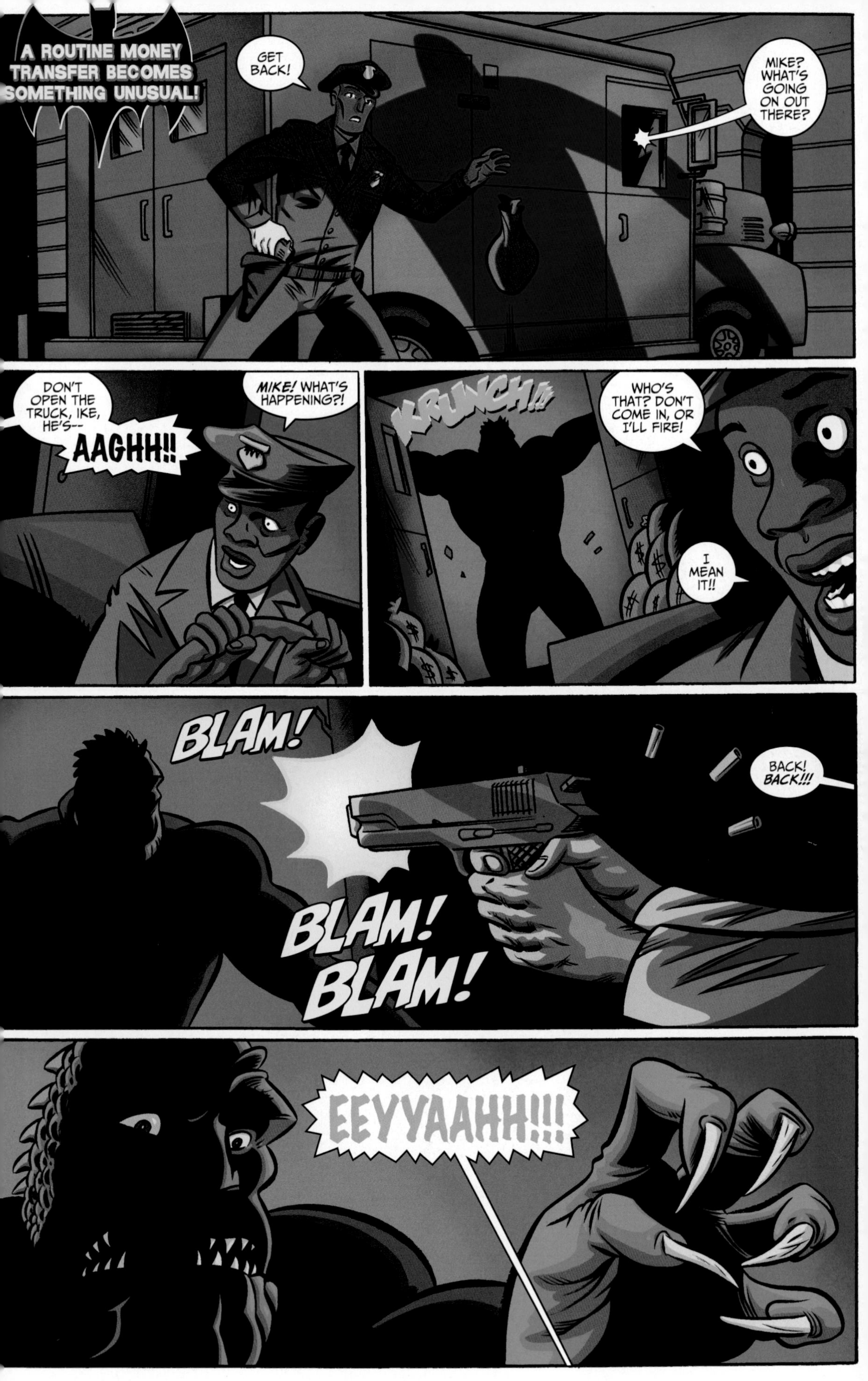
A ROUTINE MONEY TRANSFER BECOMES SOMETHING UNUSUAL!
GET BACK!
MIKE? WHAT'S GOING ON OUT THERE?
DON'T OPEN THE TRUCK, IKE, HE'S--
AAGHH!!
MIKE! WHAT'S HAPPENING?!
KRUNCH!!
WHO'S THAT? DON'T COME IN, OR I'LL FIRE!
I MEAN IT!!
BLAM!
BACK! BACK!!!
BLAM!
BLAM!
EEYYAAHH!!!

BEEP
BEEP
BEEP

I'M SORRY, COMMISSIONER. THE BATMAN IS ON PATROL IN TOWN TONIGHT.

THANK YOU, MYSTERY ATTENDANT. I'LL TRY OTHER MEANS.

BEEN A WHILE SINCE WE USED THE BAT-SIGNAL.

HEAVEN HELP US IF IT DOESN'T WORK, CHIEF.

PLEASE LOOK TO THE SKIES, MASKED MANHUNTER!

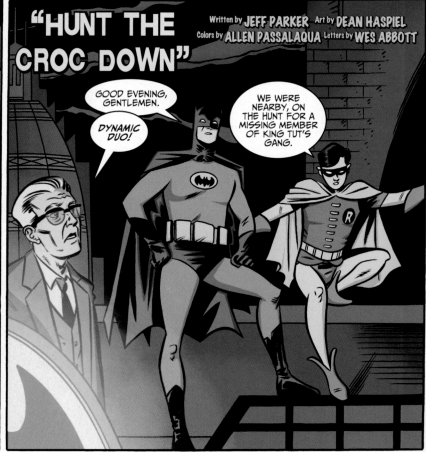

# "HUNT THE CROC DOWN"

Written by **JEFF PARKER**   Art by **DEAN HASPIEL**
Colors by **ALLEN PASSALAQUA**   Letters by **WES ABBOTT**

GOOD EVENING, GENTLEMEN.

DYNAMIC DUO!

WE WERE NEARBY, ON THE HUNT FOR A MISSING MEMBER OF KING TUT'S GANG.

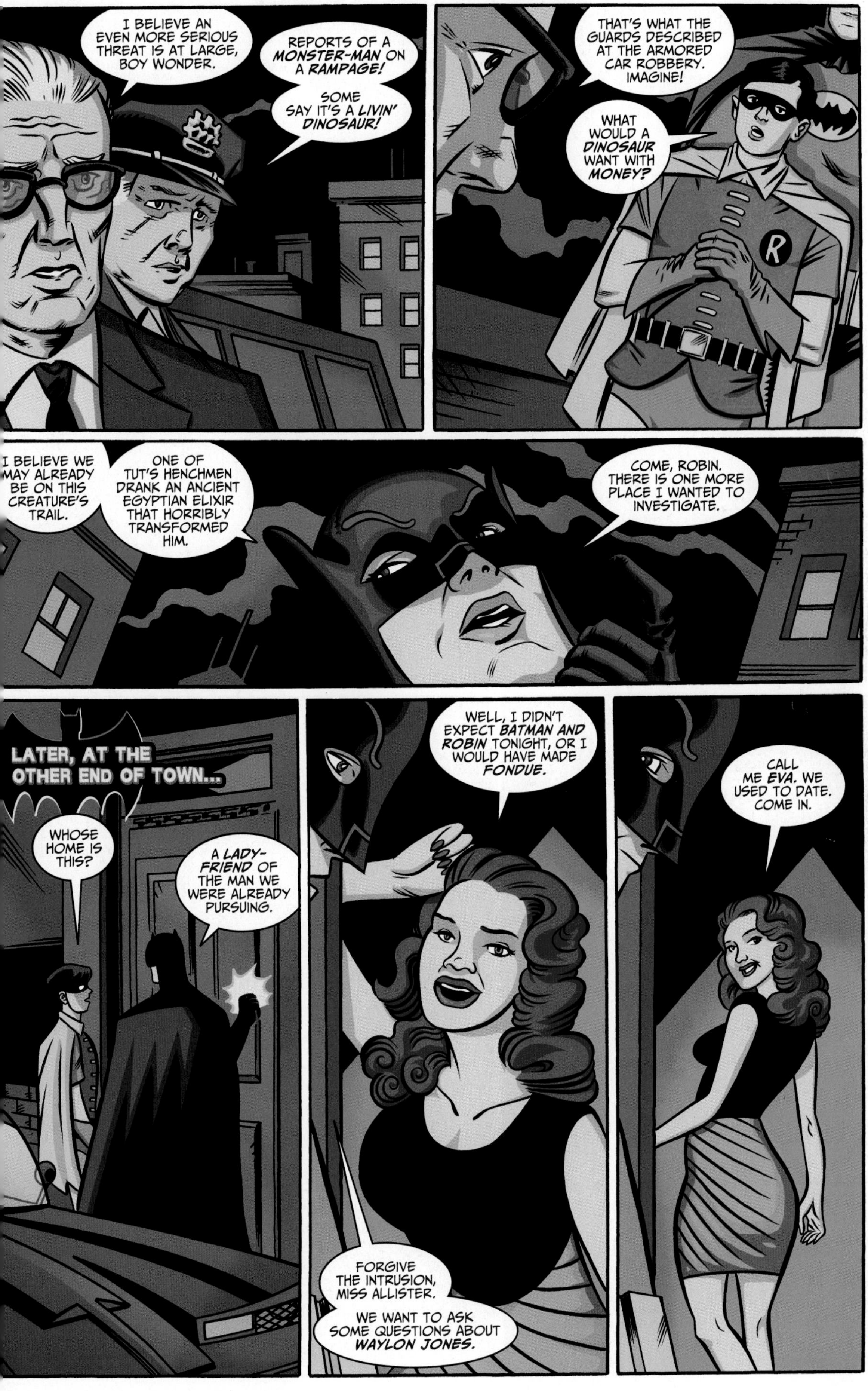
I BELIEVE AN EVEN MORE SERIOUS THREAT IS AT LARGE, BOY WONDER.
REPORTS OF A MONSTER-MAN ON A RAMPAGE!
SOME SAY IT'S A LIVIN' DINOSAUR!
THAT'S WHAT THE GUARDS DESCRIBED AT THE ARMORED CAR ROBBERY. IMAGINE!
WHAT WOULD A DINOSAUR WANT WITH MONEY?
I BELIEVE WE MAY ALREADY BE ON THIS CREATURE'S TRAIL.
ONE OF TUT'S HENCHMEN DRANK AN ANCIENT EGYPTIAN ELIXIR THAT HORRIBLY TRANSFORMED HIM.
COME, ROBIN. THERE IS ONE MORE PLACE I WANTED TO INVESTIGATE.
LATER, AT THE OTHER END OF TOWN...
WHOSE HOME IS THIS?
A LADY-FRIEND OF THE MAN WE WERE ALREADY PURSUING.
WELL, I DIDN'T EXPECT BATMAN AND ROBIN TONIGHT, OR I WOULD HAVE MADE FONDUE.
FORGIVE THE INTRUSION, MISS ALLISTER.
WE WANT TO ASK SOME QUESTIONS ABOUT WAYLON JONES.
CALL ME EVA. WE USED TO DATE. COME IN.

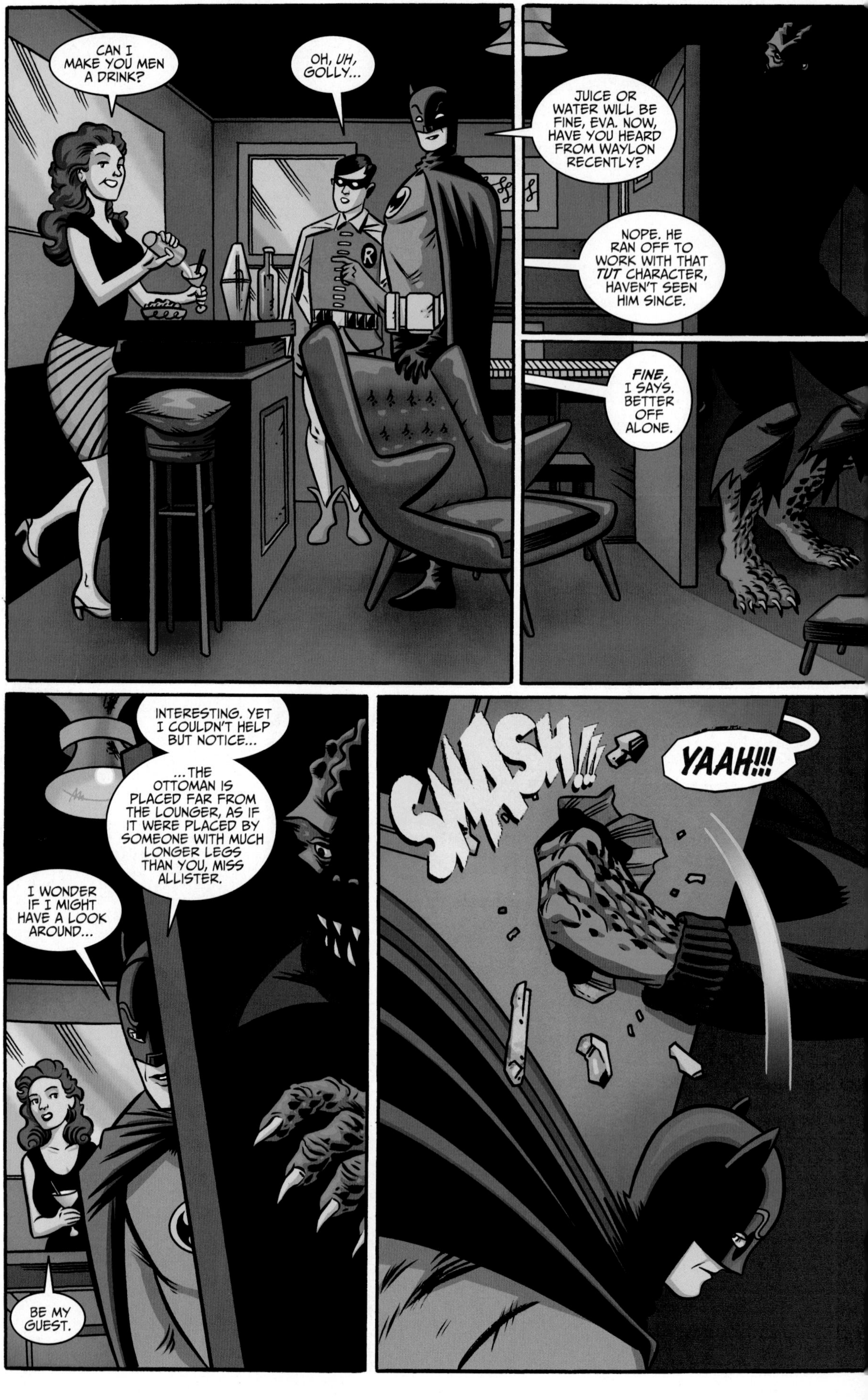
CAN I MAKE YOU MEN A DRINK?
OH, UH, GOLLY...
JUICE OR WATER WILL BE FINE, EVA. NOW, HAVE YOU HEARD FROM WAYLON RECENTLY?
NOPE. HE RAN OFF TO WORK WITH THAT TUT CHARACTER, HAVEN'T SEEN HIM SINCE.
FINE, I SAYS. BETTER OFF ALONE.
INTERESTING. YET I COULDN'T HELP BUT NOTICE...
...THE OTTOMAN IS PLACED FAR FROM THE LOUNGER, AS IF IT WERE PLACED BY SOMEONE WITH MUCH LONGER LEGS THAN YOU, MISS ALLISTER.
I WONDER IF I MIGHT HAVE A LOOK AROUND...
BE MY GUEST.
SMASH!!!
YAAH!!!

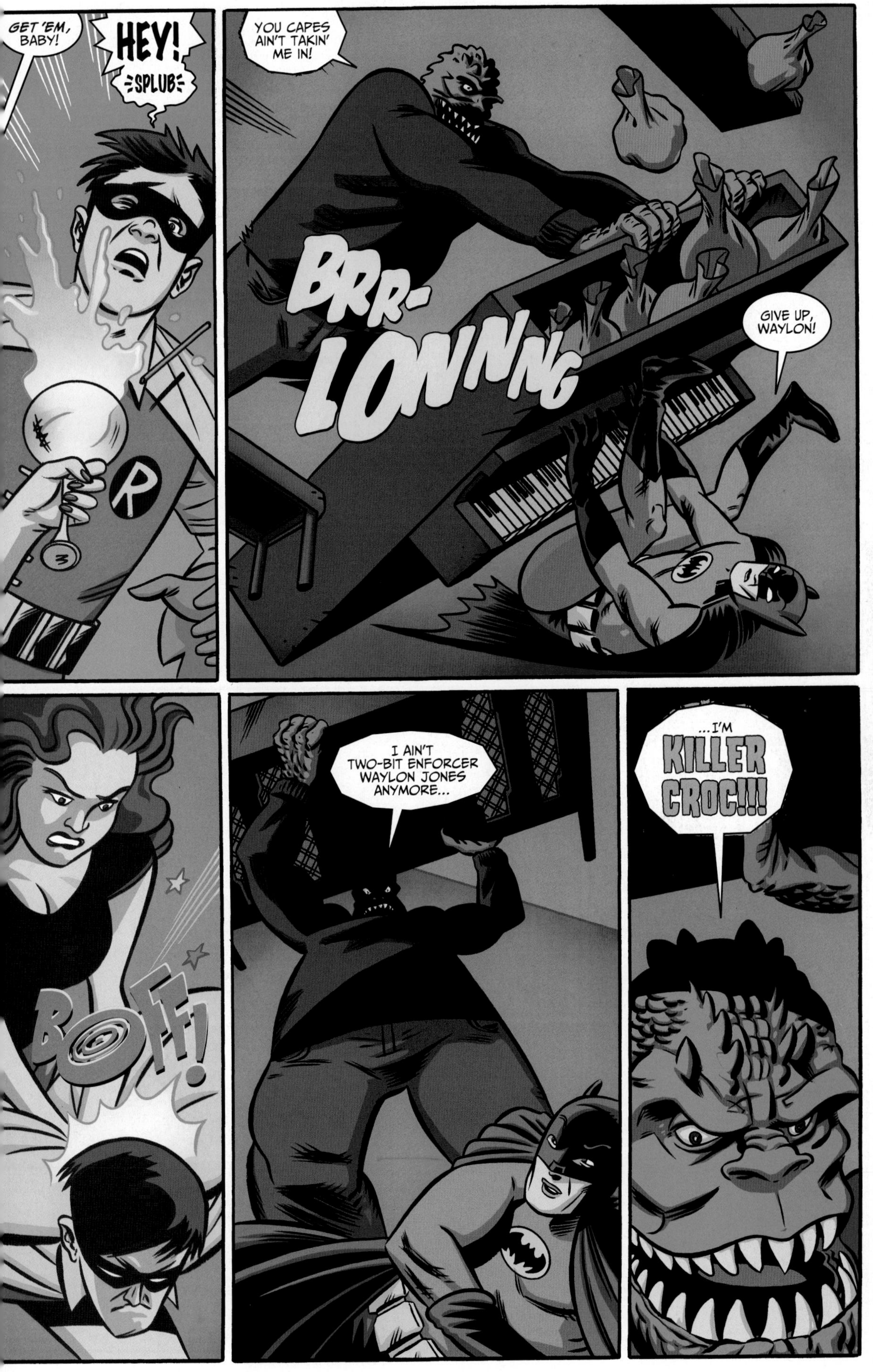
GET 'EM, BABY!
HEY!
SPLUB
YOU CAPES AIN'T TAKIN' ME IN!
BRR-LONNNG
GIVE UP, WAYLON!
BOFF!
I AIN'T TWO-BIT ENFORCER WAYLON JONES ANYMORE...
...I'M KILLER CROC!!!

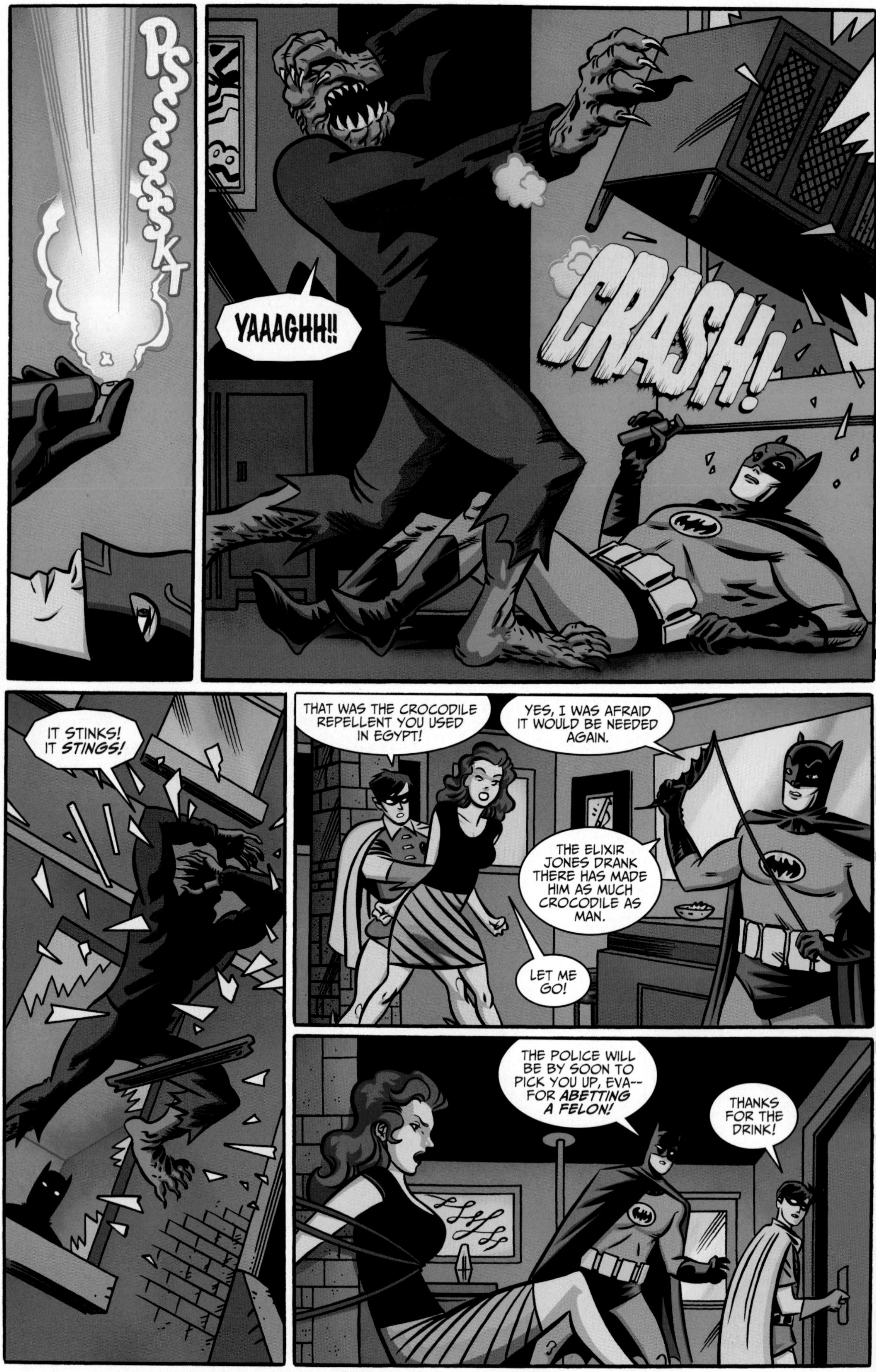
PSSSSSSKT
YAAAGHH!!
CRASH!
IT STINKS! IT STINGS!
THAT WAS THE CROCODILE REPELLENT YOU USED IN EGYPT!
YES, I WAS AFRAID IT WOULD BE NEEDED AGAIN.
THE ELIXIR JONES DRANK THERE HAS MADE HIM AS MUCH CROCODILE AS MAN.
LET ME GO!
THE POLICE WILL BE BY SOON TO PICK YOU UP, EVA-- FOR ABETTING A FELON!
THANKS FOR THE DRINK!

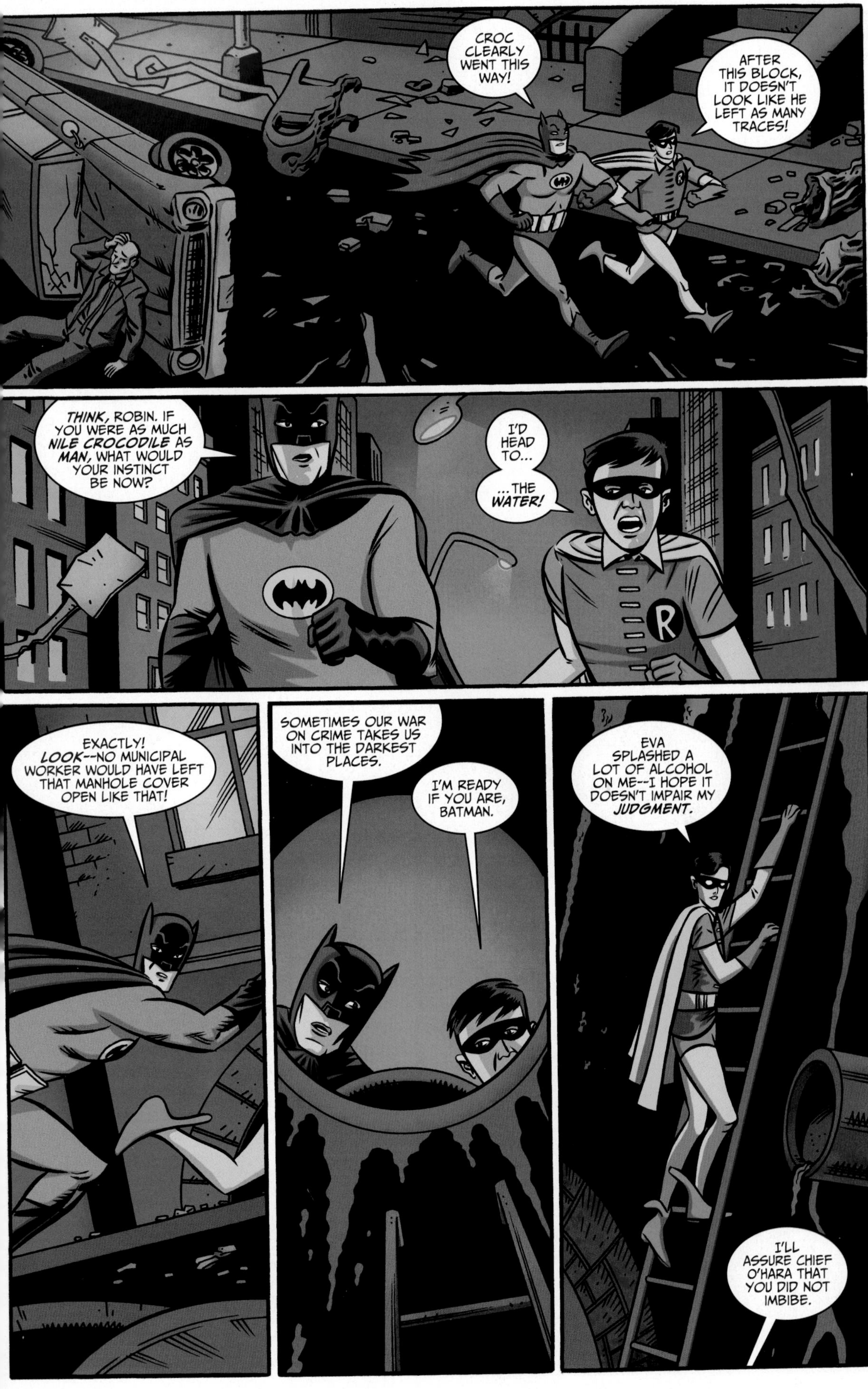

CROC CLEARLY WENT THIS WAY!
AFTER THIS BLOCK, IT DOESN'T LOOK LIKE HE LEFT AS MANY TRACES!
THINK, ROBIN. IF YOU WERE AS MUCH NILE CROCODILE AS MAN, WHAT WOULD YOUR INSTINCT BE NOW?
I'D HEAD TO...
...THE WATER!
EXACTLY! LOOK--NO MUNICIPAL WORKER WOULD HAVE LEFT THAT MANHOLE COVER OPEN LIKE THAT!
SOMETIMES OUR WAR ON CRIME TAKES US INTO THE DARKEST PLACES.
I'M READY IF YOU ARE, BATMAN.
EVA SPLASHED A LOT OF ALCOHOL ON ME--I HOPE IT DOESN'T IMPAIR MY JUDGMENT.
I'LL ASSURE CHIEF O'HARA THAT YOU DID NOT IMBIBE.

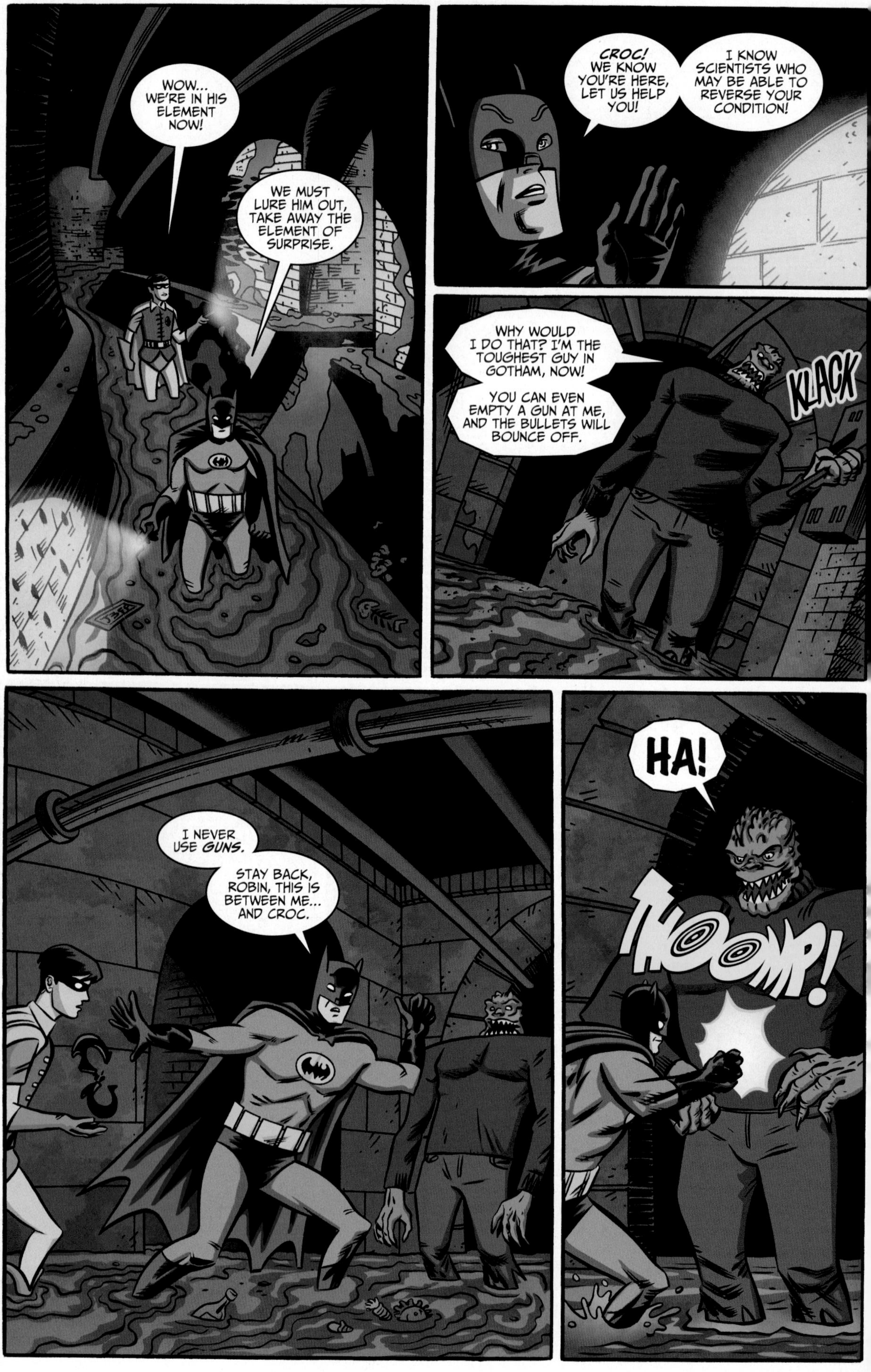
WOW... WE'RE IN HIS ELEMENT NOW!
WE MUST LURE HIM OUT, TAKE AWAY THE ELEMENT OF SURPRISE.
CROC! WE KNOW YOU'RE HERE, LET US HELP YOU!
I KNOW SCIENTISTS WHO MAY BE ABLE TO REVERSE YOUR CONDITION!
WHY WOULD I DO THAT? I'M THE TOUGHEST GUY IN GOTHAM, NOW!
YOU CAN EVEN EMPTY A GUN AT ME, AND THE BULLETS WILL BOUNCE OFF.
KLACK
I NEVER USE GUNS.
STAY BACK, ROBIN, THIS IS BETWEEN ME... AND CROC.
HA!
THOOMP!

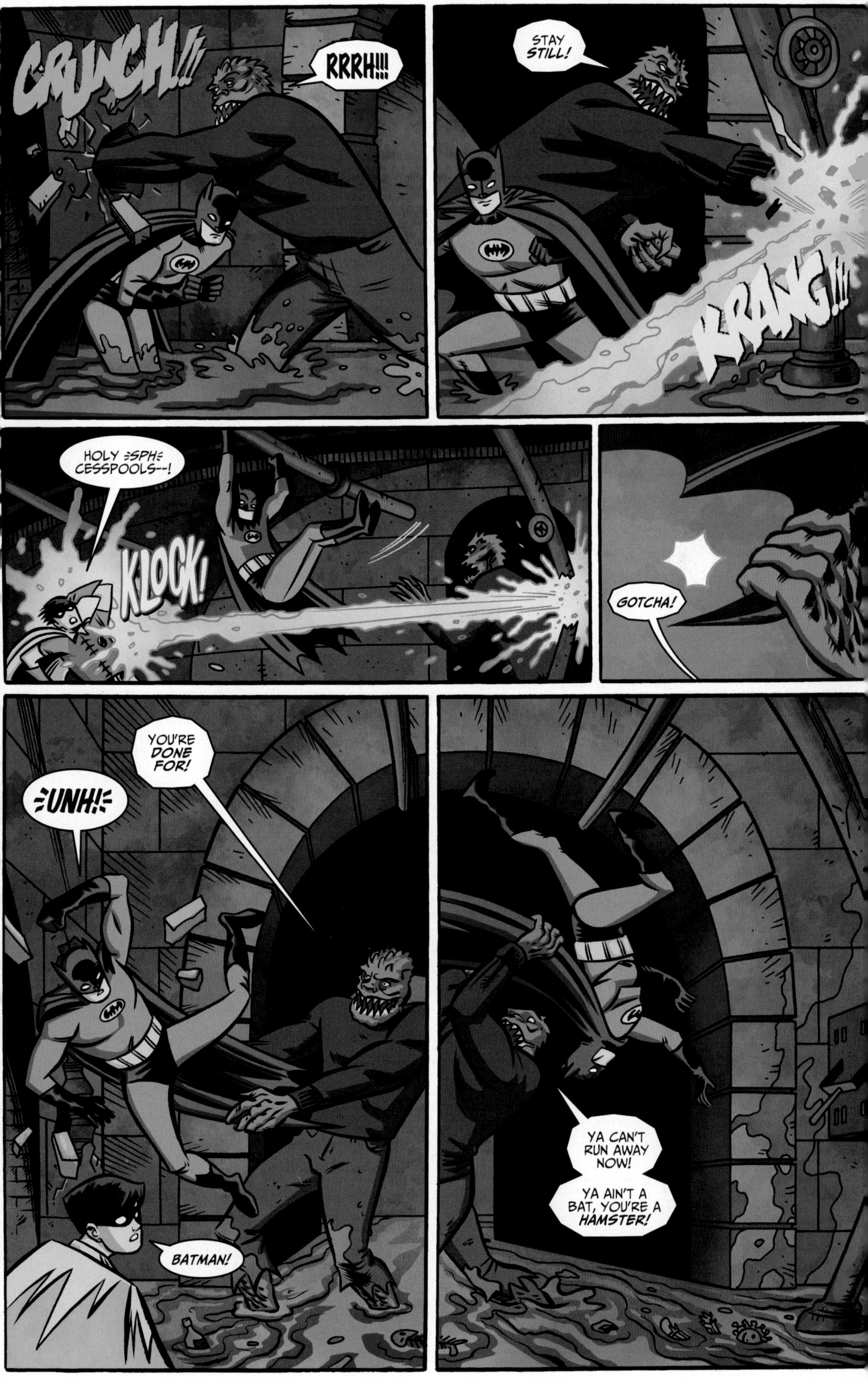
CRUNCH!!
RRRH!!!
STAY STILL!
KRANG!!!
HOLY =SPH= CESSPOOLS--!
KLOCK!
GOTCHA!
YOU'RE DONE FOR!
=UNH!=
BATMAN!
YA CAN'T RUN AWAY NOW!
YA AIN'T A BAT, YOU'RE A HAMSTER!

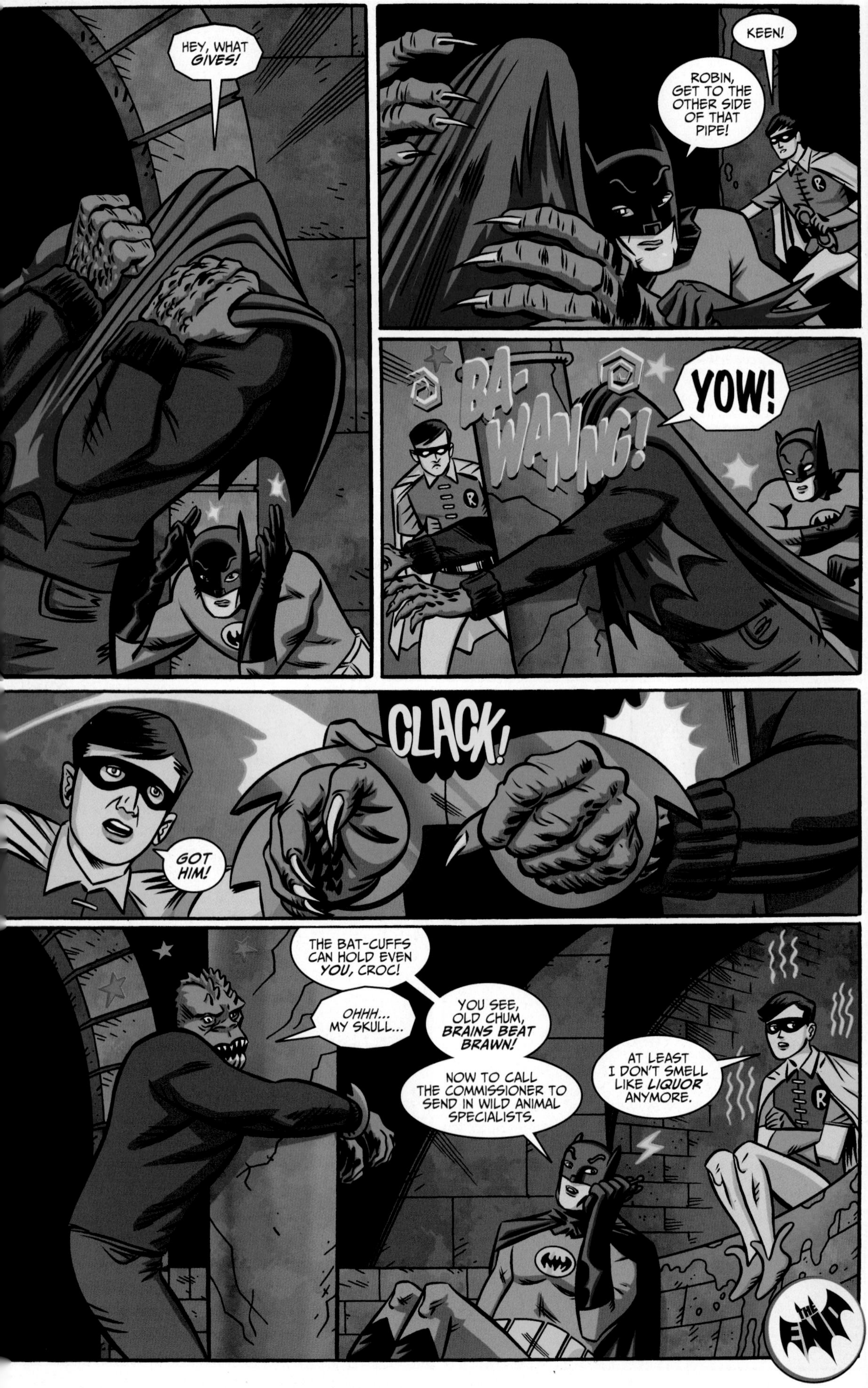
HEY, WHAT GIVES!
KEEN!
ROBIN, GET TO THE OTHER SIDE OF THAT PIPE!
BA-WANNG!
YOW!
CLACK!
GOT HIM!
THE BAT-CUFFS CAN HOLD EVEN YOU, CROC!
OHHH... MY SKULL...
YOU SEE, OLD CHUM, BRAINS BEAT BRAWN!
NOW TO CALL THE COMMISSIONER TO SEND IN WILD ANIMAL SPECIALISTS.
AT LEAST I DON'T SMELL LIKE LIQUOR ANYMORE.
THE END

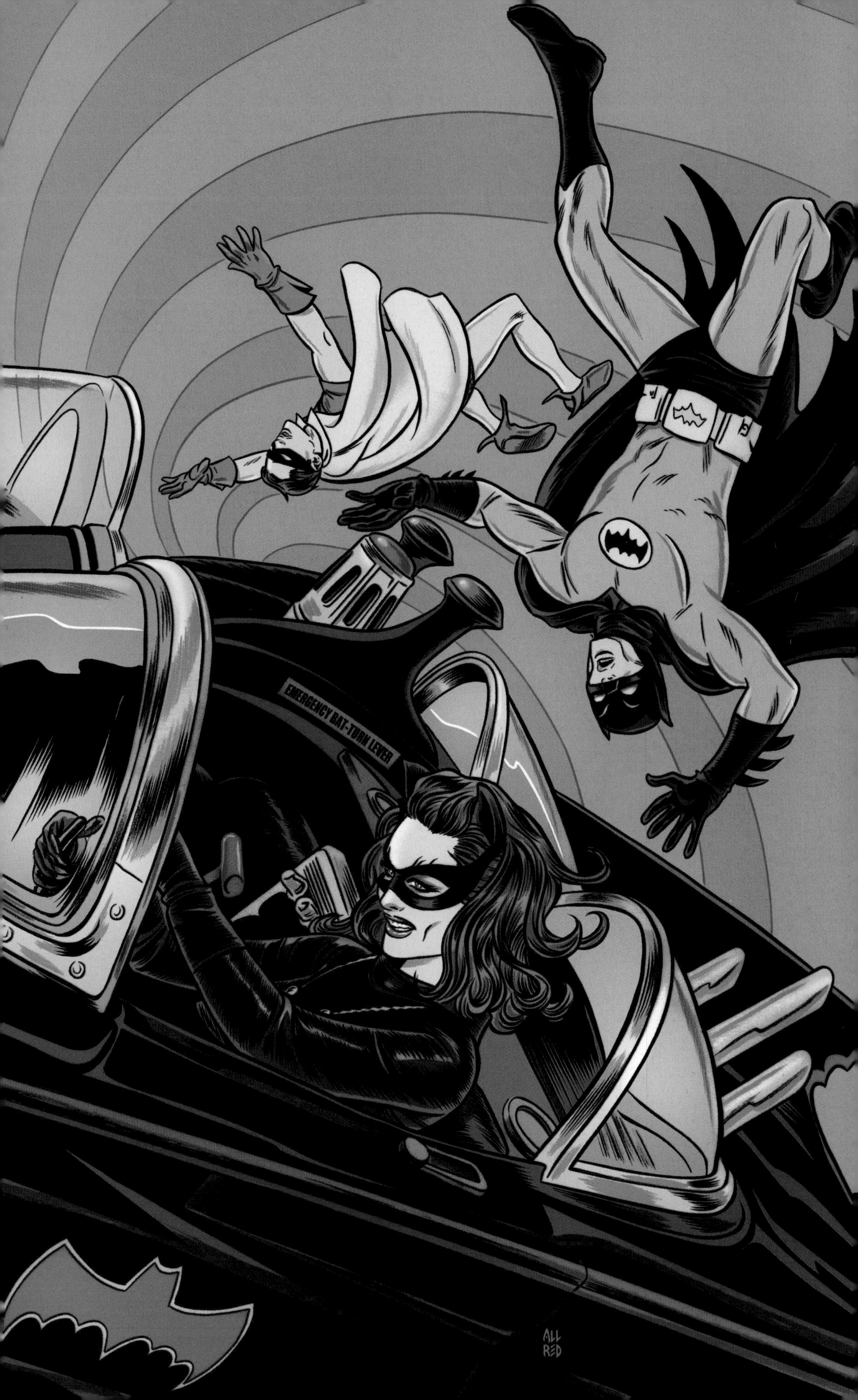
EMERGENCY BAT-TURN LEVER

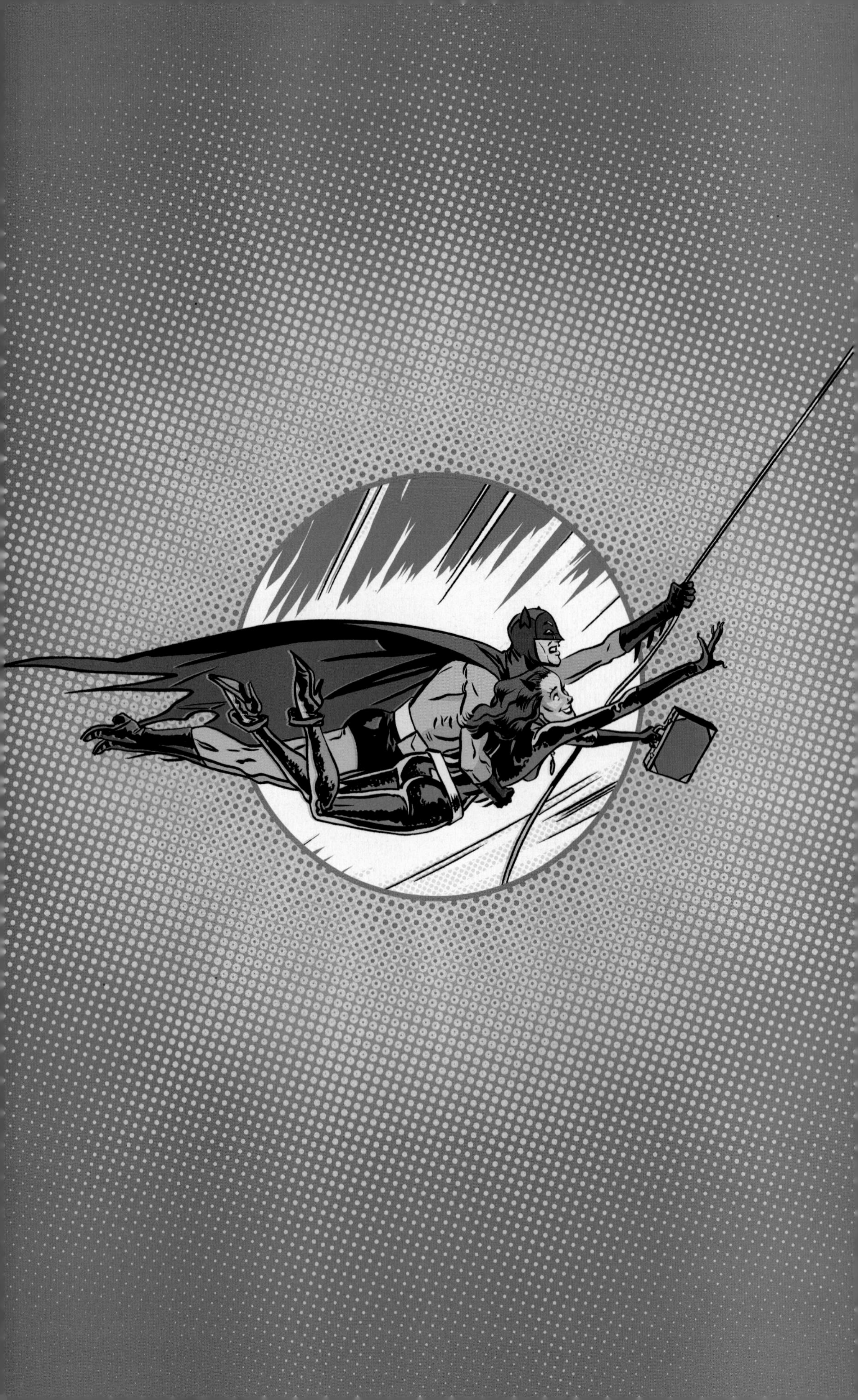

AND HOW DID WE COME TO THIS, READERS? LOOK BACK TO EARLIER TODAY!

RIOT! AT THE WOMEN'S PRISON! GOOD LUCK, CAPED CRUSADER!

THIS IS THE LAST OF 'EM.

I LIKE THEM *LEGS*, BOY WONDER! HAW, HAW!

GOSH!

THANKS FOR COMING OUT, DYNAMIC DUO, BUT AS YOU SEE, WE HAVE IT UNDER CONTROL, NOW.

INDEED, WARDEN.

STILL...COULD WE VISIT THE CELL OF THE MOTHERLY MOBSTER, MA PARKER?

I CAN'T BELIEVE IT! HER *DAUGHTER* IS GONE, TOO!

HOW DID YOU KNOW, BATMAN?

RIOTS ARE A HALLMARK OF MA PARKER'S PRISON BEHAVIOR. SHE KNOWS BETTER THAN ANYONE HOW TO START ONE.

WE SENT HER HERE SIX MONTHS AGO. JUDGING BY THE SIZE OF THE PRISON GROUNDS, THAT WOULD BE ENOUGH TIME...

...TO DIG AN *ESCAPE* TUNNEL.

TUNNELS! ON *MY* PRISON GROUNDS!

SO LONG SUCKE

YEP! WE WENT THIS WAY

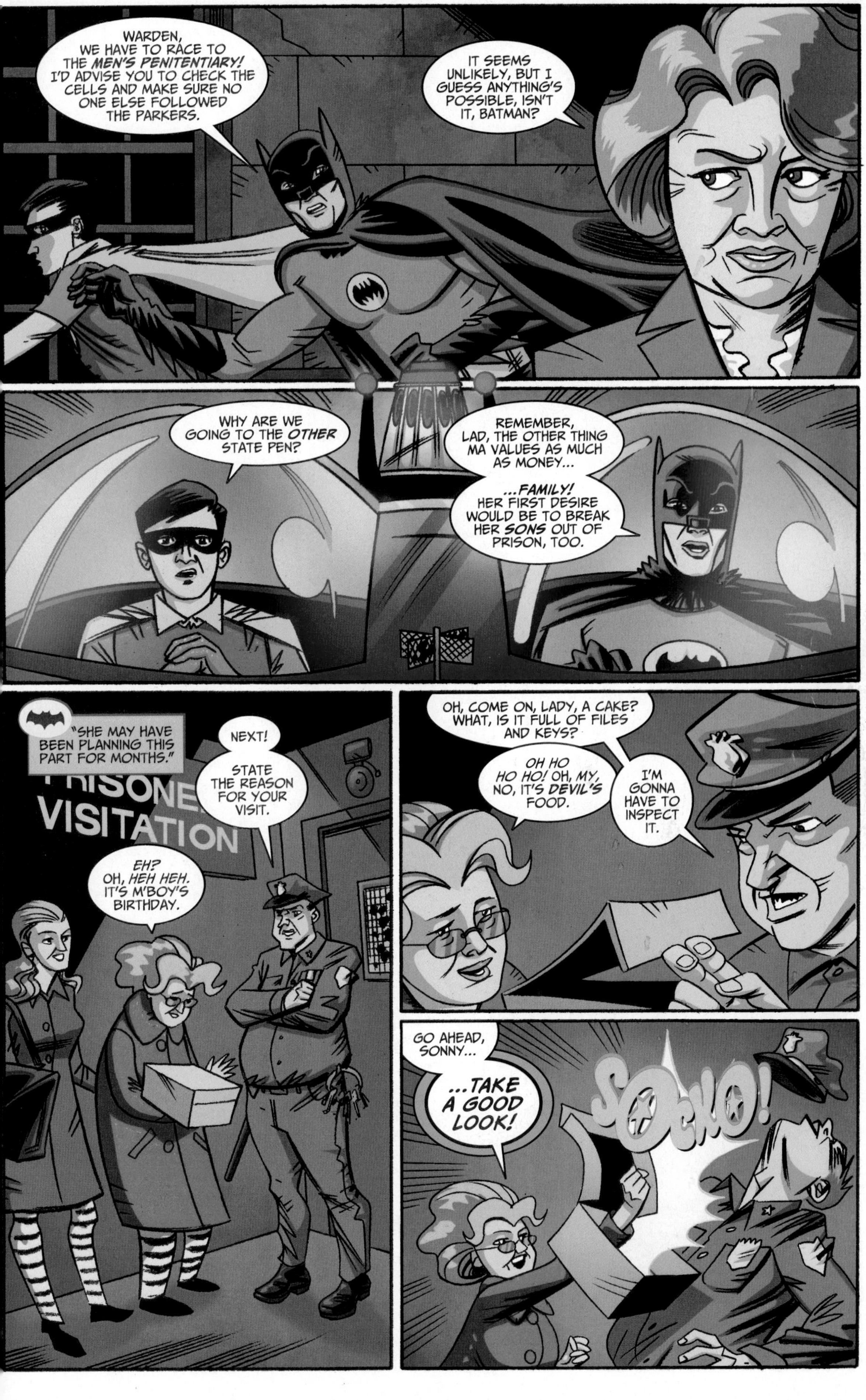
WARDEN, WE HAVE TO RACE TO THE MEN'S PENITENTIARY! I'D ADVISE YOU TO CHECK THE CELLS AND MAKE SURE NO ONE ELSE FOLLOWED THE PARKERS.
IT SEEMS UNLIKELY, BUT I GUESS ANYTHING'S POSSIBLE, ISN'T IT, BATMAN?
WHY ARE WE GOING TO THE OTHER STATE PEN?
REMEMBER, LAD, THE OTHER THING MA VALUES AS MUCH AS MONEY...
...FAMILY! HER FIRST DESIRE WOULD BE TO BREAK HER SONS OUT OF PRISON, TOO.
"SHE MAY HAVE BEEN PLANNING THIS PART FOR MONTHS."
NEXT!
STATE THE REASON FOR YOUR VISIT.
VISITATION
EH? OH, HEH HEH. IT'S M'BOY'S BIRTHDAY.
OH, COME ON, LADY, A CAKE? WHAT, IS IT FULL OF FILES AND KEYS?
OH HO HO HO! OH, MY, NO, IT'S DEVIL'S FOOD.
I'M GONNA HAVE TO INSPECT IT.
GO AHEAD, SONNY...
...TAKE A GOOD LOOK!
SOCKO!

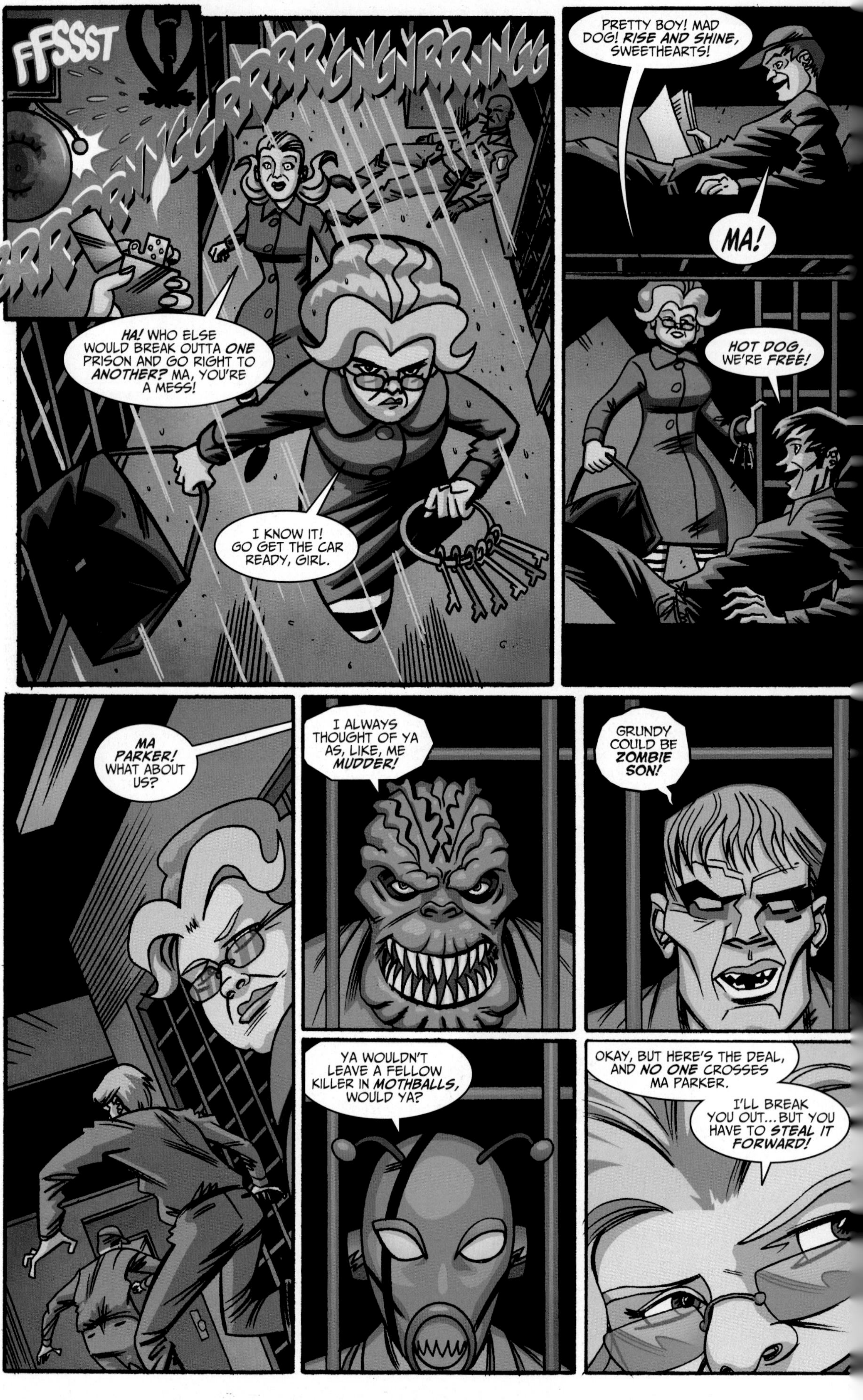
FFSSST
BRRRRRRRNGGRRRRRRNGNGNRRRNNGG
HA! WHO ELSE WOULD BREAK OUTTA ONE PRISON AND GO RIGHT TO ANOTHER? MA, YOU'RE A MESS!
I KNOW IT! GO GET THE CAR READY, GIRL.
PRETTY BOY! MAD DOG! RISE AND SHINE, SWEETHEARTS!
MA!
HOT DOG, WE'RE FREE!
MA PARKER! WHAT ABOUT US?
I ALWAYS THOUGHT OF YA AS, LIKE, ME MUDDER!
GRUNDY COULD BE ZOMBIE SON!
YA WOULDN'T LEAVE A FELLOW KILLER IN MOTHBALLS, WOULD YA?
OKAY, BUT HERE'S THE DEAL, AND NO ONE CROSSES MA PARKER.
I'LL BREAK YOU OUT...BUT YOU HAVE TO STEAL IT FORWARD!

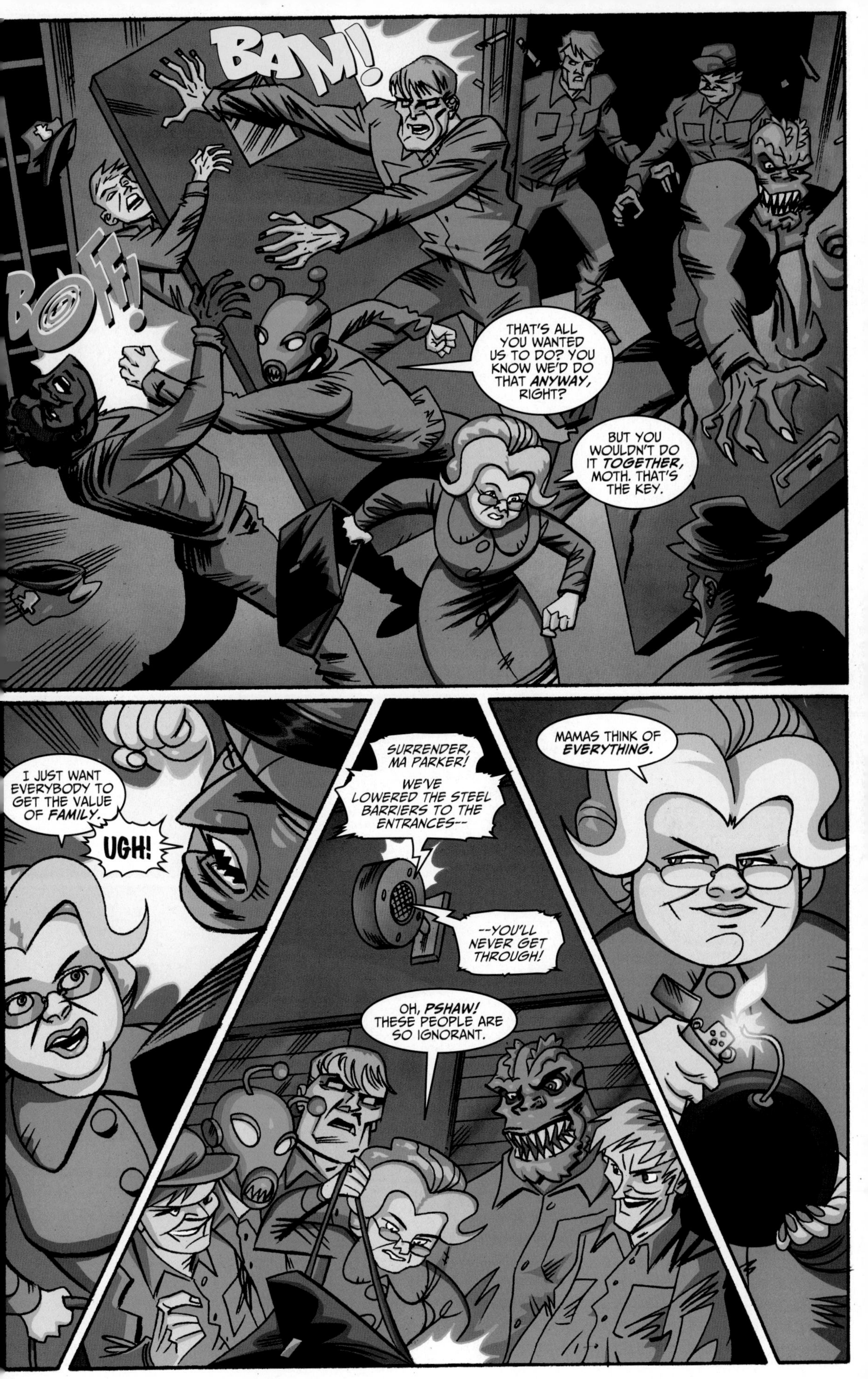
BAM!
BOFF!
THAT'S ALL YOU WANTED US TO DO? YOU KNOW WE'D DO THAT *ANYWAY*, RIGHT?
BUT YOU WOULDN'T DO IT *TOGETHER*, MOTH. THAT'S THE KEY.
I JUST WANT EVERYBODY TO GET THE VALUE OF *FAMILY*.
UGH!
*SURRENDER, MA PARKER!*
*WE'VE LOWERED THE STEEL BARRIERS TO THE ENTRANCES--*
*--YOU'LL NEVER GET THROUGH!*
OH, *PSHAW!* THESE PEOPLE ARE SO IGNORANT.
MAMAS THINK OF *EVERYTHING*.

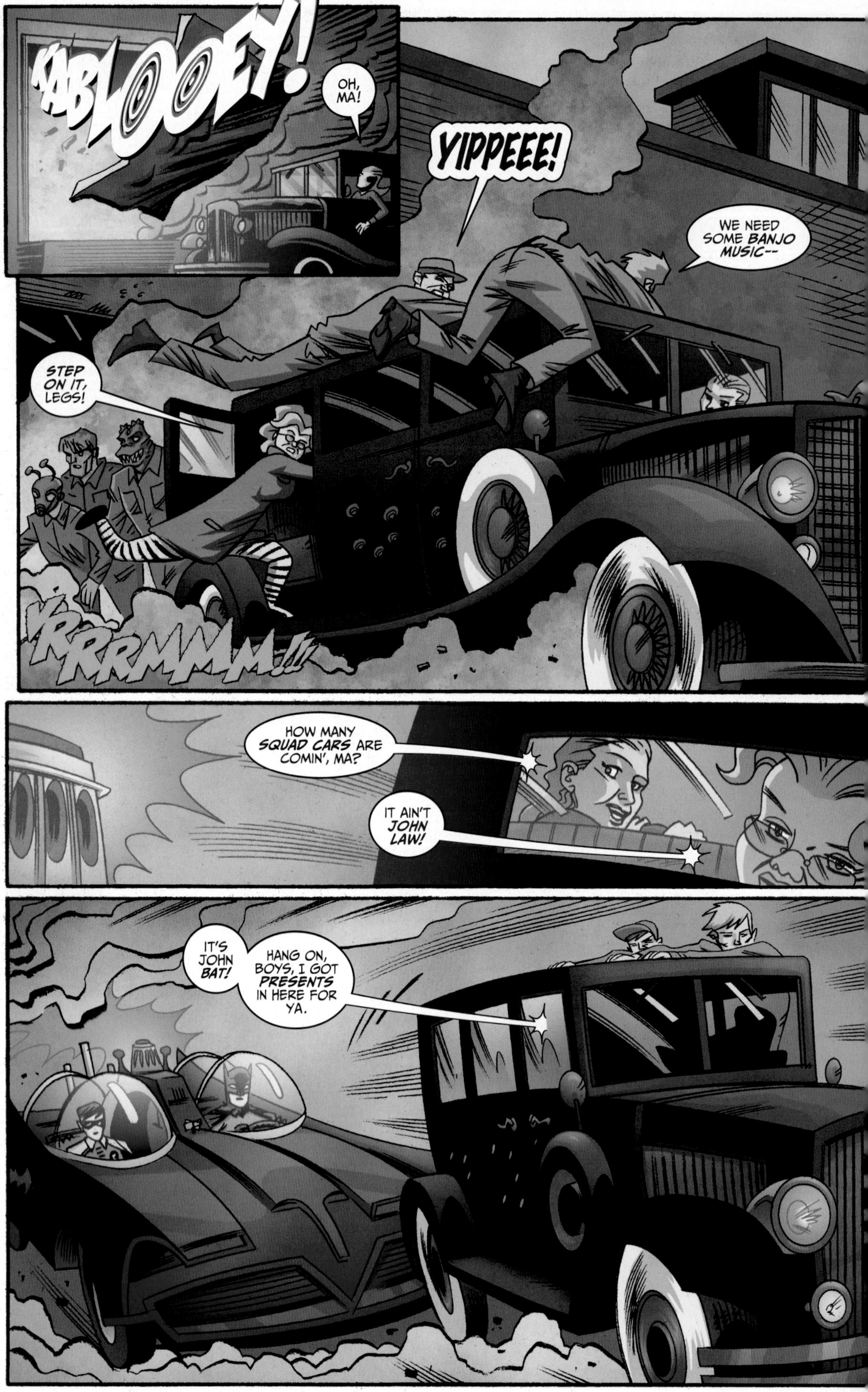
KABLOOEY!
OH, MA!
YIPPEEE!
WE NEED SOME BANJO MUSIC--
STEP ON IT, LEGS!
VRRRMMM!!!
HOW MANY SQUAD CARS ARE COMIN', MA?
IT AIN'T JOHN LAW!
IT'S JOHN BAT!
HANG ON, BOYS, I GOT PRESENTS IN HERE FOR YA.

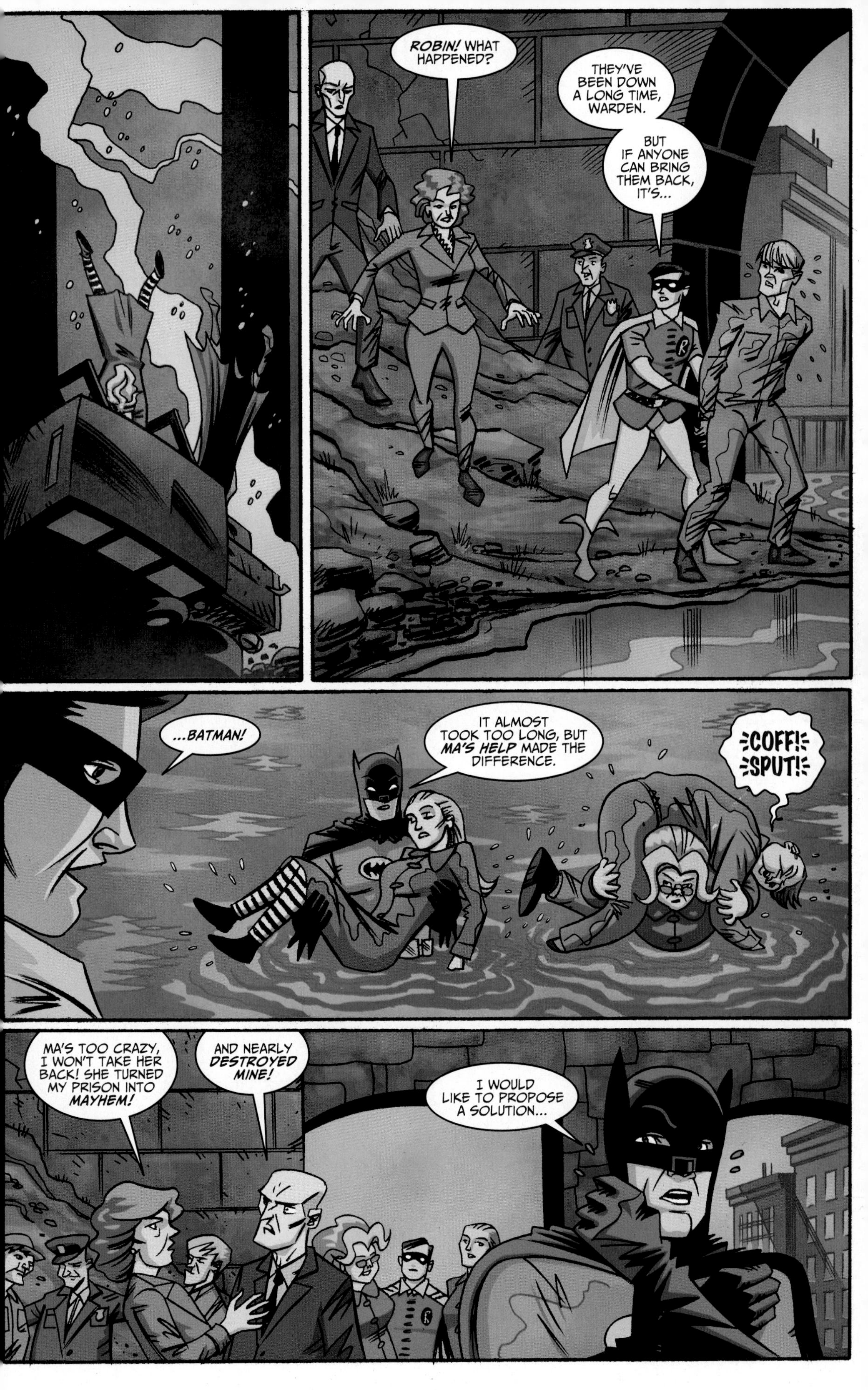

ROBIN! WHAT HAPPENED?
THEY'VE BEEN DOWN A LONG TIME, WARDEN.
BUT IF ANYONE CAN BRING THEM BACK, IT'S...
...BATMAN!
IT ALMOST TOOK TOO LONG, BUT MA'S HELP MADE THE DIFFERENCE.
COFF! SPUT!
MA'S TOO CRAZY, I WON'T TAKE HER BACK! SHE TURNED MY PRISON INTO MAYHEM!
AND NEARLY DESTROYED MINE!
I WOULD LIKE TO PROPOSE A SOLUTION...

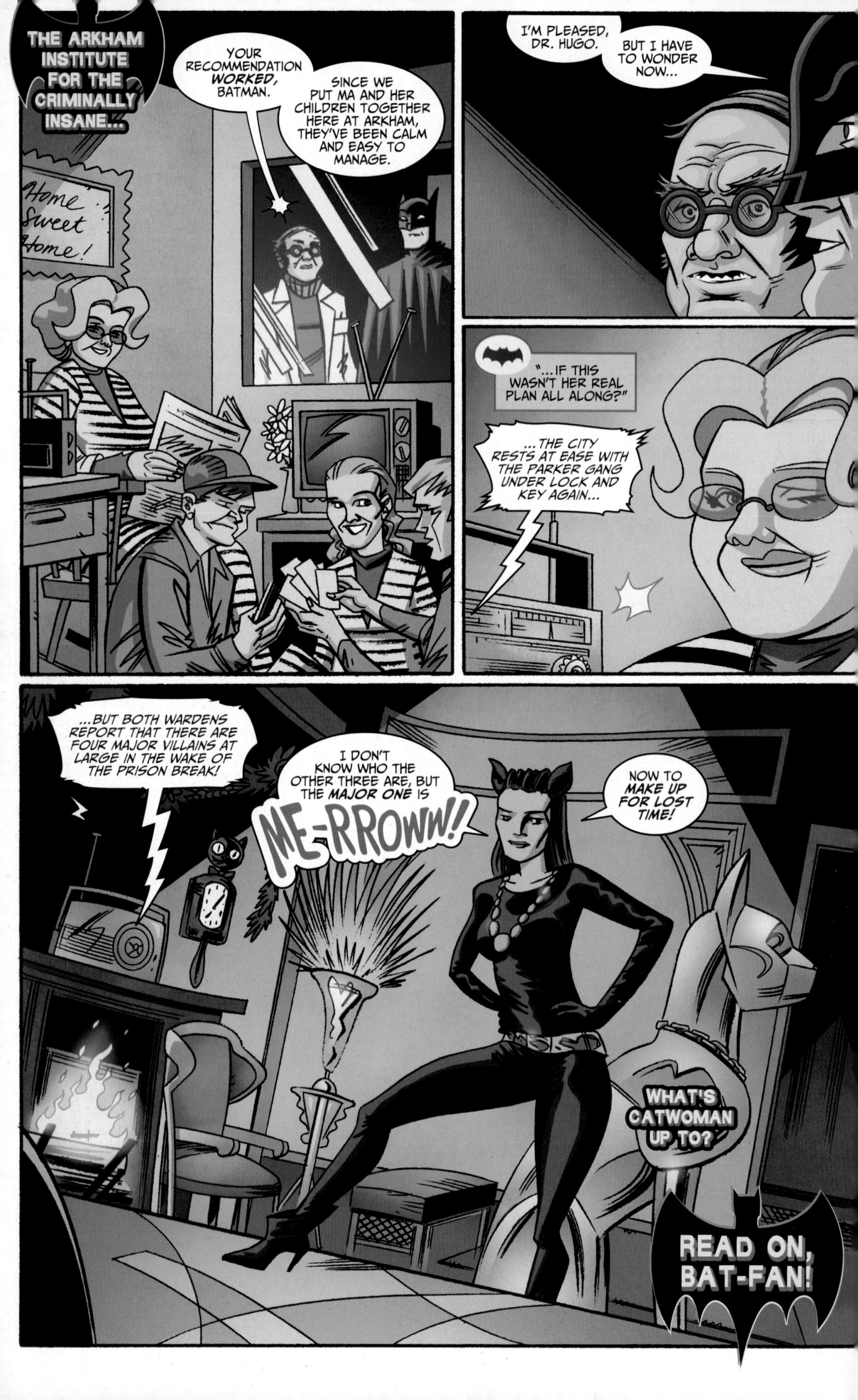

THE ARKHAM INSTITUTE FOR THE CRIMINALLY INSANE...
YOUR RECOMMENDATION WORKED, BATMAN.
SINCE WE PUT MA AND HER CHILDREN TOGETHER HERE AT ARKHAM, THEY'VE BEEN CALM AND EASY TO MANAGE.
Home Sweet Home!
I'M PLEASED, DR. HUGO.
BUT I HAVE TO WONDER NOW...
"...IF THIS WASN'T HER REAL PLAN ALL ALONG?"
...THE CITY RESTS AT EASE WITH THE PARKER GANG UNDER LOCK AND KEY AGAIN...
...BUT BOTH WARDENS REPORT THAT THERE ARE FOUR MAJOR VILLAINS AT LARGE IN THE WAKE OF THE PRISON BREAK!
I DON'T KNOW WHO THE OTHER THREE ARE, BUT THE MAJOR ONE IS
ME-RROWW!
NOW TO MAKE UP FOR LOST TIME!
WHAT'S CATWOMAN UP TO?
READ ON, BAT-FAN!

"CATWOMAN COMES ABOUT!"

Written by JEFF PARKER

Art and Colors by JONATHAN CASE

Letters by WES ABBOTT

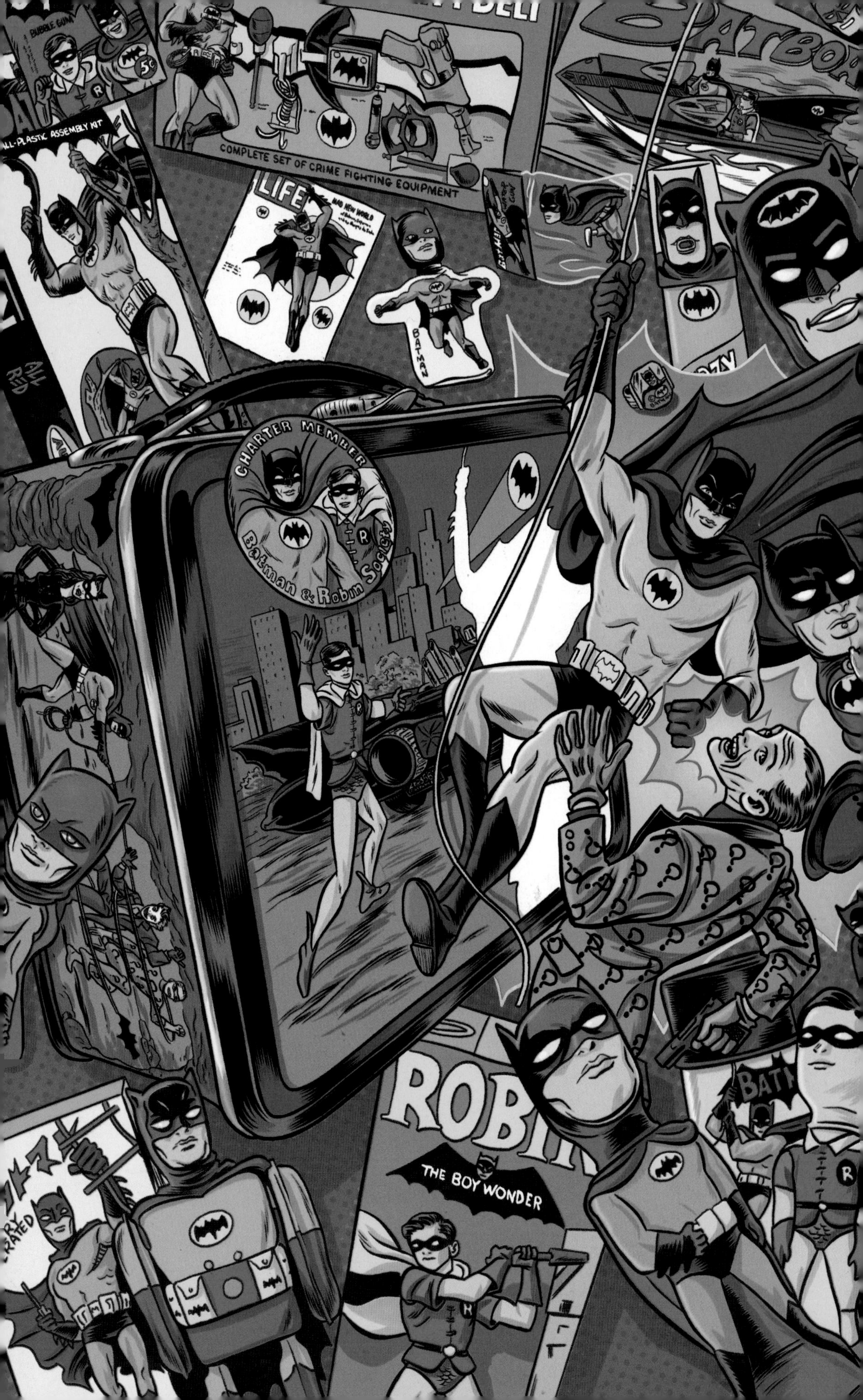
BUBBLE GUM
5¢
ALL-PLASTIC ASSEMBLY KIT
COMPLETE SET OF CRIME FIGHTING EQUIPMENT
LIFE
BATMAN
CHARTER MEMBER
Batman & Robin Society
ROBIN
THE BOY WONDER

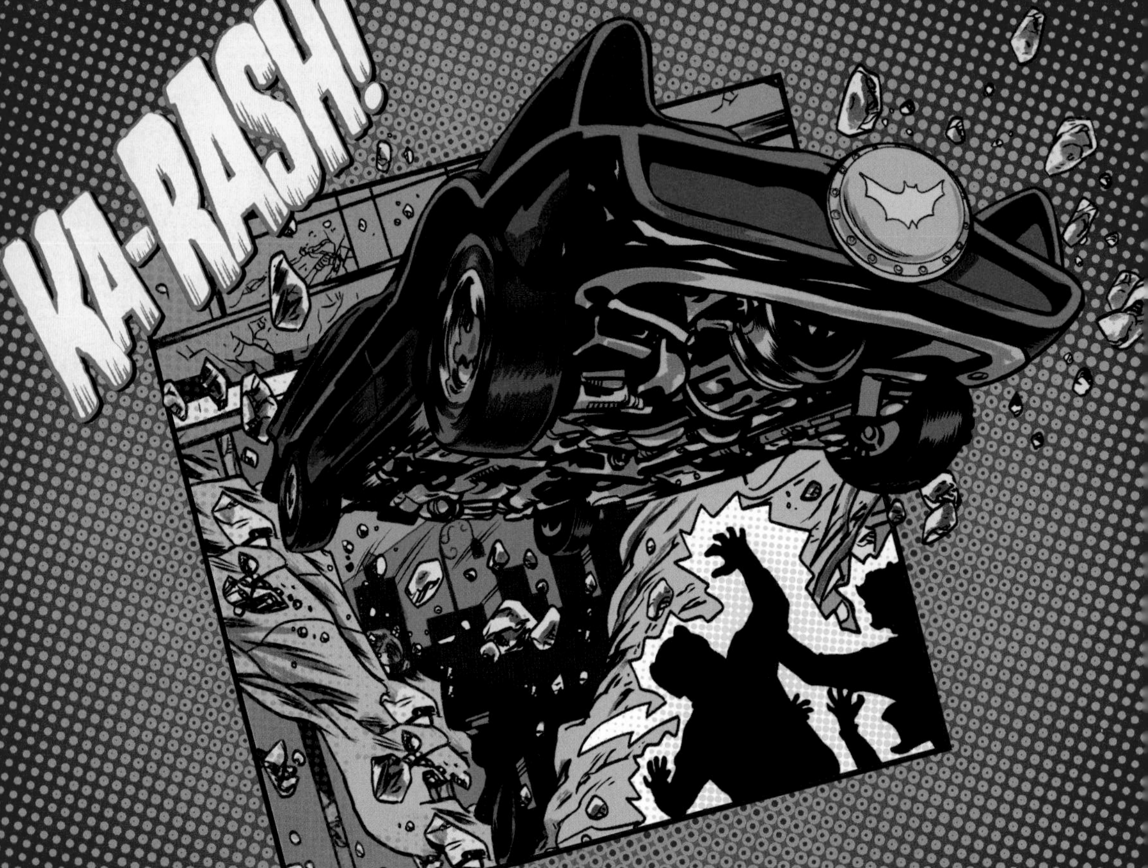
KA-RASH!

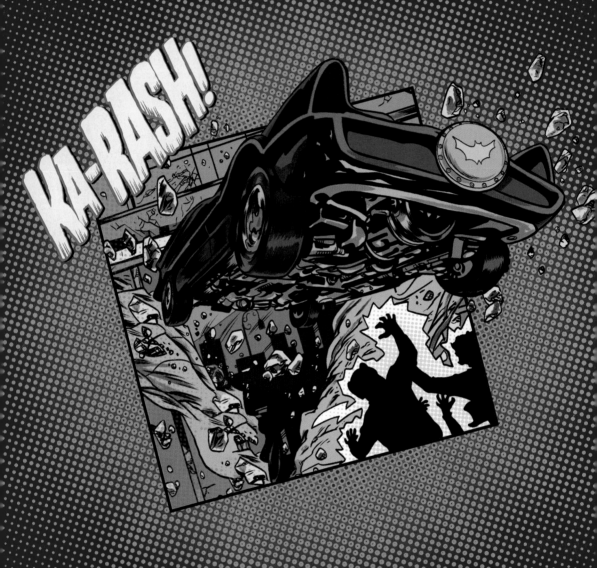

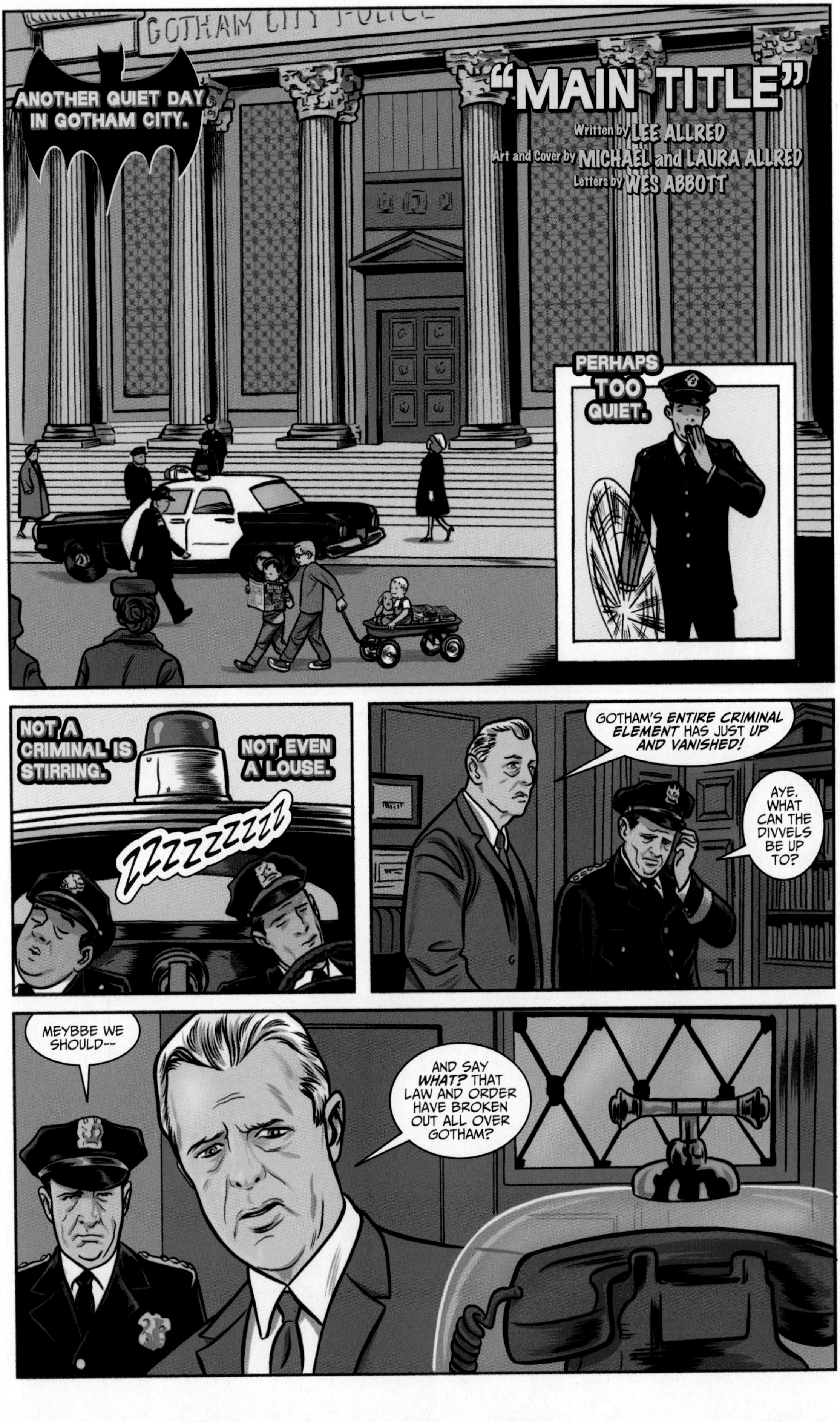
GOTHAM CITY POLICE
ANOTHER QUIET DAY IN GOTHAM CITY.
"MAIN TITLE"
Written by LEE ALLRED
Art and Cover by MICHAEL and LAURA ALLRED
Letters by WES ABBOTT
PERHAPS TOO QUIET.
NOT A CRIMINAL IS STIRRING.
NOT EVEN A LOUSE.
ZZZZZZZZ
GOTHAM'S ENTIRE CRIMINAL ELEMENT HAS JUST UP AND VANISHED!
AYE. WHAT CAN THE DIVVELS BE UP TO?
MEYBBE WE SHOULD--
AND SAY WHAT? THAT LAW AND ORDER HAVE BROKEN OUT ALL OVER GOTHAM?

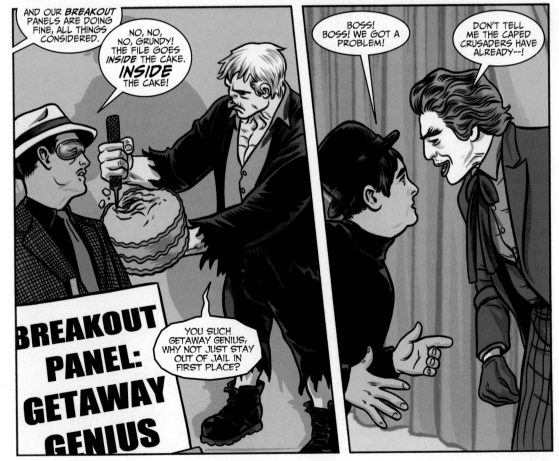

"NO SOAP, BOSS!

I DONE LIKE YOU SAID. I TALK TO PENGUIN, I TALK TO CATWOMAN, I EVEN TALK TO JOKER-- WHICH IS NO *TREAT*, LET ME TELL YOU!

THEY ALL REFUSED-- AN' WIT' *EXTREME PREJUDICE!*--A LET YOU ATTEND THEIR LITTLE CONFAB.

THEY TELL ME YOU MIGHT AS WELL BE WORKING FOR *BATMAN*, YOU AND YOUR RIDDLES.

I DO NOT THINK THEY LIKES YOU NONE, BOSS.

THEY

DARE

BLACKBALL

ME?

ME?!?

*RIDDLE ME THIS*--WHY IS *REVENGE* LIKE A *BOWL OF ICE CREAM?* BECAUSE IT'S A DISH *BEST SERVED COLD!*

I HAVE A LITTLE DELIVERY FOR YOU TO MAKE, *JIGSAW...*

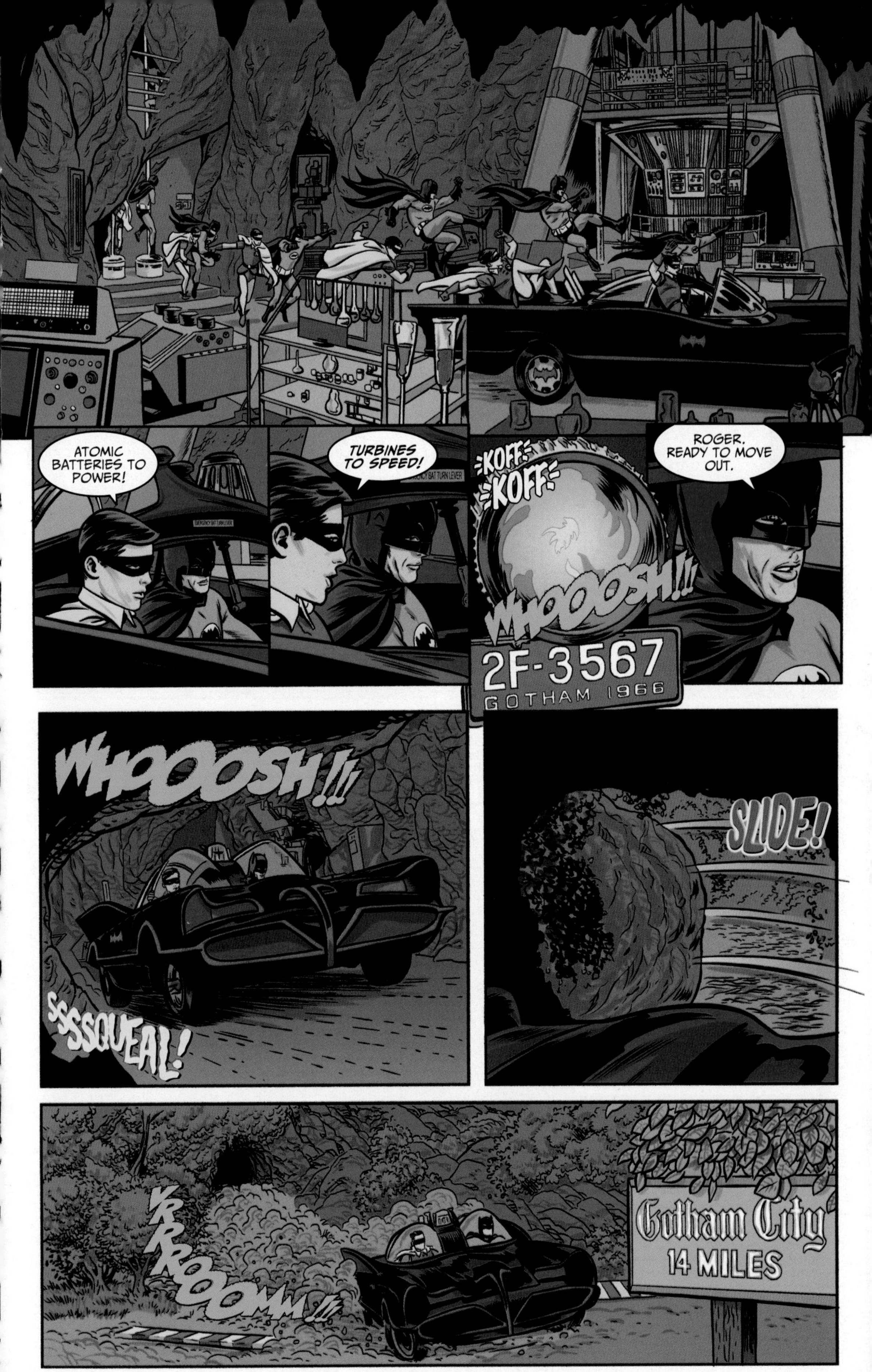
ATOMIC BATTERIES TO POWER!
TURBINES TO SPEED!
KOFF
KOFF
WHOOOSH!!!
2F-3567
GOTHAM 1966
ROGER. READY TO MOVE OUT.
WHOOOSH!!!
SSSSQUEAL!
SLIDE!
VRRROOOMM!!
Gotham City
14 MILES

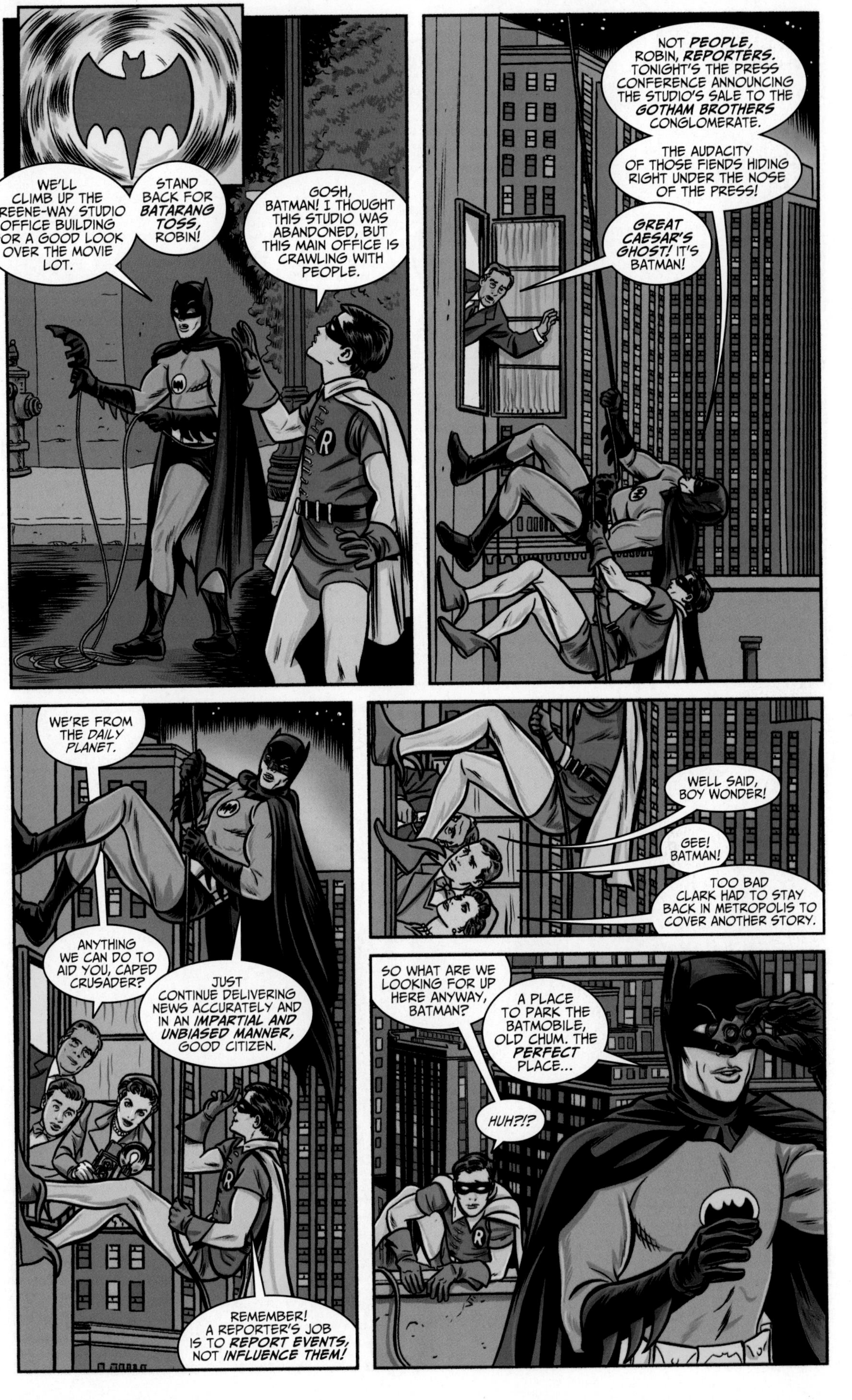

WE'LL CLIMB UP THE GREENE-WAY STUDIO OFFICE BUILDING FOR A GOOD LOOK OVER THE MOVIE LOT.
STAND BACK FOR *BATARANG TOSS*, ROBIN!
GOSH, BATMAN! I THOUGHT THIS STUDIO WAS ABANDONED, BUT THIS MAIN OFFICE IS CRAWLING WITH PEOPLE.
NOT *PEOPLE*, ROBIN, *REPORTERS.* TONIGHT'S THE PRESS CONFERENCE ANNOUNCING THE STUDIO'S SALE TO THE *GOTHAM BROTHERS* CONGLOMERATE.
THE AUDACITY OF THOSE FIENDS HIDING RIGHT UNDER THE NOSE OF THE PRESS!
*GREAT CAESAR'S GHOST!* IT'S BATMAN!
WE'RE FROM THE *DAILY PLANET*.
ANYTHING WE CAN DO TO AID YOU, CAPED CRUSADER?
JUST CONTINUE DELIVERING NEWS ACCURATELY AND IN AN *IMPARTIAL AND UNBIASED MANNER,* GOOD CITIZEN.
REMEMBER! A REPORTER'S JOB IS TO *REPORT EVENTS,* NOT *INFLUENCE THEM!*
WELL SAID, BOY WONDER!
GEE! BATMAN!
TOO BAD CLARK HAD TO STAY BACK IN METROPOLIS TO COVER ANOTHER STORY.
SO WHAT ARE WE LOOKING FOR UP HERE ANYWAY, BATMAN?
A PLACE TO PARK THE BATMOBILE, OLD CHUM. THE *PERFECT* PLACE...
*HUH?!?*

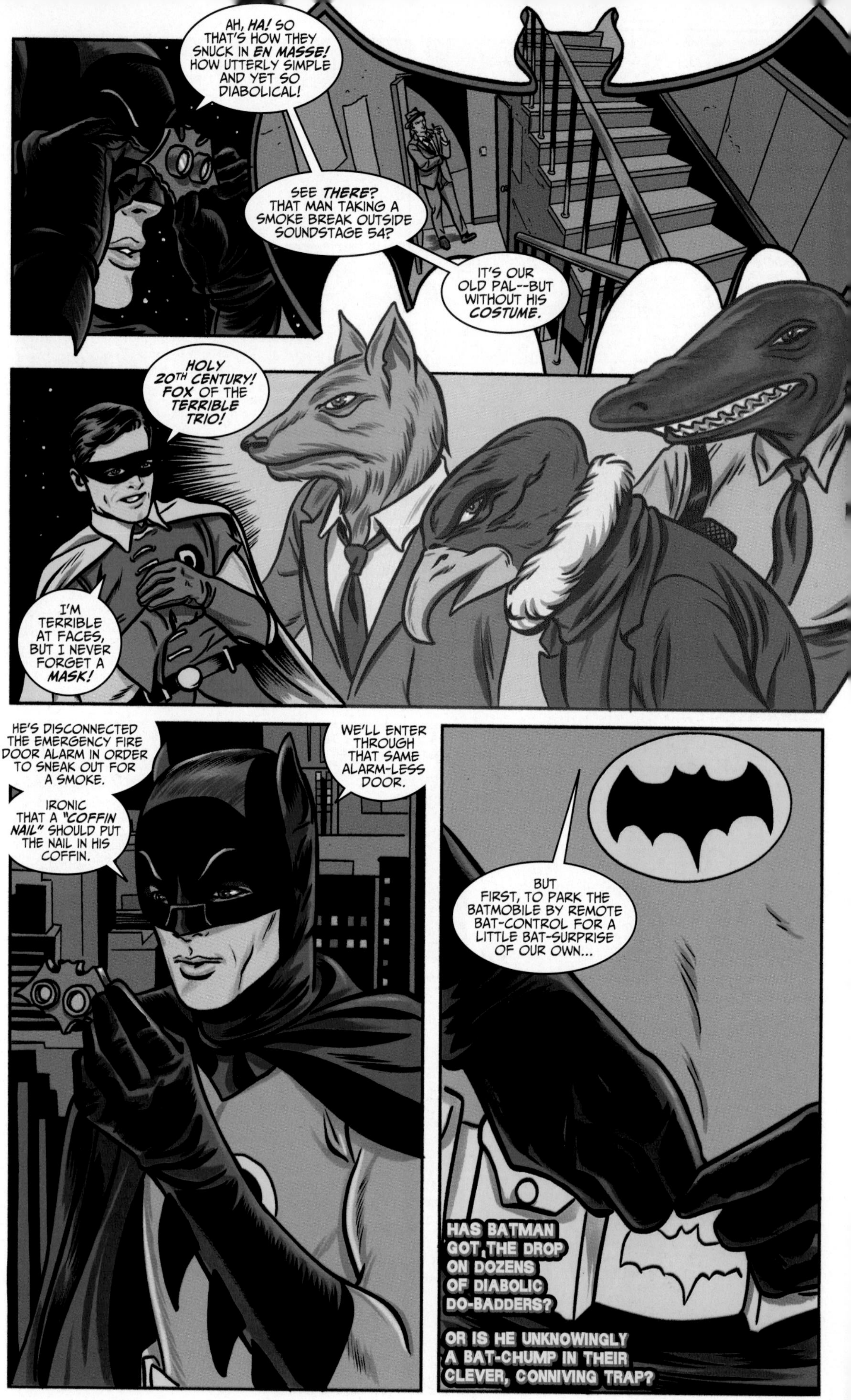
AH, HA! SO THAT'S HOW THEY SNUCK IN EN MASSE! HOW UTTERLY SIMPLE AND YET SO DIABOLICAL!
SEE THERE? THAT MAN TAKING A SMOKE BREAK OUTSIDE SOUNDSTAGE 54?
IT'S OUR OLD PAL--BUT WITHOUT HIS COSTUME.
HOLY 20TH CENTURY! FOX OF THE TERRIBLE TRIO!
I'M TERRIBLE AT FACES, BUT I NEVER FORGET A MASK!
HE'S DISCONNECTED THE EMERGENCY FIRE DOOR ALARM IN ORDER TO SNEAK OUT FOR A SMOKE.
IRONIC THAT A "COFFIN NAIL" SHOULD PUT THE NAIL IN HIS COFFIN.
WE'LL ENTER THROUGH THAT SAME ALARM-LESS DOOR.
BUT FIRST, TO PARK THE BATMOBILE BY REMOTE BAT-CONTROL FOR A LITTLE BAT-SURPRISE OF OUR OWN...
HAS BATMAN GOT THE DROP ON DOZENS OF DIABOLIC DO-BADDERS?
OR IS HE UNKNOWINGLY A BAT-CHUMP IN THEIR CLEVER, CONNIVING TRAP?

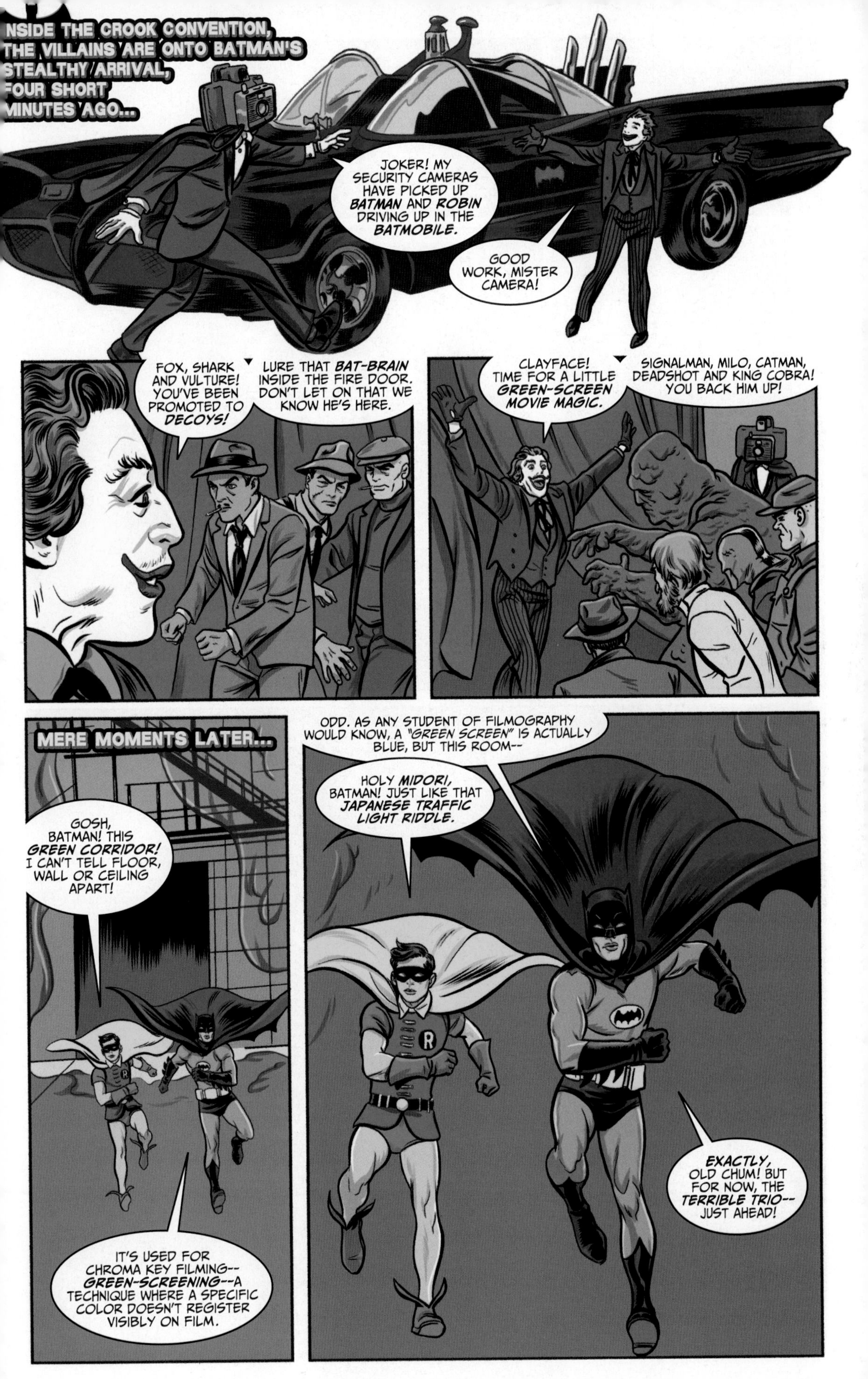
INSIDE THE CROOK CONVENTION, THE VILLAINS ARE ONTO BATMAN'S STEALTHY ARRIVAL, FOUR SHORT MINUTES AGO...
JOKER! MY SECURITY CAMERAS HAVE PICKED UP BATMAN AND ROBIN DRIVING UP IN THE BATMOBILE.
GOOD WORK, MISTER CAMERA!
FOX, SHARK AND VULTURE! YOU'VE BEEN PROMOTED TO DECOYS!
LURE THAT BAT-BRAIN INSIDE THE FIRE DOOR. DON'T LET ON THAT WE KNOW HE'S HERE.
CLAYFACE! TIME FOR A LITTLE GREEN-SCREEN MOVIE MAGIC.
SIGNALMAN, MILO, CATMAN, DEADSHOT AND KING COBRA! YOU BACK HIM UP!
MERE MOMENTS LATER...
GOSH, BATMAN! THIS GREEN CORRIDOR! I CAN'T TELL FLOOR, WALL OR CEILING APART!
IT'S USED FOR CHROMA KEY FILMING--GREEN-SCREENING--A TECHNIQUE WHERE A SPECIFIC COLOR DOESN'T REGISTER VISIBLY ON FILM.
ODD. AS ANY STUDENT OF FILMOGRAPHY WOULD KNOW, A "GREEN SCREEN" IS ACTUALLY BLUE, BUT THIS ROOM--
HOLY MIDORI, BATMAN! JUST LIKE THAT JAPANESE TRAFFIC LIGHT RIDDLE.
EXACTLY, OLD CHUM! BUT FOR NOW, THE TERRIBLE TRIO--JUST AHEAD!

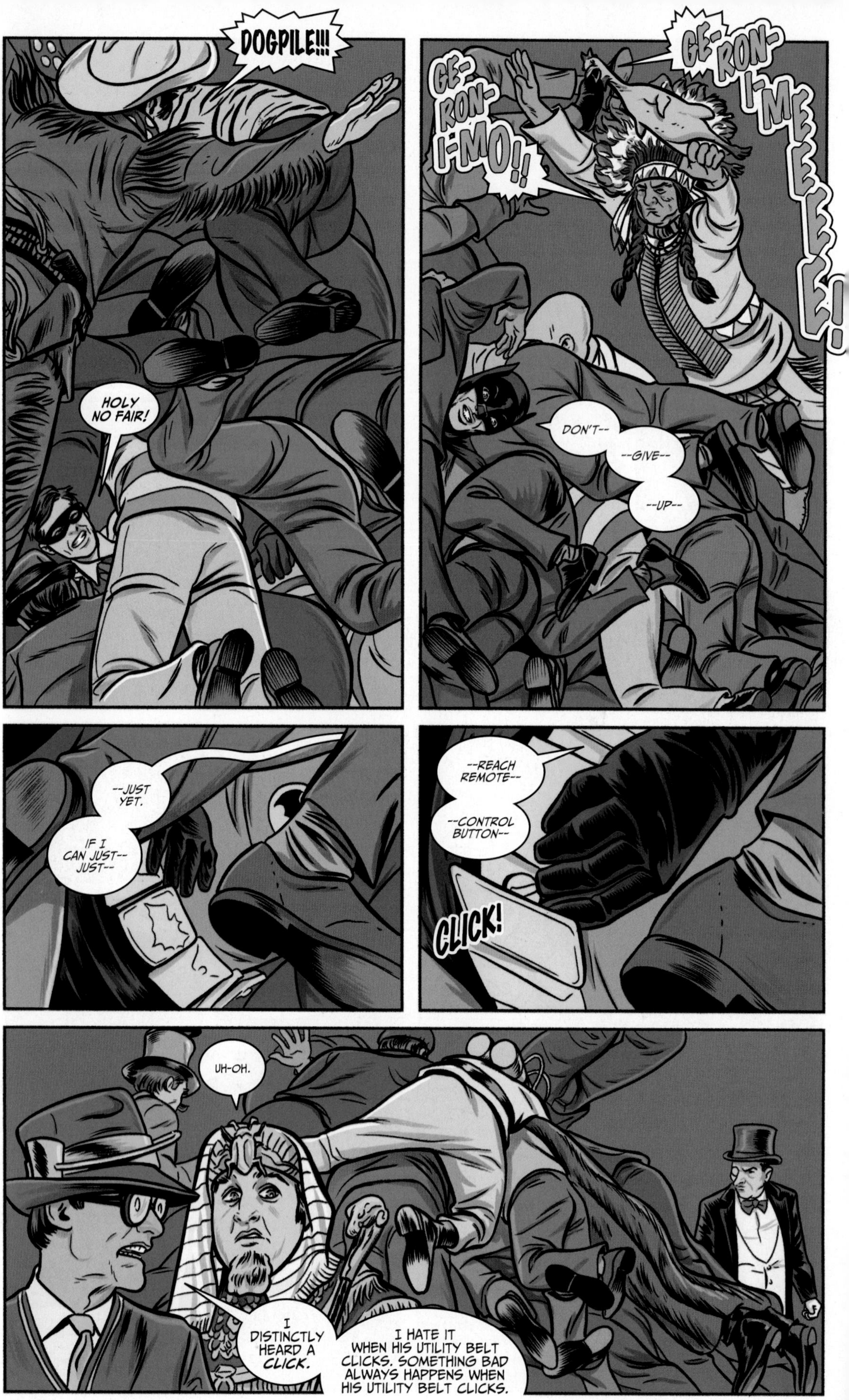
DOGPILE!!!
HOLY NO FAIR!
GE-RON-I-MO!!
GE-RON-I-MEEEE!
DON'T--
--GIVE--
--UP--
--JUST YET.
IF I CAN JUST-- JUST--
--REACH REMOTE--
--CONTROL BUTTON--
CLICK!
UH-OH.
I DISTINCTLY HEARD A CLICK.
I HATE IT WHEN HIS UTILITY BELT CLICKS. SOMETHING BAD ALWAYS HAPPENS WHEN HIS UTILITY BELT CLICKS.

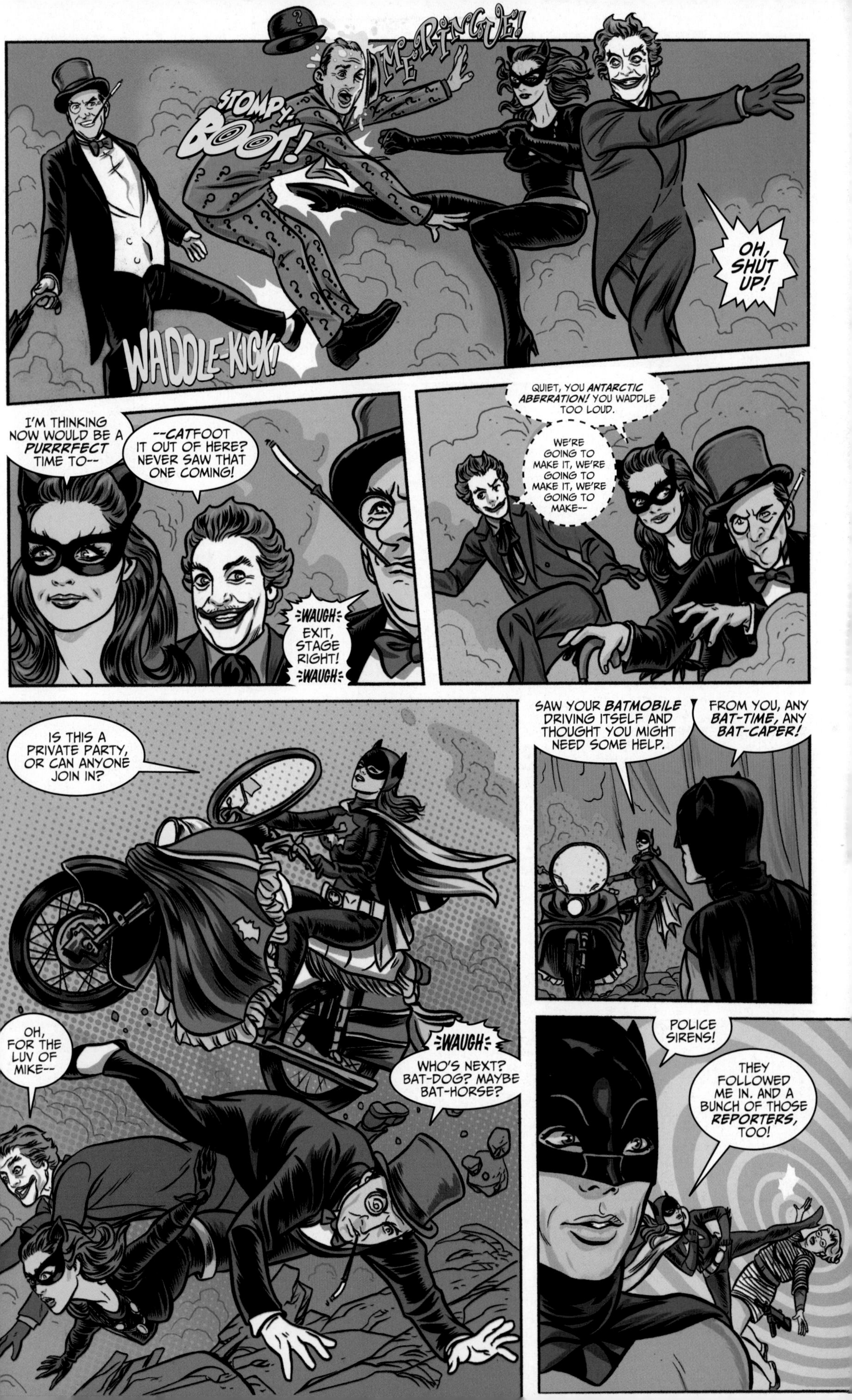
MERINGUE!
STOMPY-BOOT!
OH, SHUT UP!
WADDLE-KICK!
I'M THINKING NOW WOULD BE A PURRRFECT TIME TO--
--CATFOOT IT OUT OF HERE? NEVER SAW THAT ONE COMING!
WAUGH EXIT, STAGE RIGHT! WAUGH
QUIET, YOU ANTARCTIC ABERRATION! YOU WADDLE TOO LOUD.
WE'RE GOING TO MAKE IT, WE'RE GOING TO MAKE IT, WE'RE GOING TO MAKE--
IS THIS A PRIVATE PARTY, OR CAN ANYONE JOIN IN?
OH, FOR THE LUV OF MIKE--
WAUGH WHO'S NEXT? BAT-DOG? MAYBE BAT-HORSE?
SAW YOUR BATMOBILE DRIVING ITSELF AND THOUGHT YOU MIGHT NEED SOME HELP.
FROM YOU, ANY BAT-TIME, ANY BAT-CAPER!
POLICE SIRENS!
THEY FOLLOWED ME IN. AND A BUNCH OF THOSE REPORTERS, TOO!